194

Global Economic Prospects

D1430231

Managing the Next
Wave of Globalization

2007

ISBN-10: 0-8213-6727-7
ISBN-13: 978-0-8213-6727-8
eISBN-10: 0-8213-6728-5
eISBN-13: 978-0-8213-6728-5
DOI: 10.1596/978-0-8213-6727-8

ISSN: 1014-8906

Cover photo: Pallava Bagla/Corbis

The cutoff date for data used in this report was November 22, 2006. Dollars are current U.S. dollars unless otherwise indicated.

Contents

Tables

Boxes

Foreword

GLOBAL ECONOMIC PROSPECTS reports have customarily aimed to stand back from the Bank's day-to-day work and explore existing or emerging debates in the international arena that are of critical importance to developing countries. We have endeavored to focus on areas in which the Bank's researchers and technical experts may provide insights based on their cross-country and global knowledge. Thus, past reports have helped to deepen the Bank contribution to policy debates in areas such as international and regional trade, investment, and, last year, migration and remittances.

The strong performance of the global economy—and of developing countries in particular—in recent years led us to ask whether these higher rates of growth could be sustained for the long term. And if so, what would the implications be for the global economy and for the world's poor? Answering those questions leads us to explore the nature of the "next globalization."

Three features are likely to be particularly prominent in the next wave of globalization. First is the growing economic weight of developing countries in the international economy, notably the emergence of new trading powerhouses such as China, India, and Brazil. Second is the potential for increased productivity that is offered by global production chains, particularly in services, arguably the most dynamic sector of trade today. Third is the accelerated diffusion of technology, made possible through falling communications costs and improved access to telecommunications and the Internet, as well as through innovative forms of business organization, often linked to foreign investment.

The next globalization—deeper integration with the world economy through trade, flows of information technology, finance, and migration—will offer renewed and enhanced opportunities to increase productivity and raise incomes. Producers participating in bigger international markets will be able to produce on a larger scale, access the most appropriate technology and knowledge, and participate in increasingly integrated global production chains. Consumers everywhere will have access to the latest international products.

However, along with rising average incomes may come dislocations and environmental pressures. This *Global Economic Prospects* analyzes three possible consequences— growing inequality, pressures in labor markets, and threats to the global commons. All are evident in the current globalization, but in coming years they are likely to become more acute. If these forces are left unchecked, they could slow or even derail globalization and thus adversely affect growth and development in many developing countries. The report is premised on the idea that the threats to continued global growth and poverty reduction from environmental damage, social unrest, or new increases in protectionist sentiment are potentially serious, and it is worth exploring ways that these disruptive forces might be addressed now if we wish to see sustainable global growth in the future.

To analyze these problems, the report employs a series of projections and simulations built around a central scenario of the evolution of the global economy. The objective of the scenario-based approach is to analyze the benefits and stresses of integration. The purpose is not to predict the future—the actual numbers for global or country performance may turn out to be higher or lower—but to think about dynamics in the global economy in a coherent analytical framework.

Focusing on the future helps bring into sharper relief the choices facing policy makers in managing global integration today.

National policy makers must decide how best to respond to globalization—because the growth and long-term competitiveness of their countries are at stake. And international policy makers must devise ways for nations to work together to ensure that growth is sustained and widely shared, and does not cause irreparable damage to the environment.

François Bourguignon
Senior Vice President and Chief Economist
The World Bank

Acknowledgments

THIS REPORT WAS produced by staff from the World Bank's Development Prospects Group. Richard Newfarmer was the lead author and manager of the report. The principal author of chapter 1 was Andrew Burns. Chapter 2 was written by Dominique van der Mensbrugghe, with written contributions from Dilek Aykut and Sanket Mohapatra and with support from Sebnem Sahin. Chapter 3 was written by Maurizio Bussolo and Denis Medvedev, with the benefit of guidance from Francisco Ferreira and with support from Victor Sulla and Rafael De Hoyos. Chapter 4 was written by Julia Nielson, Paul Brenton, and Mombert Hoppe, with guidance from Gordon Betcherman. Chapter 5 was written by consultants Peter Sturm and William Shaw, with written contributions from Maureen Cropper and Philippe Ambrosi and with analytic work by Mombert Hoppe. The accompanying online publication, *Prospects for the Global Economy (PGE)*, was produced by a team led by Andrew Burns and comprising Sarah Crow, Cristina Savescu, and Shuo Tan, with technical support from Gauresh Rajadhyaksha.

The report was produced under the guidance of Uri Dadush and François Bourguignon. Several reviewers offered extensive advice and comment throughout the conceptualization and writing stages. These included Nancy Birdsall, Cornelis de Hann, Shahrokh Fardoust, Alan Gelb, Lidvard Gronnevet, Bernard Hoekman, Robert Holzmann, Eriko Hoshino, Kieran Kelleher, Jeffrey Lewis, William Maloney, Branko Milanovic, Moisés Naím, Ian Noble, Stefano Scarpetta, David Wheeler, and Roberto Zagha.

Several people contributed substantively to the various chapters. In chapter 1, the Global Trends Team, under the leadership of Hans Timmer, was responsible for the projections, with contributions from John Baffes, Maurizio Bussolo, Betty Dow, Annette De Kleine, Donald Mitchell, Denis Medvedev, Mick Riordan, Cristina Savescu, and Shane Streifel. In chapter 2, the poverty numbers originated with Shaohua Chen and Martin Ravallion from the Development Research Group.

In addition, Steven Kennedy and Bruce Ross Larsen edited the report. Dorota A. Nowak and Nigar Farhad Aliyeva managed the publication process for the Development Prospects Group, and Merrell Tuck managed the dissemination activities. Book production was coordinated by the World Bank Office of the Publisher.

Overview

THE INTENSE PACE of globalization has improved living standards worldwide on an unprecedented scale—but not for everyone. Some countries and some social groups have been left behind. Even in countries that have benefited greatly from globalization, tensions in labor markets have simmered, at times boiling over into civil disturbances. Meanwhile economic growth, while essential to improving living standards, is damaging what many call the "global commons," giving rise to concerns about the sustainability of long-term growth.

These pressures are likely to intensify in coming years. Why? Because as markets integrate, competition among countries—and their firms and workers—increases. Developing countries, once at the periphery of the global economy, are now moving to center stage and are becoming serious competitors in the markets of high-income countries and in each other's markets. Concerns about competition from China and other low-wage suppliers now pepper the headlines in rich and poor countries alike. The loss of white-collar jobs from global sourcing of services, often to India and other developing countries, provides fodder for heated debate on talk shows and as the theme of several best-selling books.[1]

Will global integration—of trade, finance, technology, ideas, and people—continue into the foreseeable future? If so, what will it mean for developing countries and for today's high-income countries? How will global integration, interacting with demography, technical change, and other forces, affect the distribution of income and labor markets in rich and poor countries? How will it affect the global environmental and health threats that cloud long-term growth prospects?

Global Economic Prospects 2007 explores the next wave of globalization. The organizing vehicle for discussion is a set of growth scenarios covering the years 2006 to 2030. The objective of the scenario-based approach is to analyze the opportunities and stresses of integration. The purpose is not to predict the future but to bring into sharper relief the choices facing the world today. National policy makers must decide how best to respond to globalization—because the growth and long-term competitiveness of their countries are at stake. And international policy makers must devise ways for nations to work together to ensure that growth can continue without becoming destabilizing.

Prospects for 2007 and 2008— bright, with a few dim spots

The medium-term outlook for the world economy remains fairly bright (chapter 1). While the pace of economic expansion is slowing, developing economies are projected to grow by 7.0 percent in 2006, more than twice as fast as high-income countries

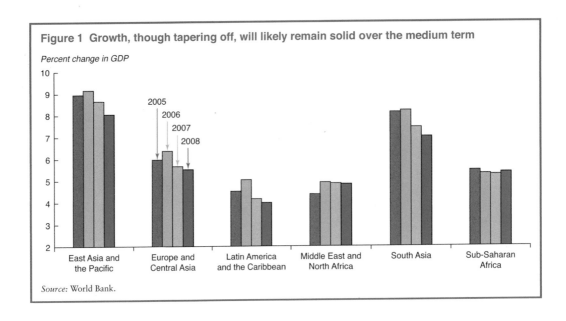

Figure 1 Growth, though tapering off, will likely remain solid over the medium term

Percent change in GDP

Source: World Bank.

(3.1 percent), with all developing regions growing by about 5 percent or more (figure 1). Looking forward, limited inflationary pressures and high savings among oil exporters and in Europe (as Europeans prepare to meet the challenges of their aging societies) are expected to keep long-term interest rates low. As a result, while growth in developing countries may slow somewhat over the next two years, it is expected to remain very robust—at more than 6 percent in 2007 and 2008. Increases in supplies of key commodities, in combination with demand-side substitution and conservation measures, should allow for some easing of prices, including those for oil, but continuing strong global growth is expected to keep commodity prices high by historical standards.

Even though a tapering down of growth to a sustainable but robust rate remains most likely, this positive outlook is subject to significant risks. Efforts to temper the expansion in some of the fastest-growing developing countries may not succeed, leading to stronger growth in the short term but a sharper slowdown later. A faster-than-expected weakening of housing markets in high-income countries could brake the economy much more abruptly than expected, thus weakening global demand.

Disruptions in oil markets are always possible. And the unwinding of the U.S. current account deficit and its mirror surpluses in oil-exporting countries and East Asia could also be disruptive if sudden movements in capital markets, perhaps abetted by collective policy inaction, drive the rebalancing. Even so, these risks appear manageable, and the promising environment for growth makes this an opportune time to focus on long-term issues.

Globalization's next 25 years—incomes up, poverty down, three big threats to growth

Demographic trends will be a major driver of future events. The Earth's current population of some 6.5 billion is expected to rise to 8.0 billion by 2030, an average increase of 60 million annually. More than 97 percent of this growth will take place in developing countries. Both the European Union and Japan are likely to experience a decline in population, and most of the increase in other rich countries will be due to migration. The largest country in the world, China, will see its population continue to grow, but at a slower pace than the rest of the developing world. With more rapid population growth, India will likely surpass China as the world's most populous country sometime during this period. The global labor force will increase from just over 3 billion today to 4.1 billion in 2030, a rate of increase greater than that of population. Meanwhile the dependency ratio is likely to fall, providing a sustained boost to world growth.

If this report's central scenario materializes, global economic growth will be somewhat faster in 2006–30 than in 1980–2005. But growth in the global economy will be powered increasingly by developing countries, where per capita incomes will rise 3.1 percent a year on average, up from 2.1 percent over the earlier period. That rate of increase will produce average per capita incomes in the developing world of $11,000 in 2030, compared with $4,800 today,[2] roughly the level of the Czech Republic and the Slovak Republic today. Average income in rich countries will also rise dramatically: the average income of the children of today's baby boomer is likely to be nearly twice that of their parents.

The output of the global economy will rise from $35 trillion in 2005 to $72 trillion (at constant market exchange rates and prices) in 2030, an average annual increase of about 3 percent—2.5 percent for high-income countries and 4.2 percent for developing countries. Though the incomes of developing countries will still be less than one-quarter those in rich countries in 2030, they will continue to converge with those of wealthy countries (figure 2). This would imply that countries as diverse as China, Mexico, and Turkey would have average living standards roughly comparable to Spain today.

This is good news for the world's poor. The implications of sustained growth for reducing poverty around the world are nothing short of astounding. Despite population growth, the number of people living in dire poverty—below the $1-a-day poverty line—is likely to fall to 550 million from 1.1 billion today. Similarly, the number of people living on less than $2 a day should fall below 1.9 billion, 800 million fewer than today. The bottom line? Poverty will decline, despite continuing population growth.

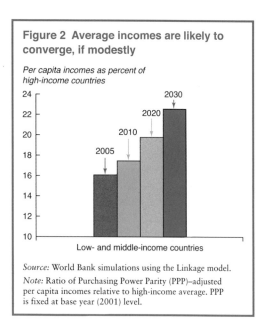

Figure 2 Average incomes are likely to converge, if modestly

Per capita incomes as percent of high-income countries

Source: World Bank simulations using the Linkage model.
Note: Ratio of Purchasing Power Parity (PPP)–adjusted per capita incomes relative to high-income average. PPP is fixed at base year (2001) level.

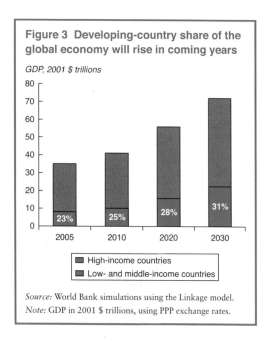

Figure 3 Developing-country share of the global economy will rise in coming years

GDP, 2001 $ trillions

Source: World Bank simulations using the Linkage model.
Note: GDP in 2001 $ trillions, using PPP exchange rates.

Developing countries, once considered the periphery of the global economy, will become main drivers. Overall, developing countries' share in global output will increase from about one-fifth of the global economy to nearly one-third (figure 3). Their share of global purchasing power would surpass half. Today, six developing countries have populations greater than 100 million and an annual gross domestic product (GDP) of more than $100 billion. By 2030, under reasonable assumptions of economic growth, at least 10 countries will reach the twin 100s thresholds.[3]

Global integration is likely to enter a new phase. In virtually every growing economy the importance of trade—captured by the ratio of trade to GDP—will rise, continuing the trend of the past two decades. The growth in the trade ratio over the next 25 years will be powered by a new dynamism in services trade. Global trade in goods and services, growing faster than output, is likely to rise more than threefold to $27 trillion in 2030 (figures 4 and 5).

Roughly half that increase will come from developing countries. This means that a growing share of global production of goods and services will be performed in those developing countries able to take advantage of

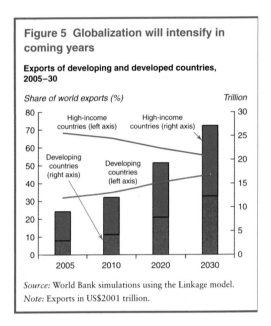

Figure 5 Globalization will intensify in coming years

Exports of developing and developed countries, 2005–30

Source: World Bank simulations using the Linkage model.
Note: Exports in US$2001 trillion.

new opportunities. For example, agriculture now accounts for about 2 percent of the economic value added of most rich countries; that share will shrink to boutique niches. A few resource-rich regions and countries, including Latin America and Australia, will be the source of 90 percent of the world's sugar, 50 percent of its grain, and 40 percent of its dairy products. Whether countries exceed projections—or fall short—depends heavily on the policies they adopt over this long period.

Several factors could alter this relatively sanguine outcome for better or worse. The central long-term scenario in this report is robust enough to resist periodic recessions, isolated regional conflicts, and even many of the destabilizing crises the world has experienced in the past 30 years. These threats are likely to affect particular regional or national economies more than the world economy, and if history is a guide, are likely to be of relatively short duration. Between 1980 and 2005 the world economy grew at a steady pace despite several major disruptions—including the Latin American debt crisis, the demise of the Soviet Union, the East Asia

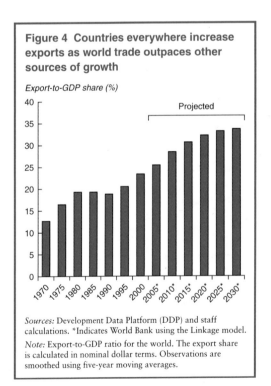

Figure 4 Countries everywhere increase exports as world trade outpaces other sources of growth

Export-to-GDP share (%)

Sources: Development Data Platform (DDP) and staff calculations. *Indicates World Bank using the Linkage model.
Note: Export-to-GDP ratio for the world. The export share is calculated in nominal dollar terms. Observations are smoothed using five-year moving averages.

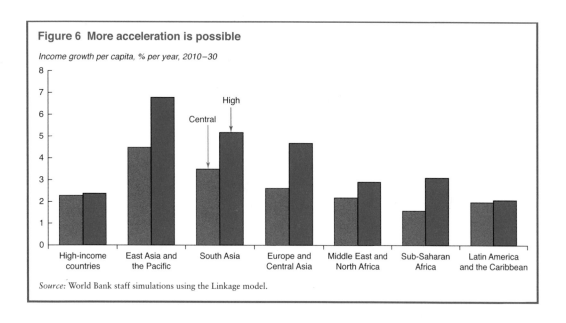

Figure 6 More acceleration is possible

Income growth per capita, % per year, 2010–30

Source: World Bank staff simulations using the Linkage model.

crisis, two global downturns, and the tragedy of September 11, 2001. These events had only short-term effects on global growth and a marginal impact on the steady advance of globalization, even though regional ripples continued for years afterward. This suggests that the basic long-term trends discussed here, if not the assumed growth rates, are fairly impervious to all but the most severe and sustained shocks.

At the same time, the possibility exists that the world will be even better than envisioned in the central scenario—thanks possibly to unanticipated technological improvements, more innovation in business processes that allow for an acceleration of globalization, and widespread adoptions of good policies within countries. Indeed, greater integration promotes knowledge about policies that work. It also shortens the duration of bad policies, as investment capital and human resources can more readily flee poorly performing nations. That discipline is likely to become more effective as financial, merchandise, and technological markets continue to integrate. The upside

scenario in this report (figure 6) is based on the assumption that countries perform closer to their full potential over a longer period of time. Predicated on maintaining the solid growth rates of the last half-decade, the high-growth scenario sketched here would lead to incomes in 2030 that are some 45 percent higher than those projected under the central scenario and to declines in absolute poverty ($1 per day) from about 20 percent of the world's population today to less than 4 percent in 2030.

Two points emerge from the discussion of scenarios (chapter 2). First, policy matters. The right domestic and international policies, sustained over long periods, have the power to raise incomes around the world, especially in certain countries. Second, whether the underlying growth rates are low or high, the dynamics underpinning any likely scenario will generate stresses that require policy attention today. The report analyzes in detail three main stresses in the global economy that could threaten growth: widening inequality, growing tensions in labor markets, and new environmental pressures.

Income inequality could widen— among and within countries

The benefits of globalization are likely to be uneven across regions and countries (chapter 3). Africa, because of underlying growth trends and the presence of many fragile states, is the region most likely to fall farther behind. But, it also has the most to gain from integration, because it can take advantage of technology and wage gaps to propel higher sustained growth.

Of equal concern, strong forces in the global economy may tend to increase inequality in many national economies. Even though a large segment of the developing world is likely to enter what can be called the "global middle class," some social groups may be left behind or even marginalized in the growth process. Unskilled workers, in particular, may fall farther behind. Technological progress, by generating demand for greater skills, tends to widen the gap between the wages of skilled and unskilled workers. Demographic patterns that affect social dependency ratios (the ratio of workers to youth and retirees) and educational attainment are also important.

Trade per se has been found generally to have no systematic effect across countries as a direct channel for wage-gap widening. However, in combination with technological change and, to a lesser extent, foreign investment, these globalization-related forces may combine to increase inequality in many countries—at the same time as they are raising average incomes.

A global middle class will emerge

By 2030, fully 1.2 billion people in developing countries—15 percent of the world population—will belong to the global middle class, up from 400 million today. Families of four in that class earn between $16,000 and $68,000 in PPP dollars (figure 7). (Because the definition used here is absolute and based on a global scale, most of those who consider themselves middle class in high-income

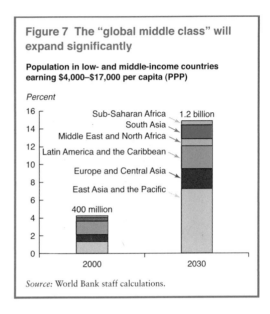

Figure 7 The "global middle class" will expand significantly

Population in low- and middle-income countries earning $4,000–$17,000 per capita (PPP)

Percent

Sub-Saharan Africa
South Asia
Middle East and North Africa
Latin America and the Caribbean
Europe and Central Asia
East Asia and the Pacific

1.2 billion
400 million

2000   2030

Source: World Bank staff calculations.

countries are classified as rich in a global context, while many people viewed as wealthy in developing countries are members of the global middle class.) This large group will participate actively in the global marketplace, demand world-class products, and aspire to international standards of higher education. That is, they would have the purchasing power to buy automobiles (perhaps second-hand), purchase many consumer durables, and travel abroad.

While still a minority in their own countries, the new members of the global middle class will place new and quite different demands on domestic political structures. Their livelihoods and standards of consumption are likely to be connected to the global market, so, as the studies reviewed in chapter 3 show, their political predilection may be more likely to favor access to the international market, if not greater openness itself. They also are more likely to demand transparency in political and corporate governance, certainty of contracts, and property rights—all hallmarks of an improving investment climate.

Most who enter the middle class will do so because they are able to move from agriculture into manufacturing and services or acquire valuable skills faster than their compatriots. For a given rate of growth, policies that allow mobility across sectors and that provide broader access to education can accelerate economic growth by creating the opportunity and incentives for all citizens to develop their productive potential.

Africa and some groups within countries may lag behind

Sub-Saharan Africa will have to make a strong effort, with the support of the international community, if it is to avoid being left behind (figure 8). Today, half of the poorest tenth of the world population lives in Asia; by 2030 Asia's share in the lowest tenth will be reduced to one-fifth under the central scenario. By contrast, Africa, now home to one-third of the poorest people, is likely to see its share of the lowest tenth double by 2030. To be sure, the region has the potential for more rapid growth, and sustained improvements in policy and investment climate could bring out that

potential. Most fundamental is a cessation of crippling civil conflicts that have stunted development in several regions of Sub-Saharan Africa. In the high-case scenario explored in chapter 2, Africa's income could be twice as high as projected in the central scenario (see figure 6).

While developing countries are closing the income gap with rich countries, as many as two-thirds—more than 80 percent of the developing world outside China—may experience a worsening of within-country inequality, thus muting the poverty-reducing effects of growth and fanning social tensions that could derail growth. Demography plays a role, as aging societies tend to become more unequal. But the main driver is the widening difference in earning potential between skilled and unskilled workers (figure 9). This is because investments in capital and technology create a more rapidly growing demand for skilled workers. The simulations in this report suggest that the combined effects of all these forces—technology, globalization, demography, and demand for skilled labor—may widen income distribution in as many as two-thirds of all countries,

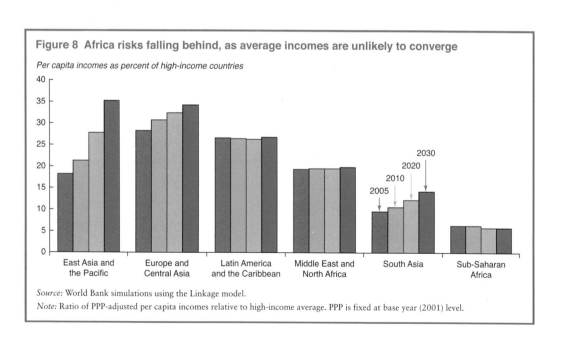

Figure 8 Africa risks falling behind, as average incomes are unlikely to converge

Per capita incomes as percent of high-income countries

Source: World Bank simulations using the Linkage model.
Note: Ratio of PPP-adjusted per capita incomes relative to high-income average. PPP is fixed at base year (2001) level.

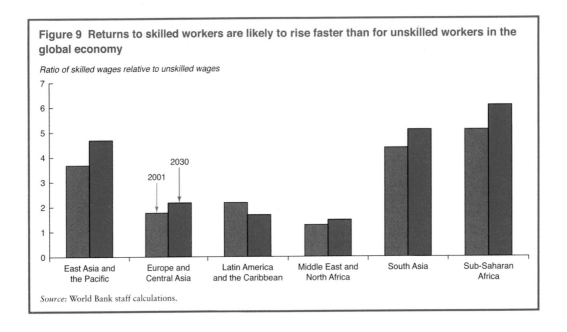

Figure 9 Returns to skilled workers are likely to rise faster than for unskilled workers in the global economy

Ratio of skilled wages relative to unskilled wages

Source: World Bank staff calculations.

including many of the most populous developing countries.

Since in some countries, girls are deprived of schooling, women in these countries are more likely to enter the labor market without skills. This discrimination in effect foredooms them to be denied access to the opportunities afforded by global integration, and means the widening skill premium is likely to affect them disproportionately.

Several policies can lead to more egalitarian countries and a more egalitarian world. Governments can create new opportunities for the poor through additional investments in education. Investments in girls' education can be an important complement to reducing gender discrimination in the workplace. Additional resources for education and other pro-poor investments are likely to become available from a tax base centered on a growing middle-class. Moreover, increasing development assistance for lagging regions and the poorest countries—and making that assistance more effective—is critical. Particularly important are investments to overcome bottlenecks in infrastructure, education, and

health. Finally, increasing the access of poor countries to global markets (and thus raising living standards) by completing the now-suspended Doha Round of world trade negotiations and lowering barriers unilaterally could boost incomes in poor countries. Measures to expand trade should be coupled with aid to overcome supply-side constraints that now weigh down the trade of poor developing countries. Of these constraints, counterproductive domestic policies are often the most binding.

China, India, and global sourcing will put pressure on labor markets, especially for the unskilled

Rapid technological progress, burgeoning trade in goods, and growing international sourcing of services have come together to put new pressures in labor markets, pressures that will only become more acute in the next 25 years (chapter 4). Globalization offers opportunities for export growth and access to a wider range of cheaper imported products that can fuel productivity growth and raise average living standards. But by creating a progressively more integrated global market for labor, it imposes adjustment costs on certain groups within countries, exerting downward pressure on some wages, decreasing job security, and making retraining and relocation necessary. Even though wages of unskilled workers in virtually all countries have risen as productivity has increased with globalization, the unskilled have received wage increases that are lower than those for skilled workers—and they have experienced greater difficulty in sustaining their employment. The projections in this report offer little reason to believe that this will change in the coming decades.

Particularly challenging is the rise of China, India, and other developing countries as manufacturing powerhouses, and, with growing tradability of services, as suppliers of services to the global market. While the qualitative implications of increasing exports of manufactured products from China and India are the same as for the emergence of the Asian tigers more than a decade ago, their sheer size raises the specter of intense export competition. Imports of high-income countries from all developing countries have rise from below 15 percent in the 1970s to nearly 40 today—but more important, their share is expected to rise to more than 65 percent in 2030 (figure 10). This has already exposed workers in rich countries to competition from low-wage countries, a pressure that will only intensify over the next 25 years.

Many developing countries fear that exports from these large new players may swamp their domestic markets, squeeze them out of the global export market, foreclose avenues of diversification in manufactures as a road to higher growth, and soak up the pool of foreign direct investment (FDI). High-income countries worry that if the large emerging economies can readily acquire and master the newest technologies, their exports may soon take over high-tech markets.

Global sourcing of services exerts similar pressures. The transfer to firms in developing

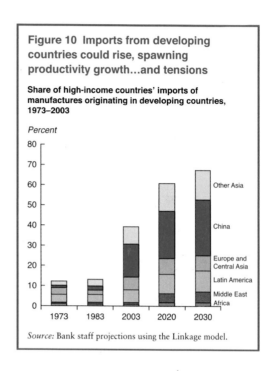

Figure 10 Imports from developing countries could rise, spawning productivity growth...and tensions

Share of high-income countries' imports of manufactures originating in developing countries, 1973–2003

Source: Bank staff projections using the Linkage model.

countries of formerly nontradable service activities imperils white-collar employment in these activities in both high-income countries and advanced developing countries. Services exports have grown by leaps and bounds in many developing countries (figure 11), creating opportunities for productivity gains in both high-income and developing countries— but have led to more rapid job turnover in formerly nontraded white-collar jobs. The global sourcing of such relatively high-paying skilled jobs, in contrast to the displacement of low-skilled manufactures, has the potential to destroy the investments of white-collar workers in firm-specific knowledge.

The analysis in this report suggests that three factors are likely to mitigate these effects in the medium and even the long term.

- First, the growth of the Chinese, Indian, and other emerging markets offers enormous offsetting opportunities for other developing and developed countries to increase exports. As China and India increase their exports, they will have

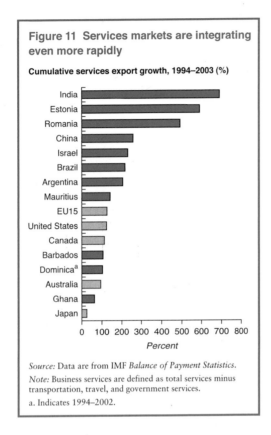

Figure 11 Services markets are integrating even more rapidly

Cumulative services export growth, 1994–2003 (%)

Source: Data are from IMF *Balance of Payment Statistics.*

Note: Business services are defined as total services minus transportation, travel, and government services.

a. Indicates 1994–2002.

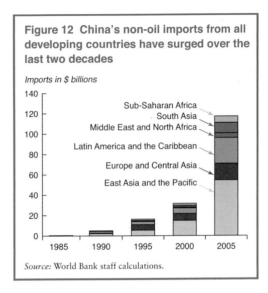

Figure 12 China's non-oil imports from all developing countries have surged over the last two decades

Imports in $ billions

Sub-Saharan Africa
South Asia
Middle East and North Africa
Latin America and the Caribbean
Europe and Central Asia
East Asia and the Pacific

Source: World Bank staff calculations.

to increase imports of intermediate inputs, energy, technology, and investment goods. Driven by Chinese demand, Asia was the principal destination for accelerated export growth for Africa and Latin America during the late 1990s and the early years of this decade (figure 12).

- Second, as exports and domestic living standards rise in these emerging economies, wages (and exchange rates) rise as well, creating space for low-income countries to move into low-skill activities abandoned by producers in the large emerging countries. Wages already have risen in China faster than in many other developing countries, a trend expected to continue (figure 13).

- Third, developing the social institutions that support a dynamic market economy in China and India will take time, providing an opportunity for smaller,

more flexible countries to progress faster in institutional development and for rich countries to continue to lead in productivity-enhancing innovation. The flow of service activities from rich to poor countries, which entails some transfer of know-how, will be slowed to the extent that institutional frameworks fail to protect the ownership of such assets and thus discourage FDI.

Despite this sanguine conclusion, the policy response of countries will determine whether they will be among those able to take advantage of the new opportunities and improve their living standards—or fall behind. Policies to embrace, rather than resist, global integration will lay the foundations for future growth and job creation. Openness to trade and FDI will become ever more critical if the poorest countries are to absorb technologies and know-how from abroad and seize the opportunities created by rising demand from, and production shifts in, China and India. But openness alone will not be sufficient to foster integration in the absence of an attractive investment climate, with sound institutions and policies that allow resources (labor, capital,

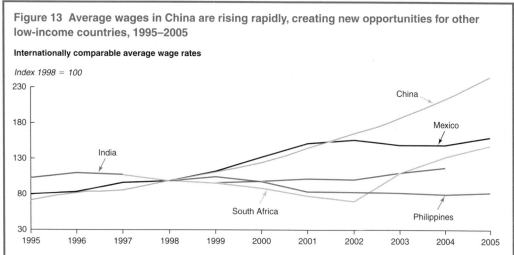

Figure 13 Average wages in China are rising rapidly, creating new opportunities for other low-income countries, 1995–2005

Internationally comparable average wage rates

Index 1998 = 100

Sources: China Statistical Yearbook 2005, People's Bank of China, International Labour Organization (the Philippines, South Africa), IBGE (Brazil), Banco de Mexico, Ministry of Statistics and Programme Implementation (India); exchange rates from IMF *International Financial Statistics*.

Note: Wages are average wages for China, the Philippines, and South Africa, average private sector wages in Brazil, and manufacturing wages for India and Mexico. Wages for 1998–2000 for the Philippines have been estimated using observed wages from 2001 and projecting them backward using GDP per capita growth rates.

and knowledge) to flow from low-return sectors to high-return sectors. Developing knowledge-intensive activities as future drivers of growth will require investing in the institutions and policy frameworks that foster innovation and providing effective education and lifelong learning for all workers.

Even in the most propitious economic environments, policies are needed to cushion the adjustment costs associated with rapidly changing work force demands and involuntary dislocation. Projections indicate that returns to skilled labor will continue to increase more quickly than those to unskilled labor, extending today's natural wage-widening tendencies evident in many, if not most, countries, and underscoring the need for public policies to support workers at the low end of the scale. Together, both volatility and rising wage inequality argue for labor-market policies focused on protecting workers rather than protecting jobs. These trends also argue for creating opportunities for low-income people through educational and infrastructure investments while eschewing subsidies to inefficient activities.

Environmental threats will demand much more multilateral collaboration

The gains from growth and globalization could be undermined by their environmental side effects. Because increases in production magnify cross-border pollution, while improvements in technology make it possible to expand or intensify exploitation of scarce global resources, decisions at the national level are having a growing impact on other countries. International institutions will thus be required to play a larger role in a wide spectrum of issues—all involving global public goods[4]—where exclusive reliance on the decisions of individual governments or the private market can lead to adverse outcomes. As developing countries enlarge their role on the global stage, their integration as full partners in multilateral solutions to global problems will be essential.

Mitigating climate change, containing infectious diseases, and preserving marine fisheries are three prominent global public goods that demonstrate the need for—and benefits of—international policy cooperation.

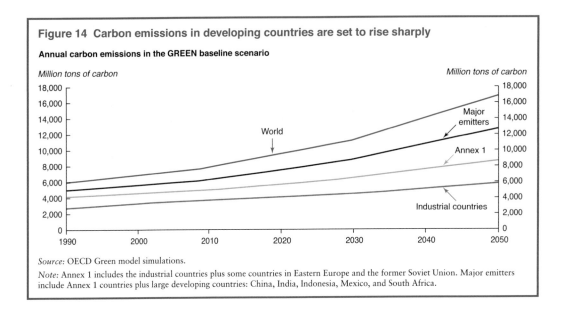

Figure 14 Carbon emissions in developing countries are set to rise sharply

Annual carbon emissions in the GREEN baseline scenario

Source: OECD Green model simulations.

Note: Annex 1 includes the industrial countries plus some countries in Eastern Europe and the former Soviet Union. Major emitters include Annex 1 countries plus large developing countries: China, India, Indonesia, Mexico, and South Africa.

- Rising industrial output means that, based on current trends with existing technologies, annual emissions of greenhouse gasses (GHGs) will increase roughly 50 percent by 2030 and will increase twofold by 2050 (figure 14). This necessarily would sharply increase the concentrations of GHGs in the atmosphere, with substantial risks of detrimental effects on future productivity and—more generally—on human welfare around the globe. The problem is how best to provide energy necessary for growth, while at the same time reducing emissions toward levels that will eventually stabilize atmospheric concentrations. Even in the next decade or two, scientists underscore the possibility—though still low probability—that global warming could cause natural disruptions severe enough to push growth rates perilously below historic trends. While decades will pass before the most severe effects of climate change will begin to be felt, the collective response of today's global leaders is almost certain to have far-reaching

implications for the welfare of future generations.
- Technological progress and rising demand have increased efforts to harvest fish from the open seas, degrading ocean environments and driving some valuable species to near-extinction. Fish catches already have leveled off (see figure 15).

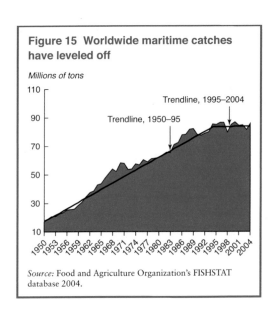

Figure 15 Worldwide maritime catches have leveled off

Source: Food and Agriculture Organization's FISHSTAT database 2004.

Recent scientific calculations project near-complete depletion by 2048 in the absence of collective international efforts to limit fishing to sustainable levels (see Worm and others 2006). Long-standing efforts to limit marine catches to sustainable levels have met with only a few successes, as institutional weaknesses, technical difficulties, and inappropriate incentives, such as fishing subsidies, impede sustainable management.

- The growing interaction of national economies through trade and movements of people, while broadly beneficial, has increased the risk of spreading contagious diseases. HIV/AIDS (human immunodeficiency virus/acquired immune deficiency syndrome) is one example. The severe acute respiratory syndrome (SARS) is another. The most prominent current threat is posed by the avian influenza virus.

These examples of the side effects of globalization—one long-term, one medium-term, and one immediate—pose risks to the progressive expansion of the global economy, and to developing countries in particular. Some of the more catastrophic climate-change scenarios, if they materialize, could undermine the development prospects of whole countries and even regions through their effects on agriculture, water, and ecosystems. According to the United Kingdom government's recent comprehensive analysis, the *Stern Review*, failure to address climate change could—potentially—lead to huge reductions in welfare (cuts in per capita consumption of 5–20 percent), while the cost of stemming the rise in GHG concentrations at a reasonable level could be about 1 percent of annual GDP by 2050 (U.K. 2006). These estimated costs of inaction are substantially higher than previous estimates. The report concludes that an international framework should include emissions trading to encourage energy efficiency, technological cooperation to ensure more rapid adoption, action to reduce deforestation, and assistance to poor developing countries to promote adaptation to permanent climatic changes.

Similarly, failure to contain an epidemic could suddenly brake global commerce, isolate some populations, and impose huge losses on affected developing countries. Unrestrained marine fishing, while less potentially calamitous than climate change or a flu pandemic, could permanently degrade a critical global food source and destroy irreplaceable deep-sea habitats and biodiversity.

Effective multilateral collaboration is needed to ensure that economic growth and poverty reduction proceed without causing irreparable harm to future generations. Developing countries are central to the management of these risks. Though these countries are relatively small contributors to global warming today, the projections in this report imply that soon enough they will become large contributors; moreover, if no action is taken, the standard of living that they could otherwise expect may well be put at risk. Similarly, given the limited supply of medical facilities and nursing care in the developing world, a flu pandemic could have horrific consequences. In many developing countries people depend on fish for an important share of their diet, and the poor would suffer if the price of fish, as well as substitutes, were to skyrocket as supplies dwindled.

The three cases differ in the degree of agreement among policy makers—and, to less degree, scientists—regarding the risks involved. There is a large international consensus on the need to protect against the spread of (selected) contagious diseases, and on the right methods of doing so. The potential for exhausting marine fisheries is well understood, although disagreement remains on the amount of resources to commit, the limits on fishing to impose, and how to allocate access to fisheries. There is an international consensus that human activity is contributing to climate change, and that industrial emissions are directly related to atmospheric concentrations of GHGs, although the precise implications of different levels of GHG concentrations for climate change remain uncertain. While disagreements over the facts in each case have hampered efforts at international cooperation, they have not been the major impediment to progress.

The greatest policy challenge in safeguarding the global commons involves strengthening international agreements and institutions. The World Health Organization has addressed the threat of global pandemics effectively. The basic legal framework is in place to safeguard the sustainability of marine fishing, but is often inadequately enforced by weak institutions. Even more work is required to establish the global institutions capable of reducing the risks from climate change. Discussions aimed at replacing the Kyoto Protocol, which expires in 2012, with a more comprehensive and ambitious agreement are underway within the framework of the United Nations Framework Convention on Climate Change. Meanwhile, it may be useful to start putting in place other vehicles, such as a global system for trading emission permits and better means of monitoring emissions in both high-income and developing countries, so as to allow a rapid implementation of effective policies, once these are agreed. Achieving policy consensus is difficult, but it is now urgent.

The world in 2030

All these developments are pieces of the new burden lying on the shoulders of national policy makers: to manage globalization or risk being run over by it. This requires government policies to ensure that the poor are incorporated into the growth process through pro-poor investments in education, infrastructure, and transfers. Similarly, it requires policies to support and invest in

workers—all the while promoting change, not fighting it.

Deepening economic interdependence also places a new burden on the collective actions of the international community. Several positive responses are clear. First, increasing the amount and effectiveness of development assistance through both multilateral and bilateral institutions can ease the tendency of globalization to produce uneven growth. Second, liberalizing trade in the framework of the World Trade Organization can create new opportunities for poor countries and poor people. The most immediate task is to reactivate the Doha Round and conclude an agreement that lowers trade barriers to the products the world's poor produce, especially agriculture and labor-intensive manufactures. And third, deepening institutional mechanisms to deal with threats to the global commons can ensure that globalization is not undone by its own success—by providing forums in which disagreements about how to provide global public goods in which all nations ultimately have an interest can be resolved. Multilateral cooperation will be even more important in the integrating world of tomorrow than it is today. The way the international community, acting together, manages the process of integration will determine whether the world of 2030 will realize its potential.

Notes

1. Several recent and provocative books deal with these themes or variations, and from quite different perspectives. See, for example, Dervis (2005), Friedman (2005), Goldin and Reinert (2006), Mishkin (2006), Stiglitz (2006), and Wolf (2004) as well as various issues of *Foreign Policy*.

2. This is measured in constant dollars adjusted for purchasing power parity.

3. Today the six countries are Brazil, China, India, Indonesia, the Russian Federation, and, most recently, Mexico. By 2030, Bangladesh, Nigeria, Pakistan, the Philippines, and Vietnam will reach both thresholds. Already today the populations of Bangladesh, Nigeria, and Pakistan exceed 100 million.

4. Examples of global public goods, in addition to protecting the environment, include ensuring global security, keeping the trading system open and nondiscriminatory, and maintaining global financial stability. A useful overview of many of these can be found in Bhargava 2006.

References

Bhargava, Vinay. 2006. *Global Issues for Global Citizens: An Introduction to Key Development Challenges.* Washington, DC: World Bank.

Dervis, Kemal. 2005. *A Better Globalization: Legitimacy, Governance and Reform.* Washington, DC: Center for Global Development.

Friedman, Thomas. 2005. *The World Is Flat: A Brief History of the 21st Century.* New York: Farrar, Straus and Giroux.

Goldin, Ian, and Kenneth Reinert. 2006. *Globalization for Development: Trade, Finance, Aid, Migration, and Policy.* Washington, DC: World Bank.

Mishkin, Frederic S. 2006. *The Next Great Globalization.* Princeton: Princeton University Press.

Stiglitz, Joseph. 2006. *Making Globalization Work.* New York: Norton.

U.K. Government. 2006. *Stern Review: Economics of Climate Change.* London: Government of the United Kingdom.

Wolf, Martin. 2004. *Why Globalization Works.* New Haven: Yale University Press.

Worm, Boris, E. Barbier, N. Beaumont, J. Duffy, C. Folke, B. Halpern, J. Jackson, H. Lotze, F. Micheli, S. Palumbi, E. Sala, K. Selkoe, J. Stachowicz, and R. Watson. 2006. "Impacts of Biodiversity Loss on Ocean Ecosystem Services." *Science* 314 (5800): 787–90.

Abbreviations

ALMP	Active labor market program
APEC	Asia-Pacific Economic Cooperation
BOP	Balance of payments
CGE	Computable general equilibrium (economic models)
CPIA	Country Policy and Institutional Assessment
DDA	Doha Development Agenda
DDP	Development data platform
DPRs	Diversified Payment Rights
EU	European Union
FCC	Federal Communications Commission
FDI	Foreign direct investment
GDP	Gross domestic product
GATT	General Agreement on Tariffs and Trade
GATS	General Agreement on Trade in Services
GHG	Greenhouse gas
GTAP	Global Trade Analysis Project
IMF	International Monetary Fund
IPPC	Intergovernmental Panel on Climate Change
ITA	Information Technology Agreement
MDG	Millennium Development Goal
MNEs	Multinational enterprises
NAFTA	North American Free Trade Agreement
NIEs	Newly industrialized economies
ODA	Official development assistance
OECD	Organisation for Economic Co-operation and Development
OPEC	Organization of the Petroleum Exporting Countries
PPP	Purchasing Power Parity
RTAs	Regional trade agreements
TAA	Trade adjustment assistance
TFP	Total factor productivity
UNCTAD	United Nations Conference on Trade and Development
WHO	World Health Organization
WTO	World Trade Organization

Prospects for the Global Economy

Summary of the medium-term outlook

Despite high commodity prices, rising short-term interest rates, and a bout of financial market volatility, global growth accelerated in the first half of 2006. While there are indications that the pace of the expansion is already slowing, developing economies are projected to expand by 7 percent for the year as a whole, more than twice as fast as high-income countries (3.1 percent), with all developing regions growing by close to or more than 5 percent.

The very fast growth of developing countries over the past five years has been fueled by low interest rates and abundant global liquidity. This has led to rising commodity prices and overheating in some high-income and developing countries. This, in turn, has provoked a tightening of monetary policy that is in part responsible for the slowdown that has already begun. However, in most countries strong productivity growth, due in part to the absorption of China and the former Eastern Bloc countries into the global economy, has checked inflationary pressures.

Limited inflationary pressures and high savings among oil exporters and in Europe (as Europeans prepare to meet the challenges of their aging society) are expected to keep long-term interest rates low. Moreover, improved fundamentals have boosted trend growth rates in many developing countries. Together these factors suggest that, while developing-country growth is projected to slow over the next two years, it should remain robust at 6.1 percent in 2008. Mainly because of the continued expansion of developing economies, global growth will remain robust and this should keep commodity prices high. Nevertheless, increases in supply, combined with demand-side substitution and conservation measures, should allow for some easing of commodity prices, including that of oil.

This positive outlook is subject to significant risks. Past episodes of fast growth and favorable financial conditions have been followed by sharp and largely unanticipated reversals. While stronger fundamentals in most developing countries reduce the likelihood that a hard landing would be as severe as in the past, countries need to take particular care to ensure that their fiscal, monetary, and structural policies are in order so as to minimize the domestic consequences of external shocks—a point driven home by the financial market turbulence observed in the spring of 2006, which affected most sharply those countries whose fundamentals were most out of balance.

A soft landing remains likely, but the global economy has reached a turning point and many factors could result in a more pronounced slowdown. A faster-than-expected weakening of housing markets in high-income countries could generate a much sharper downturn and even recession, with potentially significant effects for developing countries. Much slower growth would likely cause commodity prices to weaken more than already projected, potentially placing many developing countries that have so far avoided current-account problems in difficulty. In addition, demand is expanding unsustainably rapidly in many developing countries. Should efforts to contain growth in these countries fail, their economies could overheat, yielding initially stronger growth outcomes and additional inflation, but a much sharper slowdown later on. An oil-sector supply shock could be similarly disruptive, driving up oil prices even further, while simultaneously slowing growth and weakening the prices of non-oil commodities. Finally, although global imbalances appear to be stabilizing, they remain large. There is a continuing risk that they will be resolved in a more disruptive manner than is assumed in the baseline scenario outlined here.

Global growth surged to 3.9 percent in 2006

Despite oil prices that topped $75 a barrel during the course of the year, world gross domestic product (GDP) growth is estimated to have strengthened in 2006, coming in at 3.9 percent, compared with 3.5 percent in 2005 (table 1.1). To a significant degree, this strong global performance reflects the very rapid expansion in developing economies, which grew by 7 percent—more than twice as fast as high-income countries (3.1 percent). Overall, 38 percent of the increase in global output originated in developing countries, far exceeding their 22 percent share in world GDP. As discussed in chapter 2, continued faster growth among developing countries over the next two decades is expected to lift their share of world output to about 31 percent in 2030.

Very strong growth (10.4 percent) in China played a significant role in the recent strength of developing countries, contributing an expected 0.5 percentage points to global growth. Nevertheless, the pickup was broadly based. Even excluding China and India, developing countries

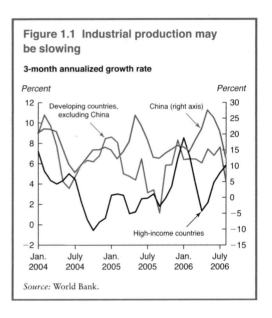

Figure 1.1 Industrial production may be slowing

3-month annualized growth rate

Source: World Bank.

grew 5.5 percent (5 percent for small oil exporters), and all regions are expected to have grown by close to, or more than, 5 percent.

Most of the acceleration in global growth was concentrated in the first half of the year. World industrial production grew 6.7 percent in the first six months of 2006, compared with 4.3 percent in 2005 (figure 1.1). Among developing countries, rates of growth of industrial production eased in the second and third quarters, although this was partially offset by stronger growth among high-income countries. Order books and business sector confidence are strong in both Europe and Japan, suggesting that industrial activity should remain robust for the remainder of the year, while in the United States there are clear signs that industrial production is slowing.

In the United States, the acceleration in industrial output was mirrored by GDP, which began 2006 expanding by a torrid 5.6 percent. However, responding to higher short-term interest rates, residential investment spending has fallen sharply and a cooling housing market has moderated consumer demand.[1] As a result, the economy slowed in the third quarter to a 1.6 percent annualized growth rate, with most of the slowdown restricted to the

Table 1.1 The global outlook in summary

Percentage change from previous year, except interest rates and oil price

	1960–80	1980–2000	2004	2005	Estimate 2006	Forecast 2007	2008	2008–30
Global conditions								
World trade volume	—	5.8	10.4	7.7	9.7	7.5	7.8	
Consumer prices								
G-7 countries[a,b]			1.8	2.2	2.5	2.1	1.7	
United States			2.7	3.4	3.4	2.5	2.1	
Commodity prices (US$)								
Non-oil commodities			17.5	13.4	20.6	−4.5	−8.4	
Oil price (US$ per barrel)[c]			37.7	53.4	64.0	55.9	52.7	
Oil price (percent change)			30.6	41.5	19.9	−12.7	−5.7	
Manufactures unit export value[d]			6.9	0.8	2.4	3.8	0.4	
Interest rates								
$, 6-month (percent)			1.6	3.6	5.4	5.7	5.0	
€, 6-month (percent)			2.1	2.2	3.0	3.6	4.2	
Real GDP growth[e]								
World	4.7	3.0	4.1	3.5	3.9	3.2	3.5	2.9
Memo item: World (PPP weights)[f]			5.2	4.7	5.1	4.5	4.6	
High-income	4.5	2.9	3.3	2.7	3.1	2.4	2.8	2.4
OECD countries			3.2	2.6	3.0	2.3	2.7	
Euro Area			1.7	1.4	2.4	1.9	1.9	
Japan			2.7	2.6	2.9	2.4	2.5	
United States			4.2	3.2	3.2	2.1	3.0	
Non-OECD countries			6.4	5.8	5.3	4.7	4.8	
Developing countries	6.2	3.4	7.2	6.6	7.0	6.4	6.1	4.0
East Asia and the Pacific	5.5	8.5	9.0	9.0	9.2	8.7	8.1	5.1
China			10.1	10.2	10.4	9.6	8.7	
Indonesia			5.1	5.6	5.5	6.2	6.5	
Thailand			6.2	4.5	4.5	4.6	5.0	
Europe and Central Asia	10.7	0.6	7.2	6.0	6.4	5.7	5.5	2.7
Poland			5.3	3.4	5.4	5.1	5.2	
Russian Federation			7.2	6.4	6.8	6.0	5.5	
Turkey			8.9	7.4	6.0	5.0	5.0	
Latin America and the Caribbean	5.5	2.2	6.0	4.5	5.0	4.2	4.0	3.0
Argentina			9.0	9.2	7.7	5.6	4.0	
Brazil			4.9	2.3	3.5	3.4	3.8	
Mexico			4.4	3.0	4.5	3.5	3.5	
Middle East and North Africa	5.9	4.0	4.8	4.4	4.9	4.9	4.8	3.6
Algeria			5.2	5.3	3.0	4.5	4.3	
Egypt, Arab Rep. of			4.2	4.9	5.8	5.6	5.8	
Iran, Islamic Rep. of			5.1	4.4	5.8	5.0	4.7	
South Asia	3.7	5.4	8.0	8.1	8.2	7.5	7.0	4.7
Bangladesh			6.3	6.2	6.7	6.2	6.5	
India			8.5	8.5	8.7	7.7	7.2	
Pakistan			6.4	7.8	6.6	7.0	6.5	
Sub-Saharan Africa	4.4	2.2	5.2	5.5	5.3	5.3	5.4	3.3
Kenya			4.9	5.8	4.9	5.1	4.9	
Nigeria			6.5	6.2	4.8	5.1	5.4	
South Africa			4.5	4.9	4.6	3.9	4.3	
Memorandum items								
Developing countries								
excluding transition countries	5.1	4.2	7.3	6.8	7.0	6.4	6.1	
excluding China and India	6.6	2.3	6.1	5.1	5.5	4.9	4.9	

Source: World Bank.

Note: PPP = purchasing power parity.
a. Canada, France, Germany, Italy, Japan, the United Kingdom, and the United States.
b. In local currency, aggregated using 2000 GDP weights.
c. Simple average of Dubai, Brent, and West Texas Intermediate.
d. Unit value index of manufactured exports from major economies, expressed in U.S. dollars.
e. GDP in 2000 constant dollars; 2000 prices and market exchange rates.
f. GDP measured at 2000 PPP weights.

housing sector. Importantly profits, non-residential investment, and consumption remain robust and inflation and unemployment low. As a consequence, although growth is expected to remain subdued, it should not decline in the fourth quarter and the strong first quarter means that output for the year as a whole is expected to increase 3.2 percent.

In high-income Europe, following several years of weakness, growth also accelerated in the first half of 2006. GDP expanded by about 3.3 percent in the first two quarters of the year, as private consumption and investment spending took over from exports as the main drivers of the recovery. Growth slowed to a 2 percent pace in the third quarter, with growth in France having stalled as investment expenditures turned negative and exports weakened. However, both in France and in the rest of Europe, consumer demand remained robust and consumer and business surveys suggest that economic activity should be robust in the fourth quarter, leading to an estimated 2.5 percent increase in GDP for the year as a whole (2.4 percent for the Euro Area).

In Japan, the acceleration in output that began in 2005 has continued, with GDP

estimated to have expanded by 2.9 percent in 2006. A slowdown in exports contributed to weaker growth in the second quarter of the year, but growth rebounded in the third quarter led by a surge in investment spending. As of August, exports were up 11 percent from a year earlier, partly reflecting a 25.6 percent increase in sales to China, where import volumes have strengthened markedly.

Developing economies grew 7 percent in 2006. Much stronger European and continued robust Japanese growth, combined with low real interest rates and interest rate spreads, made for robust activity among the world's developing economies, which are expected to have expanded by 7 percent in 2006. This represents the fourth consecutive year that their growth rates have exceeded 5 percent.

The expansion was particularly robust in China and India, where output is estimated to have increased by 10.4 and 8.7 percent, respectively. But the strong performance was broadly based, with all developing regions growing by close to or by more than 5 percent (figure 1.2). Despite further substantial increases in the price of oil during the first half of the year, growth among the remaining oil-importing developing countries actually

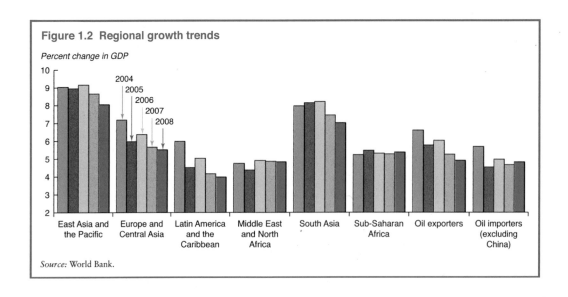

Figure 1.2 Regional growth trends

Percent change in GDP

Source: World Bank.

strengthened and is expected to come in at 5 percent for the year as a whole.

Developing economies to outperform high-income countries in 2007–08

High oil prices are expected to continue to weigh on growth in industrialized countries. The slowdown that they and higher interest rates (working through residential investment and household consumption) have already initiated in the United States is projected to continue into the first half of 2007 before an expected relaxation of monetary policy permits the economy to pick up. Overall, GDP in the United States is projected to increase 2.1 percent in 2007 and 3 percent in 2008. Weaker domestic demand is expected to be reflected in slower import growth and should result in a decline in the trade and current account deficits of the United States, with the latter coming in around 5.5 percent of GDP in 2008.

Continued accommodative macroeconomic policy and pent-up investment demand following several years of very weak growth should maintain the pace of the expansion in most European countries, without exacerbating underlying inflationary pressures. However, a planned 3 percent increase in the German value-added tax (VAT) is projected to slow demand in that country in 2007, with knock-on effects elsewhere in the continent. The higher VAT can also be expected to prompt a one-time increase in inflation, although its effect should be attenuated by slower growth. Overall, GDP in high-income Europe is projected to slow to about 2.1 percent (1.9 percent for the Euro Area) in 2007 and 2008.

In Japan, vigorous growth in developing East Asia, renewed consumer and business confidence, and reduced drag from consolidation are positive factors expected to maintain growth at about 2.5 percent in 2007 and 2008. The recent return to positive inflation is projected to persist, allowing short-term interest rates to gradually rise to around 2 percent by the end of 2008. At the same time, domestic demand is expected to firm as unemployment

declines toward 3.5 percent of the labor force. As a result, the current account surplus should decline to about 3 percent of GDP in 2008.

In most developing regions, high oil prices, rising interest rates, and the maturation of the business cycle are expected to restrain growth in 2007–08. As a group, however, low- and middle-income countries should again outperform high-income economies by a wide margin—and this strong performance will continue to be a critical driver of global growth. Administrative restrictions on investment and slower export growth are expected to bring Chinese growth down to a more sustainable 8.7 percent by 2008. Higher interest rates and some further fiscal tightening are expected to slow the expansion in India to about 7.2 percent over the same period, helping to unwind some of the inflationary tensions that have built up in that country.

Prospects for the *remaining oil importers* are varied. Many, particularly in Eastern and Central Europe, are overheating and have entered a phase of policy tightening. These countries are expected to decelerate. Others, including Brazil and Mexico, are projected to accelerate or enjoy high but stable growth rates as they continue to benefit from a favorable external climate, including low long-term real interest rates and interest-rate spreads. Overall, developing-country oil importers, excluding China and India, are projected to enjoy broadly stable growth of about 4.8 percent in 2007–08.

For oil exporters (and other large commodity exporters) strong revenue inflows should continue to fuel robust domestic demand growth despite lower prices and less rapid increases in global demand for commodities, resulting in rapid growth of both imports and the noncommodity sectors of these economies. Overall, the pace of the expansion in developing-country oil exporters is expected to decline from 6 percent this year to 4.9 percent in 2008, as capacity constraints slow growth in the resource sector and a rising share of demand is met by imports.

Regional outlooks

More detailed descriptions of economic developments in developing regions, including regional forecast summaries and country-specific forecasts, are available online at http://www.worldbank.org/globaloutlook. Country-specific forecasts are reported in the appendix.

East Asia and the Pacific[2]

An emerging growth pole.

The economies of the East Asia and Pacific region continued to expand at robust rates in 2006, with regional GDP growth expected to accelerate to 9.2 percent in 2006 from 9 percent the year before. In China, continued rapid investment growth, in conjunction with an unexpected surge in exports as new capacity came on stream, led to a 10.7 percent year-over-year increase in GDP over the first three quarters. The overall contribution of the external sector to GDP growth was up because, even though import growth accelerated, increased output from China's import-competing sectors prevented import volumes from expanding as rapidly as exports. Investment spending has been spurred by growth in credit and the money supply as well as strong profits. Concerns about excessive investment creating potential overcapacity in specific sectors led the authorities to reinforce administrative measures aimed at containing investment growth.

The expansion in the rest of the region remains robust. A rebound in global high-tech demand and stronger import demand from China prompted an acceleration in exports that began in the second half of 2005 and continued into 2006. Vietnam's growth is expected to reach 8 percent, backed by across-the-board strength in exports, domestic consumption, and investment. In Indonesia, growth slowed in the first six months of 2006 following a substantial reduction of fuel subsidies and monetary tightening in the latter part of 2005. Activity appears to be picking up now, with monthly indicators suggesting a strong rebound in domestic consumption and investment in the third quarter. For the year as a whole, GDP is expected to increase by about 5.5 percent. Growth in Malaysia and the Philippines is also expected to come in at around 5.5 percent, while in Thailand it is expected to reach only about 4.5 percent, because, despite strong export growth, consumption and investment have been depressed by high oil prices, rising interest rates, and continued political uncertainty.

High oil prices and rapid growth have raised inflation in the region, prompting a general tightening of monetary policies during 2005. As a result, both headline and core inflation are now easing in most of the larger economies in the region. Regional equity markets were subject to the general correction affecting many emerging markets during May–June 2006. However, spreads on bonds remain low, and equity markets began recovering in August, suggesting that the earlier correction did not represent a reassessment of the region's economic fundamentals.

Growth is expected to moderate only somewhat. In China, investment growth and domestic demand are projected to remain robust. However, with investment at some 50 percent of GDP, more forceful policy action may be needed to keep credit and investment growth in check. Moreover, the country's large and persistent current account surplus suggests the need, over the longer term, to promote a more consumption-oriented pattern of growth. In Indonesia, the ongoing recovery in growth is projected to continue, with GDP expanding by 6.5 percent in 2008.

Economic pressures for the revaluation of developing Asian currencies are likely to intensify. In addition to reducing global imbalances, revaluation would also reduce inflationary pressures, improve domestic macroeconomic management capabilities, steady asset markets, and improve living standards for local populations.

Finally, the region remains susceptible to outside risks, including a worsening of the avian influenza epidemic—either through wider effects on domestic animals or because transmission to (or between) humans becomes more efficient (World Bank 2006).

Europe and Central Asia

Oil exporters and European Union integration underpin strong growth.

Economic activity in the Europe and Central Asia region is estimated to have increased by 6.4 percent in 2006, up from 6 percent in 2005. This acceleration comes despite slower growth in Turkey, where a significant tightening of monetary policy following this spring's financial market turbulence is projected to reduce growth from 7.4 percent last year to 6 percent in 2006.

Faster growth in Europe and low real interest rates have helped to maintain growth at high levels elsewhere in the region. Among the largest economies, growth in the Russian Federation is estimated to have picked up to 6.8 percent in 2006, supported by high oil prices. Improved incomes and activity in the mining sector boosted growth in Ukraine to an estimated 6 percent pace in 2006 versus 2.6 percent in 2005, while rising wages and falling unemployment increased growth in Poland from 3.4 percent in 2005 to an estimated 5.4 percent in 2006. Elsewhere, rebounding demand in industrial Europe, coupled with rapidly growing demand from regional oil exporters, notably Russia, bolstered exports among smaller oil importers, whose economies grew 6.1 percent, up from 5.8 percent in 2005. Higher oil prices and the coming on stream of oil projects lifted the GDP growth among oil exporters to 7.3 percent.

The pace of demand growth in many countries in the region continues to exceed supply and, as a result, 13 countries have current-account deficits in excess of 5 percent of GDP, and inflation is rising in 12. Strong capital inflows, predominantly in the form of foreign direct investment (FDI), coupled with extremely rapid domestic credit expansion, are at the root of excess demand in several countries (the Baltic countries, Bulgaria, Hungary, Romania, the Republic of Serbia, and Turkey). Although FDI flows are less easily reversed than portfolio and equity investments and are more likely to be associated with physical investments, more volatile capital flows are also increasing, and a substantial portion of the FDI is going into the banking sector, where it may be more volatile than in other sectors. While such flows are likely to remain strong, motivated by investment opportunities associated with European Union (EU) integration, the real-side disequilibrium that these inflows are provoking may make these countries sensitive to a change in investor sentiment. Indeed, as events in the spring of 2006 highlighted, countries with large current account deficits are particularly vulnerable—especially those with pegged exchange rates (Hungary and Latvia) and currency boards (Bulgaria, Estonia, Lithuania)—because sharp reductions in inflows may require very large and disruptive real-side adjustments. In Hungary, a budget deficit of close to 10 percent of GDP poses further challenges.

Excess demand has also contributed to inflationary pressures and a tightening of monetary policy. Overheating remains a risk both there and in Azerbaijan, the Baltic states, Belarus, Bulgaria, the Czech Republic, Kazakhstan, Romania, Russia, the Slovak Republic, Turkey, and Ukraine. Other factors contributing to the slower growth include a slump in manufacturing activity (especially mining) in Armenia, a marked deceleration of export growth in Latvia, and rising capacity constraints combined with declining competitiveness in Belarus. Growth is continuing at a modest pace in the former Yugoslav Republic of Macedonia (4 percent in 2006), where domestic demand is recovering slowly following a period of fiscal consolidation and violent conflict in 2001.

Growth in the region is expected to slow somewhat over the next two years, coming in at about 5.5 percent in 2008. Slower growth in industrialized Europe and higher short-term interest rates are expected to cause regional export growth to decline for both oil importers and oil exporters. In the case of the latter, domestic demand growth is expected to ease but remain strong, because, although oil revenues will decline, they will remain high. Lower prices will contribute to the expected slowdown in oil exporters' GDP growth from 7.3 percent in 2006 to 6.2 percent in 2008. In addition, it will also slow demand for exports from regional oil importers, which, in combination with weaker export demand from Germany and the United States in 2007, is expected to reduce their GDP growth to about 5.2 percent in 2008.

The combination of rising inflation and elevated current account deficits poses a persistent challenge for regional policy makers. To the extent that the contractionary influence of higher interest rates continues to be offset by capital inflows, further fiscal tightening may be unavoidable—even if it means pushing government balances into surplus in some countries. For many countries in the Commonwealth of Independent States, future prospects will be dependent on continued strong demand from Russia. Prospects for the poorer countries in the region will also depend on the extent to which these countries are able to strengthen domestic institutions so as to sustain high growth rates.

Latin America and the Caribbean
Improved performance but still under-performing.

Economic activity in Latin America and the Caribbean has picked up and GDP is estimated to have increased by 5 percent in 2006. The faster growth reflects favorable international financial conditions, strong commodity prices, and a relaxation of monetary policy in Brazil and Mexico, two of the region's largest economies.

In Mexico, GDP accelerated sharply in the first half of 2006, growing 5.5 and 4.7 percent (year-over-year) in the first two quarters as lower interest rates boosted domestic demand and construction activity. Stronger sales of cars to the United States and oil exports also contributed. Brazil, too, benefited from a more relaxed monetary policy stance, although real interest rates remain high at 11 percent. GDP accelerated to about 5.2 percent in the first

quarter, and although it slowed in the second quarter, growth for the year as a whole is expected at 3.5 percent.

In contrast, demand in Argentina and República Bolivariana de Venezuela, which had been expanding at unsustainable rates, slowed. Nevertheless, demand in each country remains very strong, and GDP is projected to expand by 7.7 and 8.5 percent, respectively, well beyond potential. Unsurprisingly in these conditions, inflation has picked up and now exceeds 10 percent in both countries. In each case, this surge occurred despite price freezes in a number of sectors that are hurting sectoral investment and supply (inflation of uncontrolled goods and services is running at 16 percent in Argentina). The rapid expansion of demand in República Bolivariana de Venezuela has been fueled by ballooning government transfers. The growth in supply has been concentrated in the non-oil sector, as reductions in investment by the government's oil company and by private oil firms (discouraged by high taxes and royalties and antibusiness policies) have caused oil production to decline.

Other countries in the region are also growing relatively rapidly. In Chile, a waning investment boom and higher imports have contributed to a slight slowing of growth in 2006. In Central America, growth is expected to accelerate in most countries in 2006, boosted by exports and investments associated with free trade agreements (Costa Rica, the Dominican Republic, El Salvador, Guatemala, Honduras, and Nicaragua), strong remittance inflows, increased agricultural production due to better weather, and post-hurricane investment spurts (El Salvador). In the Caribbean, growth in Jamaica and the Dominican Republic has picked up, reflecting foreign investments in the tourism and mining sectors (Jamaica) and a growth rebound following the 2003 currency crisis (Dominican Republic). Uncertainty over the results of elections in Nicaragua has hurt investor confidence, partially offsetting the beneficial effects of a relatively buoyant agricultural sector and the writing off of $975 million in debt.

Electoral uncertainty and concerns about the future path of U.S. interest-rate policy contributed to volatility in financial markets in the spring of 2006. The currencies of a number of countries depreciated, following earlier appreciations in some cases (Brazil and Colombia). Stock markets also underwent a major correction. However, the improved fiscal stance and reduced indebtedness of many countries meant that the region was not particularly affected by this episode. Risk premia, after rising somewhat, have once again declined and currently are just 20 points above their historical minimums.

Prospects for countries in the region reflect a number of offsetting influences. The projected slowdown in global activity is expected to moderate demand for commodities, resulting in a modest decline in their prices and slower volume growth. As a result, while revenues from this sector will remain elevated, they will decline, as will their contribution to the growth of domestic demand in commodity-exporting countries. Overall, GDP among commodity exporters (excluding República Bolivariana de Venezuela, see below) is projected to slow to about 3.8 percent in 2008. Commodity importers also will feel the effect of slower global and U.S. growth. In the case of Mexico, the anticipated cycle in the United States is expected to be reflected in slower exports and growth. For most commodity importers the slowdown is expected to be less marked (from 4.6 to 4 percent, excluding Mexico), in part because many countries have considerable spare capacity.

As indicated above, unsustainably rapid growth in Argentina and República Bolivariana de Venezuela, boosted by a dangerously expansionary fiscal and monetary policy, has already strained capacity in these countries. In the baseline projection, this unsustainable demand stimulus is expected to continue, with domestic demand increasing at double-digit rates. The inability of domestic supply to keep pace means that GDP will grow less quickly, declining to 4 percent in Argentina and 5.5 in República Bolivariana de Venezuela in 2008,

as imports and inflation rise rapidly. Unless significant policy restraint is introduced in the near future, these developments will result in a deterioration of current account balances, leading to an erosion of Argentina's current account surplus to about 0.9 percent of GDP and a much-reduced surplus of 7.6 percent in República Bolivariana de Venezuela by 2008. The longer the two countries' aggressively expansionary macroeconomic policies keep demand growing in excess of supply, the sharper and more disruptive will be the recession required to reestablish equilibrium.

Middle East and North Africa[3]
Riding the oil boom.

High oil prices and strong oil demand continue to be key drivers for the developing economies of the Middle East and North Africa.[4] Overall, these countries' GDP increased by an estimated 4.9 percent in 2006, the fastest pace in some four years. Among developing-country oil exporters, growth is expected to reach 4.9 percent, up from last year's 4.7 percent.

Reflecting strong investment and remittance flows from high-income oil exporters and the Euro Area, output among regional oil importers has strengthened. For the year as a whole, output is expected to come in at 5 percent. Strong Suez Canal revenues in the Arab Republic of Egypt, better crops following a drought in the Maghreb, hefty tourism receipts throughout the region, and a pickup in European demand are additional factors explaining this relative strength. An exception is Lebanon, where the war and political uncertainty weighed heavily on activity in the first three quarters. While reconstruction efforts are expected to give a fillip to growth toward the end of the year and into 2007/08, Lebanese GDP is expected to contract by about 5.5 percent in 2006.

Generous fuel subsidies are pervasive throughout the region. For countries that do not benefit from large oil revenues, these subsidies have strained fiscal balances. Countries such as Egypt, Jordan, Morocco, and Tunisia saw fiscal deficits pick up within a range of 0.5 to 2 percent of GDP over the course of 2005, in part linked to oil subsidies. Since then, Jordan reduced subsidy expenditures by 59 percent in the second quarter. In Egypt, these and other steps have helped reduce the consolidated government deficit from 9.1 percent in fiscal year 2005 to 6.5 percent in 2006. Nevertheless, such subsidies remain important in the region and threaten the fiscal sustainability of some countries. They also impede adjustment, although their balance of payments consequences have been mitigated by strong remittance and investment flows.

Rising oil prices during the first eight months of 2006 bolstered revenues of the major exporting countries in the region. Oil-related revenues were up 33 percent in the Islamic Republic of Iran and 30 percent in Algeria, and many governments boosted spending. Measures included substantial investments to augment oil-sector capacity, infrastructure projects, and other non-oil-sector investments in human and social capital, all of which should help boost future supply. However, a significant share of the additional spending, such as substantial civil service wage increases in several countries and increased spending on fuel subsidies, merely stoke demand and may prove difficult to sustain should oil prices decline further.

The surge in oil revenue and government spending among oil exporters has yet to generate substantial inflationary pressures. However, inflation is up in a number of countries, including Egypt, Jordan, Oman, and Tunisia. In the Islamic Republic of Iran, although inflation is declining, it still exceeds 10 percent. Moreover, regional stock and housing markets have appreciated enormously throughout the region. While local markets lost as much as 25–33 percent of their value in the May–June 2006 market correction, valuations remain high, and there are concerns about increased leverage in private sector balance sheets (IMF 2006).

High oil prices are expected to continue feeding domestic demand in oil-producing countries, causing imports to continue rising rapidly, even as growth of export revenue slows. Capacity constraints and strong import growth is projected to slow GDP growth among developing oil-exporting countries to 4.7 percent in 2007 and 4.5 percent in 2008. Their current account surpluses should decline from 11 percent of GDP in 2005 to about 5.3 percent of GDP in 2008. In the oil-importing economies, growth is expected to gradually pick up from 5 percent in 2006 to 5.3 percent in 2008, reflecting assumed improvements in crop conditions, stronger European growth and continued robust investment and remittance inflows from regional oil exporters.

South Asia
Rapid growth is pushing against capacity constraints.

Despite a tightening of both monetary and fiscal policy, real interest rates remain low, and growth in the South Asia region picked up to an estimated 8.2 percent in 2006. Direct and indirect subsidization of consumer energy prices have helped contain inflationary pressures but are keeping government deficits high and contributing to strong domestic demand.

With the exception of Nepal, which is only now emerging from political strife, growth throughout the region was strong in the first half of the year. In India, GDP increased by 9.3 percent in the first quarter, supported by strong industrial and service-sector production, while in Pakistan industrial production was up 12 percent. Partly reflecting improved sales of textiles and clothing after the restrictions on Chinese exports were reintroduced, merchandise exports in the region increased more than 30 percent in the first half of 2006 (on a year-over-year basis). A good start to the monsoon season suggests that agricultural output (and incomes) will be strong also. Overall, regional GDP is projected to increase by 8.2 percent for the year, or 6.4 percent if the two largest economies (India and Pakistan) are excluded. In the Maldives a rebound in tourism and post-tsunami reconstruction efforts are expected to contribute to a 19 percent expansion in GDP, while a new hydroelectric plant may help boost output in Bhutan by 10 percent.

Notwithstanding robust export demand and a first-quarter current account surplus in India, strong domestic demand is expected to result in a small further deterioration of regional current account deficits in 2006, particularly in Pakistan, where increased government spending (tied to the Kashmir earthquake and ongoing military expenditures) is projected to push the current account deficit to 3.9 percent of GDP. In contrast, strong remittance flows and robust exports are expected to propel the current account of Bangladesh toward balance.

Rapid growth and the relatively expansionary stance of fiscal and monetary policies in the region have provoked a rise in inflation. Successive hikes in policy rates in India have increased interest rates, but higher inflation means that real rates were negative in August. In Pakistan, tighter monetary policy brought inflation down to 6.2 percent in April, but it picked up again and was 8.1 percent in October. Ample domestic and international liquidity has also contributed to substantial increases in local stock market valuations (up about 45 percent in both India and Pakistan). Throughout the region, higher international oil prices have yet to be fully passed through to consumers, placing a strain on government accounts and implying significant additional inflationary pressure in the pipeline.

Despite tighter monetary and fiscal policies in India and Pakistan, and weaker export demand from the United States, low real interest rates, strong international capital inflows, and high government deficits are expected to keep domestic demand expanding rapidly. When added to the delayed pass-through of higher oil prices, this should maintain inflation pressures in the region and sustain rapid import growth. As a result, the external sector is expected to make a significant negative contribution to growth, and regional GDP growth should moderate to about 7 percent by 2008. Owing to continued strong growth, the region's current account deficit is projected to deteriorate further despite falling oil and non-oil commodity prices.

Sub-Saharan Africa
Another good year.

GDP in Sub-Saharan Africa expanded by an estimated 5.3 percent in 2006. Oil-exporting economies are expected to grow 6.9 percent in 2006, about the same as last year. Among oil importers (excluding South Africa), the expansion has been sustained, and growth is estimated to have increased 4.7 percent.

South Africa, the region's largest economy, expanded at growth rates above its potential for the third consecutive year. Household expenditure has been exceptionally strong, benefiting from low nominal interest rates, rising real incomes, and wealth effects. As a result, domestic demand and output growth in the manufacturing and service sectors have been very strong. Despite a large positive terms-of-trade shock as metal prices soared, the external sector's contribution to growth was negative, owing to strong import growth fueled by robust household consumption and the stronger rand. The surge in imports caused the current account deficit to deteriorate to 6.2 percent of GDP in the first half of 2006, which contributed to the sharp depreciation of the rand during May–June. Overall, the rand has depreciated 20 percent on a trade-weighted basis since the beginning of the year, and this has contributed to inflationary pressures. Nevertheless, consumer confidence and demand remain at historically high levels.

In Nigeria, the region's second-largest economy, attacks on oil infrastructure slowed growth, as oil production fell by 25 percent during the first five months of 2006. It has since picked up but remains down 6.5 percent from a year ago. Nevertheless, the non-oil economy is expanding rapidly (up 12.8 percent in the second quarter) and supplementary budgetary spending is expected to bolster growth, perhaps leading to a buildup in inflationary pressures.

The regional expansion is broadly based, with a third of the countries experiencing growth in excess of 5 percent. Among oil exporters, growth was particularly strong in Angola (16.9 percent), Sudan (11.8 percent), and Mauritania (17.9 percent), which began oil production in February. In addition to a strong expansion in oil production, buoyant domestic demand is projected to spur rapid growth in the non-oil sectors of most oil-exporting countries.

The aggregate stability and strength of growth among the region's oil importers reflects divergent patterns. A number of countries that recently emerged from conflict are experiencing very strong growth rates (Burundi, the Democratic Republic of Congo, Liberia, and Sierra Leone). Elsewhere strong international metal and mineral prices are generating revenue streams and prompting additional investments, which have contributed to strong growth. However, drought-related crop failure, high fuel costs, and energy rationing have resulted in weaker results for East African oil-importing countries. In addition, although both the numbers and the intensity of conflicts in Africa have subsided, the risks associated with political turmoil remain high and are undermining growth in Chad, Côte d'Ivoire, the Democratic Republic of Congo, Eritrea, Lesotho, the Seychelles, Somalia, Swaziland, and Zimbabwe.

Current accounts have come under pressure in several oil-importing economies in the region, although higher commodity prices and increased official and private transfers have helped contain the deterioration. The most notable decline in the current account came in South Africa, where an initial appreciation of the rand boosted imports and dampened exports, driving the current account deficit to 6.2 percent of GDP in the first half of 2006. Debt relief from Paris Club creditors under the Multilateral Debt Relief Initiative should reduce debt-servicing cost by substantial margins in several countries, which, in combination with the expected easing in oil prices, is projected to provide some relief to current accounts over the projection period.

Inflation is up in a number of countries because of higher international oil prices and seasonal and drought-induced increases in food prices. In the case of South Africa these factors have been exacerbated by excessive domestic demand. Inflation there is projected to exceed 6 percent, above the upper limit set by the Reserve Bank. In Nigeria, year-over-year inflation remains high but is declining rapidly, owing in part to the appreciation of the naira.

GDP growth for the region as a whole is projected to remain broadly stable, coming in at about 5.4 percent in 2008, with weaker growth in South Africa offsetting a pickup among oil exporters and stable growth among smaller oil importers. In South Africa, higher interest rates are projected to overcome strong mining and manufacturing growth in 2007, before the latter forces generate a recovery in 2008. In the baseline projection, emerging electrical shortages due to insufficient generating capacity are expected to constrain growth in Burundi, Kenya, Malawi, Rwanda, Tanzania, Uganda, and Zambia, but improved rainfall in East and West Africa should help replenish hydroelectric dams, thereby improving electrical supply and manufacturing output. An end to drought should also boost agricultural output and domestic incomes, although weaker agricultural prices and high fertilizer prices may negatively affect agricultural crops and could represent a drag on growth.

Financial markets
Some signs of emerging inflationary pressures
High oil prices and the rapid pace of global growth have contributed to a gradual increase in median inflation among developing countries, from about 1.7 percent in 2002 to 3.2 percent during the third quarter of 2006 (figure 1.3). The acceleration was not consistent across the globe. Inflation has been stable or declining in half of the developing regions over the past year, falling to an average level of 5.3 in the third quarter. In contrast, in

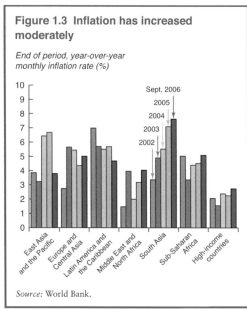

Figure 1.3 Inflation has increased moderately

End of period, year-over-year monthly inflation rate (%)

Source: World Bank.

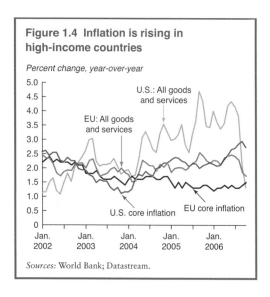

Figure 1.4 Inflation is rising in high-income countries

Percent change, year-over-year

Sources: World Bank; Datastream.

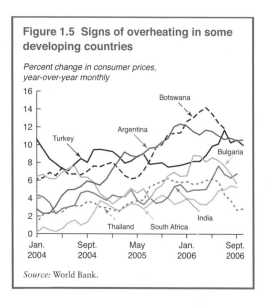

Figure 1.5 Signs of overheating in some developing countries

Percent change in consumer prices, year-over-year monthly

Source: World Bank.

high-income countries it rose from 1.3 to 2.7 percent before falling to 1.4 percent in October as oil prices declined.

Most of the increase appears to reflect the direct impact of higher oil prices. Until recently, core inflation in high-income countries has been relatively stable (figure 1.4). Core inflation in the United States was rising much of the year, but it has been easing recently and stood at 2.7 percent in October 2006. In many developing countries, inflation first picked up in response to higher oil prices, but it has since declined, reflecting both solid productivity growth and the impact of more credible monetary policies that have helped anchor inflation expectations.

However, developments in a number of low- and middle-income countries run counter to these general trends. In these countries, inflation is rising, reflecting the combined influence of several years of above-trend growth and steep increases in global commodity prices (figure 1.5). Higher inflation would appear to reflect overheating in Argentina and several countries in Europe and Central Asia, the Middle East, North Africa, and South Asia.

Inflation has also picked up in Sub-Saharan Africa. There, in addition to several years of

rapid growth, high food prices following successive droughts are playing a role. The concern is that if an inflationary spiral develops, because the credibility of monetary policy is not yet well entrenched, it could have serious consequences for macroeconomic stability and affect the ability of those economies to sustain the strong growth of the past several years.

In countries such as India, regional imbalances in the distribution of growth contribute to difficulties because inflationary pressures and capacity constraints are concentrated in rapidly growing cities and co-exist with considerable slack elsewhere in the economy.

Rising short-term interest rates

Higher inflation throughout the developed world has translated into rising short-term interest rates and the gradual removal of the monetary policy stimulus that has characterized the past several years. Although policy rates are increasing throughout the developed world, the process is most advanced in the United States, while at relatively early stages in Europe and Japan. Many developing countries also have acted to restrain credit expansion and contain inflation. Policy rates have risen sharply and appear to be slowing inflation in Bulgaria, Indonesia, Thailand, and Turkey. In others (Argentina, India, Pakistan) the tightening cycle is less advanced and, as a result, real interest rates remain low and inflation high.

Long-term interest rates (see figure 1.8) remain low and the yield curve flat, suggesting that markets are confident that the monetary authorities will be successful in containing inflationary expectations—a contention supported by the spread between inflation-indexed

bonds and nonindexed bonds, which has remained relatively stable at around 2.5 percentage points.

More volatile financial conditions for developing countries

Despite high short-term interest rates, financial conditions for developing countries remain highly favorable. Several years of very loose monetary policy, an ample supply of global savings (due to aging populations in Europe and rapidly increasing incomes among oil exporters), business-sector consolidation in the United States and Asia, and high savings rates in the fastest-growing sectors of the world economy have combined to buoy global liquidity. This helps explain the low long-term bond yields and the search for yield that has boosted the flow of private capital to developing countries. That flow, in combination with improved fundamentals, has brought interest spreads down to historically low levels.[5]

However, conditions have become more volatile (figure 1.6). The transition from a slow and widely anticipated tightening of U.S. monetary policy toward a more data-driven approach increased uncertainty in financial markets during the second quarter of 2006. Initially,

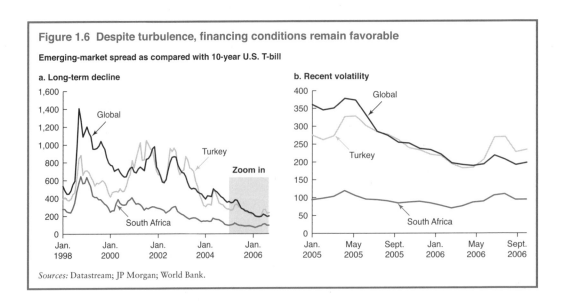

Figure 1.6 Despite turbulence, financing conditions remain favorable

Emerging-market spread as compared with 10-year U.S. T-bill

a. Long-term decline

b. Recent volatility

Sources: Datastream; JP Morgan; World Bank.

the prospect that dollar-denominated returns would no longer be rising resulted in a surge of flows into emerging market stocks, commodity markets, and currencies. As values of these assets rose, the market reassessed long-term prospects, resulting in a substantial correction.

For the most part, this volatility failed to disrupt growth, and net private capital flows to developing countries are expected to rival last year's record highs (figure 1.7). However, in some countries, particularly those with large current account deficits (such as South Africa and Turkey) and relatively heavy debt burdens, the correction was more severe and is expected to result in much slower growth in 2006 and 2007, as the real side of these economies adjusts to weaker financial inflows.

The combination of several years of low interest rates has increased global liquidity substantially (see earlier versions of *Global Economic Prospects* and *Global Development Finance*). Despite the increase in short-term interest rates, the persistence of low long-term interest rates, due in part to high savings rates among oil-exporting countries, has kept global liquidity abundant. The OECD (2006) estimates that depending on the measure employed, high-income liquidity exceeds historical norms by between 15 and 17 percent (figure 1.8). In the baseline, although interest rates are projected to rise somewhat, liquidity is projected to remain relatively abundant and continue to be a factor behind strong developing-country growth.

Global imbalances are stabilizing

The imbalances in global spending patterns that have characterized the world economy over the past five years began to show signs of

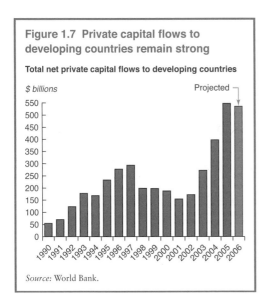

Figure 1.7 Private capital flows to developing countries remain strong

Total net private capital flows to developing countries

Source: World Bank.

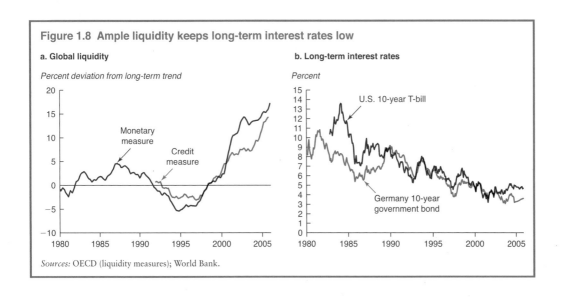

Figure 1.8 Ample liquidity keeps long-term interest rates low

a. Global liquidity

b. Long-term interest rates

Sources: OECD (liquidity measures); World Bank.

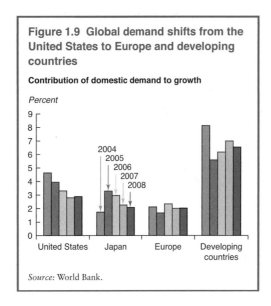

Figure 1.9 Global demand shifts from the United States to Europe and developing countries

Contribution of domestic demand to growth

Source: World Bank.

An important component of this story has been the slowing in U.S. domestic demand and the simultaneous increase in developing-country domestic demand (figure 1.9). This rotation of growth, plus the lagged effect of past depreciations, contributed to a 13 per-cent increase in the volume of U.S. exports in the first half of 2006, almost twice the growth rate for imports (7 percent). Nevertheless, the U.S. trade balance declined further, in part because of very high oil prices during the first eight months of the year. The subsequent decline in oil prices should reduce the value of U.S. imports, resulting in an improved trade balance during the fourth quarter. Because of this strong volume performance and declining oil prices, global imbalances are not expected to deteriorate significantly over the projection period—in stark contrast to the recent past, when they deteriorated sharply each year (figure 1.10).

stabilizing in 2006. Weaker domestic demand in the United States, the acceleration of eco-nomic activity in Europe, and continued recovery in Japan helped to stabilize the U.S. current account deficit, which is expected to come in at about $850 billion, roughly the same share of GDP as in 2005.

Exchange rates are broadly stable
Despite the substantial financial flows required to finance the U.S. current account deficit, the dollar has remained broadly stable against major currencies during 2006—up about 2 percent

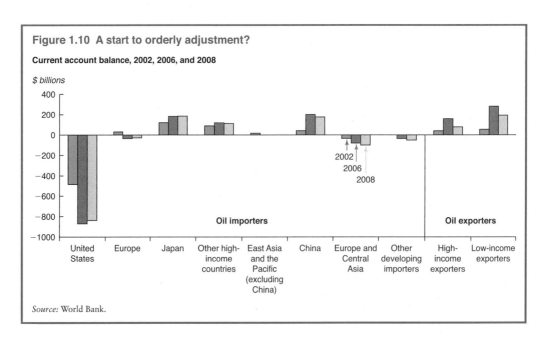

Figure 1.10 A start to orderly adjustment?

Current account balance, 2002, 2006, and 2008

Source: World Bank.

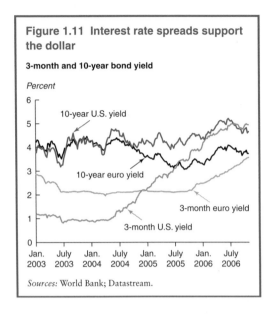

Figure 1.11 Interest rate spreads support the dollar

3-month and 10-year bond yield

Percent

10-year U.S. yield

10-year euro yield

3-month euro yield

3-month U.S. yield

Sources: World Bank; Datastream.

against the yen and depreciating by about 5 percent against the euro. In real-effective terms it has lost only 2 percent of its value. In part, this relative strength is explained because many of those countries running large current account

surpluses (China and several oil exporters) have resisted upward pressure on their currencies with respect to the dollar.

The depreciation against the euro occurred despite a substantial premium currently being offered on both short- and long-term U.S. bonds (see figure 1.11). With U.S. monetary policy nearing or at the end of its tightening cycle, these differences are expected to narrow. In the baseline forecast, this narrowing and slower growth in the United States are projected to cause the dollar to depreciate by a further 5 percent against the euro in each of 2007 and 2008, which should further facilitate the unwinding of global imbalances.

However, should downward pressures be more severe, the depreciation could be stronger or interest rates in the U.S. may have to rise further (see the section on risks).

Currency developments for the remaining developing countries were dominated by the reemergence of financial market volatility in the first half of 2006 (figure 1.12). Downward pressure on the dollar toward the end of 2005 and at the beginning of 2006 saw the currencies

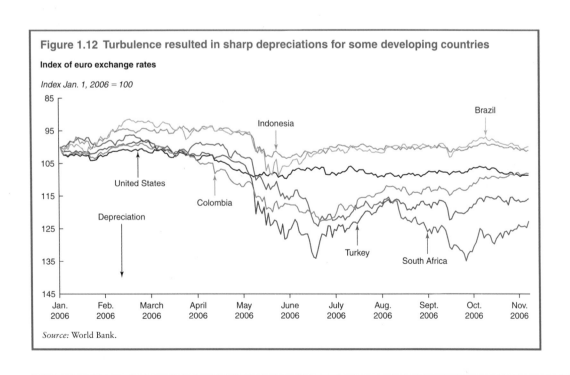

Figure 1.12 Turbulence resulted in sharp depreciations for some developing countries

Index of euro exchange rates

Index Jan. 1, 2006 = 100

Indonesia

Brazil

United States

Colombia

Depreciation

Turkey

South Africa

Source: World Bank.

of many developing countries appreciate strongly. For many countries that appreciation was reversed in May and June as investors re-assessed their positions. While disruptive, and provoking a sharp rise in interest rates in some countries, the volatility was short-lived and in most cases merely served to unwind earlier appreciations that had been out of step with countries' underlying fundamentals.

World trade

Stronger industrial activity was mirrored in world trade. Merchandise trade growth grew 11 percent during the first eight months of 2006, up from 6 percent the year before. Most of the acceleration occurred in China, Japan, and the United States and was concentrated in the first quarter. Weaker U.S. consumption and investment demand, and growing domestic demand in the developing world combined with the lagged effects of past depreciations to boost U.S. export volumes by an annualized rate of 13 percent in the first half of 2006, compared with 7 percent in the last half of 2005. Measured on the same basis and over the same period, exports in Japan

and China increased by 10 and 30 percent, respectively. Trade flows weakened in the second quarter but show signs of picking up once again in the third quarter.

Over the medium term, growth in merchandise trade volumes is projected to ease to about 9 percent, in line with slower global GDP growth. The recent relative strength of U.S. export volumes is projected to persist (figure 1.13). Those volumes are projected to rise by more than 9 percent in 2007 and 2008 as the cumulative effect of past and expected future depreciations increase the international competitiveness of U.S. products. For developing countries, weaker U.S. import demand should be partially compensated by stronger demand from Europe, but, overall, developing-country export growth is projected to slow from an estimated 12.2 percent in 2006 to 10 percent in 2008, even as countries continue to increase their market share.

Trade outlook—continued expansion
Developing-country trade reached a landmark in 2006. Following 25 years of solid growth, the value of China's exports overtook those of the United States, making China the world's

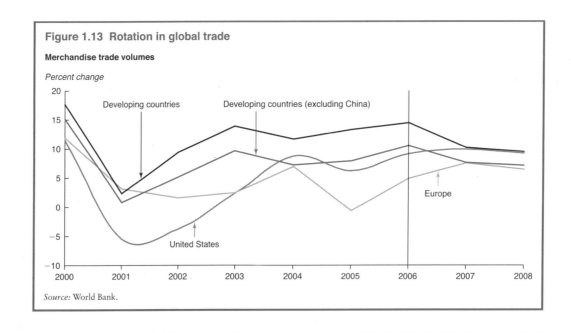

Figure 1.13 Rotation in global trade

Merchandise trade volumes

Percent change

Developing countries

Developing countries (excluding China)

Europe

United States

Source: World Bank.

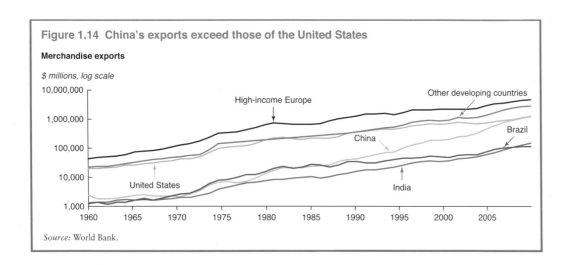

Figure 1.14 China's exports exceed those of the United States

Merchandise exports

$ millions, log scale

Source: World Bank.

second-largest exporter. Increasing exports in other developing countries, notably Brazil and India, have further increased the weight of developing countries in world trade (figure 1.14). Over the long term, as these trends continue, the share of developing countries in world trade is projected to reach some 45 percent by 2030 (see chapter 2).

While the phenomenal success that China has enjoyed in expanding its world market share since the introduction of market reforms has increased competitive pressure on both developing and developed countries (see chapter 4), Chinese imports also have grown very rapidly (up 477 percent in value terms over the past decade), and China is a growing destination for the exports of other developing countries (Dimaranan, Ianchovichina, and Martin 2006). Sixty-three percent of China's imports are intermediate goods, 31 percent in the form of parts and components. Overall, 79 percent of China's imports are sourced from developing countries. Partly as a result of China's rapid increase in imports, the value of other developing countries' non-oil exports has risen by 153 percent, and their global market share has increased by 2.3 percentage points.

In addition to these direct effects, the expansion of developing-country commerce means that these countries are increasingly

becoming privileged destinations for FDI, both as an export platform for multinational companies and because they represent the fastest-growing market segment.

The extent to which other developing countries will be able to take advantage of the expected continued strong growth of China and India (see chapter 2) will depend on their ability to expand exports. This requires eliminating the anti-export bias in their incentive framework, reducing costs of produced services, and improving customs procedures that undermine competitiveness. It also requires investments in transport systems to reduce transit times (Newfarmer 2005) and in other forms of infrastructure, such as electrical generators so as to facilitate the expansion of capacity. In addition, as discussed in chapter 4, countries need to reduce rigidities in product, labor, and financial markets so that firms can react with agility to new opportunities to expand the range of products they produce and sell.

On the multilateral front, the suspension of talks on the Doha Round in July 2006 poses significant challenges. Weakened confidence in the multilateral system could lead to trade disputes, rising protectionist sentiment, and trade diversion arising from proliferating bilateral and regional trade agreements. To capitalize on progress already made in the Doha Round, such as the offer to end agricultural export subsidies by 2013, it is important that parties return to the negotiating table with the necessary flexibility to conclude an ambitious deal.

Commodity markets

Strong global growth, and especially the rapid expansion of output in developing countries, is largely responsible for the run-up in commodity prices over the past several years. Improvements in technology and new discoveries are expected to preclude any major disruptions to growth over the long term (see chapter 2), but increased demand for energy and other natural resources may generate significant environmental pressures (see chapter 5).

Non-oil commodities
Metals and minerals take off.

While oil-price increases have received the bulk of media attention, the rise in the price of metals and minerals during the course of 2006 has been much stronger (figure 1.15). Continued rapid growth in global output, speculative demand, low stocks, and numerous supply disruptions have pushed metals and minerals prices up by some 48 percent since the beginning of 2006. Agricultural prices also posted

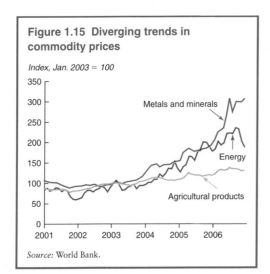

Figure 1.15 Diverging trends in commodity prices

Index, Jan. 2003 = 100

Source: World Bank.

gains in dollar terms, up 7 percent by the beginning of November, but were broadly stable if expressed in euros.

The biggest increases in metals prices were those of copper (up 64 percent), zinc (up 110 percent), and nickel (up 144 percent). High prices and continued strong demand have prompted significant destocking of copper and nickel in China—suggesting that prices may remain high even as supply disruptions ease. Nevertheless, stocks of other products such as aluminum, lead, and tin have recovered, and their prices have eased or stabilized, suggesting that a peak in the metals market may have been reached.

Financial sector activity also played a big role in price developments during 2006. Recent estimates suggest that more than $19 billion flowed into retail commodity funds during the first eight months of the year, when prices were rising. More recently, these flows have reversed sharply. Outflows from exchange-trade commodities totaled $12 billion during the first two weeks of September, when prices were falling (Norman and Shen 2006).

With global growth projected to slow somewhat but remain strong, the overall metals and minerals index is expected to decline in 2007 and 2008, but remain elevated.

Moderate gains in agricultural prices.

Agricultural prices have risen an estimated 11 percent in 2006 compared with 2005, reflecting a weaker dollar and the impact of higher energy and fertilizer prices. Other factors, such as crop-specific supply shortfalls and droughts, low carryover stocks, and strong demand growth contributed to the price increases. Real agricultural prices have increased 35 percent since their cyclical lows in 2001.[6] This increase is well below the increases in oils and metals, in part because agricultural demand is less sensitive than industrial demand to economic growth, and because agricultural supply responds more quickly to increased demand and prices.

High energy prices have contributed directly to the surge in the price of some agricultural commodities that are either used as energy crops (biofuels) or compete with synthetic products made from petroleum. The price of sugar, which is being diverted to ethanol production for automotive fuel, more than doubled from late 2004 until early 2006, while that of natural rubber (a substitute for synthetics produced from petroleum products) rose 60 percent between December and June 2006. The price of maize, which is used as the feedstock for ethanol production in the United States, is expected to rise 8 percent in 2006.

High energy costs also have contributed to increasing agricultural prices by raising the cost of fertilizers. This prompts an increase in the cost of production of agricultural goods, but also induces a reduction in yields because farmers use less fertilizer. As a result, energy- and fertilizer-intensive crops such as grains are expected to show reduced yields and higher prices in 2006. These factors, plus low carry-over stocks and poor harvests in several important producing areas, are projected to push wheat prices up 28 percent in 2006 and even higher next year before production increases enough to rebuild stocks. In the case of rice, higher costs and reduced yields are expected to boost prices by 8 percent.

In contrast, prices of fats and oils are expected to be 5 percent lower, because markets appear to be well supplied. Drought in Kenya is keeping tea prices high (up 14 percent from 2005). Robust coffee prices are expected to average 18 percent higher in 2006, a continuation of the price increases that began in 2002. Timber prices are projected to increase 14 percent owing to strong demand, particularly from China, while international supplies remain limited because of controlled logging and export quotas.

Prospects for agricultural prices in 2007 are mixed, with grains and oilseeds higher, while beverages and raw materials prices will be lower. Overall, agricultural prices are expected to decline by about 1 percent in 2007 and 2.8 percent in 2008 as higher prices begin to moderate demand and induce increased supply. Should oil prices rise further, agricultural prices could also strengthen because of

cost-push factors and because higher energy prices make biofuel more economically viable, generating an additional source of demand for products such as maize and sugar cane. Already, 20 percent of the U.S. maize crop and 50 percent of the Brazilian sugar cane crop are used to produce ethanol. Should this trend continue, demand for other commodities, especially grains, will increase to substitute for crops used for biofuels.

Oil market
Rising supply and slow demand cause prices to ease.

After showing signs of stabilizing in the fall of 2005, the price of oil shot up once again in the first half of 2006 (figure 1.16). Prices have since declined and were below $60 in late November—bringing the price of oil below the level at which it began the year. Expressed in euros, the price has declined 7 percent since the beginning of the year and stands at about the same level as before the hurricanes of last summer and fall.

High prices slowed the growth in demand for oil despite the acceleration in economic activity in 2006. Oil demand increased by 0.5 million barrels per day (mbpd) in the three quarters of 2006, compared with 3.2 mbpd

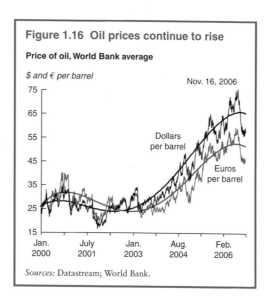

Figure 1.16 Oil prices continue to rise

Price of oil, World Bank average

Sources: Datastream; World Bank.

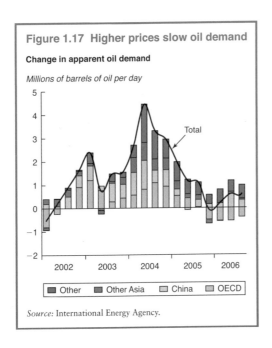

Figure 1.17 Higher prices slow oil demand

Change in apparent oil demand

Millions of barrels of oil per day

Source: International Energy Agency.

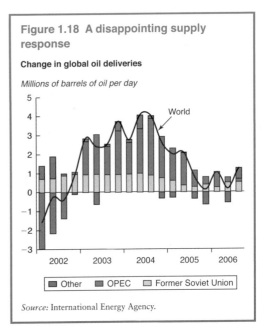

Figure 1.18 A disappointing supply response

Change in global oil deliveries

Millions of barrels of oil per day

Source: International Energy Agency.

in 2004 (figure 1.17). Demand among OECD countries actually declined by about 0.5 mbpd, and although demand in developing countries continued to increase by just under 1 mbpd, this was much slower than the increases recorded in 2003 and 2004. Econometric estimates suggest that had prices remain unchanged, oil demand would have increased by some 2–2.5 mbpd.[7]

Notwithstanding some three years of higher prices since the recent upward trend in oil prices began in early 2003, and the arrival on stream of new fields in Africa and elsewhere, aggregate non-OPEC (Organization of Petroleum Exporting Countries) oil supply was relatively slow to increase (figure 1.18).[8] Most recently, there has been a pickup in deliveries from the former Soviet Union and other non-OPEC sources, with the result that supply rose by 0.8 mbpd during the first nine months of 2006.

Despite the limited responsiveness of supply in the first half of 2006, growth of final oil demand was even weaker, and as a result inventories and global spare capacity increased somewhat (figure 1.19). However, spare capacity remains low (at just 3 mbpd), leaving

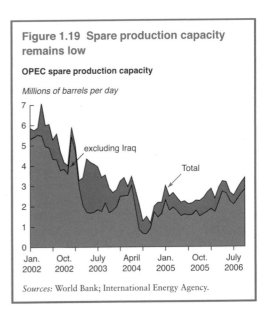

Figure 1.19 Spare production capacity remains low

OPEC spare production capacity

Millions of barrels per day

Sources: World Bank; International Energy Agency.

the world vulnerable to a significant supply shock (see the section on risks below). It is that vulnerability, plus concerns about future Middle East supplies, that provides the best explanation for the increase in oil prices observed during the spring and early summer.

Financial market speculation also likely played a role, especially in the first half of 2006, when a weakening dollar coincided with a significant run-up in emerging-market assets (among them the prices of some commodities), followed by a significant reversal in May and June. An indication of the importance that such forces may have played was the 30 percent fall in U.S. wholesale gasoline prices in August following the decision of Goldman Sachs to reduce the share of gasoline in its commodity indexes.

Over the near term, limited spare capacity and strong global growth suggest that oil prices will remain volatile. However, high prices should continue to moderate demand growth, while investments in new capacity already in the works are projected to increase output by about 15 mbpd by 2010, implying a 3 mbpd annual increase—well above expected increases in demand of between 1.5 and 2 mbpd annually. As a result, the price of oil is projected to decline modestly over the next two years, reaching an average level of $53 in 2008.

Downside risks predominate

A number of factors suggest the soft-landing scenario outlined above as the most likely outcome. Tighter monetary policy in high-income and a number of developing countries is slowing growth in those countries and should alleviate inflationary tensions. Meanwhile, still-low long-term interest rates and emerging-market spreads are expected to maintain favorable external conditions for developing countries, allowing them to grow at a slower but still robust pace of 6 percent.

While the soft landing is the most likely scenario, the global economy is at a turning point following several years of very strong growth—and such periods are fraught with risk. Indeed, as described in chapter 2, the last century began under similarly auspicious circumstances, characterized by an extended period of strong growth buoyed by technological change and ample liquidity. Rather than continuing forward as anticipated by leading economists at that time, the world plunged into the Great Depression. Thus, while much in the current environment is reassuring, a note of caution is merited.

The remainder of this chapter explores four main risks to the outlook.

Overheating could provoke a sharper slowdown

The world economy and, in particular, developing countries have been expanding at near-record rates over the past few years. So far, the inflationary effects of fast growth have been largely confined to the markets for global goods, such as commodity markets. The inflationary response at the national level has been remarkably muted. Improved monetary policy has succeeded in anchoring inflationary expectations at low levels, while competitive pressures induced by the entry into the global marketplace of the countries of the former Soviet Bloc and China, with their relatively high skills and low wages (see chapter 4), have boosted global productivity and kept the pricing power of firms in check. In the baseline projection these factors are assumed to continue to hold sway, while tightening of monetary policy and slower growth in countries where signs of a pickup of inflation have emerged are assumed to prevent inflation from rising further.

However, long-term interest rates are projected to remain low and international financial conditions relatively loose. As a result, global growth is expected to remain strong and further inflationary pressures may yet emerge. In particular, given projected levels of global demand, further price hikes in commodity markets cannot be ruled out.

Moreover, should measures to slow growth in several key developing economies (Argentina, China, India, and many European and Central Asian economies) fail, as they have to varying degrees in recent years, inflation in those countries could pick up. That could lead to a more marked slowdown later on, either because of a much sharper tightening of policy or because of endogenous factors such as a loss of external competitiveness.

A housing market crisis could cause a recession

Growth in the United States and several other high-income countries[9] has been bolstered over the past several years by rapidly rising housing prices. In the United States, rising housing prices increased household wealth by 14.6 percent of GDP between 2000 and mid-2006. The pickup in housing valuations was spurred by low interest rates and the introduction of new interest-only variable-rate mortgages. Higher valuations in turn generated a boom in home-equity withdrawals, which boosted consumer spending and residential investment.

As short-term interest rates rose, demand for variable-rate mortgages dried up, and the rate of increase of housing prices cooled substantially[10] (figure 1.20). By the third quarter of 2006, the contribution to growth of residential investment had swung from a strong 0.5 percentage points in 2005 to a strongly negative −1.1 percentage points. That swing, plus the end of the additional consumption demand generated by home-equity withdrawals, underlies the slowdown in U.S.

growth observed in the second and third quarters, which is projected to continue into the first half of 2007.

The risk is that the slowdown may be much more severe, either because house prices decline more sharply or because the indirect effects of the anticipated 9.3 percent decline in residential investment has wider impacts on the rest of the economy. A much steeper slowdown following a sharp decline in housing prices[11] could accentuate the decline in residential investment, driving it down by as much as 20 percent from its level in mid-2006, while the reversal in the trend to household wealth could cut as much as 1 percent from growth in personal consumption. On the plus side, Australia, the Netherlands, and the United Kingdom have all observed substantial decelerations and even declines in housing prices without recession (see OECD 2006 for more details).

Such a shock could prompt a recession in the United States, with growth slowing to as little as −0.2 percent of GDP in 2007 and 2.7 percent in 2008. Slower growth would weaken inflationary pressure in the United States, allowing for lower interest rates in the course of 2007, helping to spur a recovery toward the end of 2008.

Such a U.S. recession would affect developing economies through three channels: reduced exports to the United States, lower commodity and oil prices owing to slower global growth, and more favorable financing conditions. The balance of these forces would vary across regions and countries. Regions with the tightest trade ties, such as Latin America and East Asia, would suffer the greatest negative impact. The combination of weaker domestic demand in the United States and less marked slowdowns elsewhere would help to reduce global imbalances.

A disorderly unwinding of global imbalances remains possible

The rotation of growth away from the United States and increased consumption demand in Europe and the developing world are welcome developments that mark the beginning of an

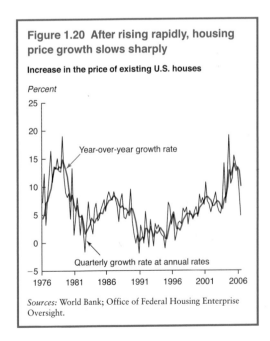

Figure 1.20 After rising rapidly, housing price growth slows sharply

Increase in the price of existing U.S. houses

Percent

Year-over-year growth rate

Quarterly growth rate at annual rates

Sources: World Bank; Office of Federal Housing Enterprise Oversight.

orderly adjustment of global imbalances. In particular, they signal an end to a troubling trend of rapidly rising U.S. current account deficits. While relative stability should reduce financial market concerns, the financing of the gap in the U.S. current account, at 6.5 percent of GDP, remains a challenge. Such a deficit is not sustainable over the long run. Each year, it augments the net international debtor position of the Unites States and its financing costs. The United States has already become the world's largest net debtor, with the value of foreign-owned U.S. assets exceeding that of U.S.-owned foreign assets by 21 percent of U.S. GDP in 2005. In addition, the balance of the interest payments on these debts was −$8.8 billion during the first three quarters of 2006, the first time in some 30 years that the United States paid out more than it received on internationally held financial assets. Unless savings in the United States increase substantially, even assuming further improvements in the trade balance, the net asset position of the United States will continue to deteriorate, potentially reaching between 65 and 48 percent of GDP by 2015 (Higgins, Klitgaard, and Tille 2005).

As long as the trend toward real-side adjustment (increased savings in the United States and increased domestic demand and imports abroad) continues, the resolution of global imbalances should proceed in an orderly manner, even though it may take several years beyond our medium-term projection period (2006–08) before the U.S. current account deficit reaches sustainable levels. That said, the medium-term risk to the global economy remains that adjustment will occur not on the real side but on the financial side, either because investors rapidly lose confidence in the dollar—thereby provoking a currency crisis, much higher U.S. interest rates, and financial market turmoil—or because they increasingly demand higher interest rates on U.S.-denominated assets. While this would help increase U.S. savings and therefore hasten adjustment compared with an orderly adjustment, it would do so at greater cost in terms of growth in high- and low-income

countries, both because of its dampening effect on investment and potential output and because a rapid adjustment would inevitably result in greater short-term misallocations of resources.

In the baseline scenario, financial sector adjustments are assumed to be benign. The expected narrowing of short-term interest-rate differentials is projected to prompt investors to continue shifting assets into euros, placing downward pressure on the dollar. This should be offset somewhat by a tendency for U.S. long-term rates to rise relative to those in Europe. While the relative depreciation of the dollar should be smooth, the dollar could weaken quickly if investors were to react nervously. That would provoke much higher U.S. interest rates and a sharper slowdown. Such a risk can be reduced by collaborative policy actions to increase public and private savings in the United States, strengthen demand in the rest of the world, and provide for more flexible management of exchange rates.

However adjustment occurs—be it a sharp adjustment led by the financial sector or a more gradual real-side adjustment—the process is likely to be relatively short-lived in the context of the 25-year projections reported in chapter 2. Although a disorderly adjustment would imply up to two years of substantially below-trend growth for the global economy, this would have minimal effects on the average long-term growth rates reported there.

An oil-sector supply shock could disrupt growth

With spare production capacity at only 3 mbpd, the world oil market remains vulnerable to a supply shock. Because no country can easily ramp up production, if output in a producing country were to fall significantly, world supply would fall, provoking a decline in economic activity.

Simulations presented in last year's *Global Economic Prospects* (World Bank 2006) suggest that a negative supply shock of two million barrels per day that caused oil prices to double for a period of three months and then remained at $80 for nine further months would cause global output to shrink initially by about 1.5 percent of GDP, as compared with the baseline scenario.[12] Inflation would pick up rapidly, and on average the current account position of oil-importing countries would deteriorate by about 1.1 percent of GDP. The impact would be more severe in large low-income and middle-income countries, both because of higher energy intensities and a greater inflationary impact, which requires a larger contraction to eliminate.

While the impact in terms of GDP for current-account-constrained low-income countries is smaller, it is more severe in terms of domestic consumption and investment. Such countries have limited access to international capital markets and their capacity to pay higher oil prices is limited by their export revenues. If these revenues are stable, such countries would be forced to reduce domestic demand and non-oil imports in order to pay their higher oil bill. As a consequence, when oil prices rise, oil consumption remains relatively constant in terms of volume (being generally inelastic in the short run), but the oil bill rises. To compensate, non-oil imports and domestic demand tend to decline in unison—leaving GDP relatively unchanged. For these countries, the terms-of-trade-shock of the initial increase in oil prices is estimated at 4.1 percent of their GDP, which would translate into a 2.7 percent decline in domestic demand, with potentially serious impacts on poverty.

Notes

1. Housing prices, which had been rising by 10 percent a year, declined at a 1.2 percent annualized pace in the third quarter of 2006. As a result, increases in household wealth slowed, and home-equity withdrawals, which boosted GDP growth by as much as 1 percentage point during 2000–05, turned negative. At the same time, the contribution of residential investment to GDP growth fell from 0.5 percentage points in 2005 to −0.7 and −1.1 percentage points in the second and third quarters of 2006, respectively.

2. In addition to the *Prospects for the Global Economy* Web site (www.worldbank.org/outlook) the World Bank's East Asia update provides more detailed information on recent developments and prospects for the East Asia and Pacific region (www.worldbank.org/eapupdate/).

3. In addition to the *Prospects for the Global Economy* Web site (www.worldbank.org/globaloutlook), which describes regional developments in more detail, the World Bank's Middle East and North Africa Web site, *Economic Developments and Prospects* (www.worldbank.org/mena) provides an even more comprehensive discussion of recent economic developments, projections, and policy priorities.

4. For the purposes of this report the developing countries of the region are Algeria, the Arab Republic of Egypt, Jordan, the Islamic Republic of Iran, Morocco, Oman, the Syrian Arab Republic, Tunisia, and the Republic of Yemen. Djibouti, Iraq, Lebanon, and Libya were excluded from the projections because of a lack of data. Important regional players such as Bahrain, Kuwait, Qatar, Saudi Arabia, and the United Arab Emirates are included in the high-income aggregate.

5. As of early November 2006, the credit ratings of 34 emerging market countries have been upgraded. Only 3 have been downgraded.

6. Agricultural prices are quoted in U.S. dollars and therefore have been deflated by U.S. inflation.

7. The short-term price elasticity of oil demand is estimated at between −0.01 and −0.2 percent (Burger 2005), implying that immediately following a 100 percent increase in oil prices, such as observed between 2002 and 2005, oil demand would be expected to decelerate by between 1 and 20 percent. Long-term elasticities are larger (between −0.2 and −0.6 percent), implying that the negative effect of higher prices over the past few years will continue to be felt.

8. In the three years following both the 1973 and 1979 oil price hikes, non-OPEC and non–former Soviet Union oil producers increased their output by some 3.5 million barrels per day. In contrast, since 2002, production from these sources has actually declined. OPEC did increase its deliveries during 2004 by drawing down its spare capacity, but so far investment to increase that capacity has been limited.

9. Robust increases in residential investment and rising housing prices have been important drivers of growth in recent years in Canada, Denmark, France, Ireland, Spain, and the United States.

10. As of September 2006 the median sales price of houses in the United States had fallen 1.2 percent (year-over-year). This measure, produced by the National Association of Realtors, differs from data provided by the OFHEO, which are reproduced in figure 1.20, because it does not control for the quality of the houses being sold.

11. Girouard and others (2006) estimate that U.S. housing prices have a more than 75 percent chance of falling if interest rates rise by 100 basis points.

12. Studies suggest that the likelihood of such a disruption occurring over the next several years may be as high as 70 percent (Beccue and Huntington 2005).

References

Beccue, Phillip C., and Hillard G. Huntington. 2005. "An Assessment of Oil Market Disruption Risks." *Final Report of Energy Modelling Forum & SR 8, Energy Modeling Forum*. October.

Burger, Victor. 2005. "House Prices in Developing Countries." World Bank, Washington, DC.

Dimaranan, Betina, Elena Ianchovichina, and Will Martin. 2006. "Competing with Giants: Who Wins, Who Loses?" In *Dancing with Giants: China, India, and the Global Economy*, ed. L. Alan Winters and Shahid Yusuf. Washington, DC, and Singapore: World Bank and Institute of Policy Studies.

Girouard, N. and others. 2006. "Recent House Price Developments: The Role of Fundamentals." OECD Economics Department Working Papers No. 475.

Higgins, Mathew, Thomas Klitgaard, and Cedric Tille. 2005. "The Implications of Rising U.S. International Liabilities." *Current Economic Issues* (Federal Reserve Bank of New York) 11(5).

Institute for International Finance. 2006. *Capital Flows to Emerging Markets*.

IMF (International Monetary Fund). 2006. *World Economic Outlook: Financial Systems and Economic Cycles*. Washington, DC: IMF.

Newfarmer, Richard. 2005. *Trade, Doha, and Development: A Window into the Issues*. Washington, DC: World Bank.

Norman, John, and Lei Shen. 2006. "How Much Money Has Left Commodities?" *Global Currency & Commodity Strategy* (JP Morgan, New York), September 18.

OECD (Organisation for Economic Co-operation and Development). 2006. *OECD Economic Outlook* 80 (December).

World Bank. 2006. *Global Development Finance 2006: The Development Potential of Surging Capital Flows*. Washington, DC: World Bank.

2

The Coming Globalization

The emergence of China, India, and the former communist-bloc countries implies that the greater part of the earth's population is now engaged, at least potentially, in the global economy. There are no historical antecedents for this development.

—Ben Bernanke, August 25, 2006

The last quarter-century, a time of unprecedented integration for the global economy, has witnessed a dramatic rise in standards of living around the world. The fall in transport and communications costs and in barriers to trade paved the way for productivity increases associated with the integration of emerging economies into global markets. Add to these forces the fall of the Berlin Wall, the subsequent lifting of the Iron Curtain, and the progressive opening of the Chinese and then Indian economies—and the stage was set for a new wave of globalization of production, trade, and finance. While the associated benefits have been uneven over time and space, average living standards across the globe have risen markedly. Global income has doubled since 1980, 450 million have been lifted out of extreme poverty since 1990,[1] and life expectancy in developing countries is now 65 on average.[2]

Can one expect these trends to continue for the next 25 years, and if so, what are the key forces that will shape the world economy of tomorrow? If globalization continues, what does it mean for the allocation of production

in rich and poor countries? What role will developing countries play—particularly those with large populations, such as China and India? Finally, what forces could accelerate growth and globalization—and what could derail them?

This chapter explores these questions by developing a long-term scenario to 2030. The scenario is anchored in trends already evident in recent years, and ones unlikely to be reversed in the foreseeable future. The results describe a world in which the gross domestic product (GDP) in high-income countries is slated to nearly double and that of developing countries will more than triple. The progressive expansions of China and India, the two largest developing economies and home to half the people of the developing world, are projected to drive the process. Their impact on the global economy will be increasingly felt as their exports and energy use, for example, approach the levels of the European Union and the United States.

The next 25 years will undoubtedly bring significant surprises that cause outcomes to deviate from the central scenario in this chapter. Growth in parts of the world may well be more robust than projected in this scenario; other countries or whole regions may face serious setbacks. Many imaginable and even unimaginable shocks are likely. The chapter thus includes a discussion of various shocks that could propel growth higher than the central scenario—or depress growth with impacts devastating for poverty. Developing countries are likely to become more important in the global economy. Indeed, if anything, the likelihood that developing countries will experience higher rises in incomes seems greater than the downside risks. Although outcomes less sanguine than those in the central scenario are possible, it would take disruptive sea-changes in the structure of the global economy to produce large deviations from, much less reversals of, the strong underlying trends toward globalization.

The good performance of developing countries in recent years, combined with the still huge difference in relative incomes between developing and developed countries, points to strong potential growth across the developing world during the coming decades. The central scenario assumes a world growth rate of 2 percent per capita, slightly faster—by 0.6 points per capita—than in 1980–2005. It also assumes growth in developing countries of 3.1 percent, compared with 1.9 percent in developed countries. There are two main reasons for this. First, policy is far better on average today in developing countries than it was earlier, say in 1980. Second, technological dissemination is far faster. Indeed, in the last five years, growth in developing countries has been substantially *higher*—4.6 percent—than the assumption of 3.1 percent in the central scenario.

Whatever the scenario, challenges will abound. Growth and integration will lead to structural changes, job losses, uneven income growth, and other painful transitions. Fast growth could lead to ever-increasing competition for scarce resources and put additional strains on the environment. And some regions could continue to lag behind, owing to weak institutions, fragile states, and inadequate infrastructure. Many of these challenges will be dealt with at the national level, but some require global leadership. Perhaps one of the biggest challenges will be shaping a new global architecture that can take into account the increasing diversity of countries and interests and allow for peaceful resolution of emerging global tensions.

The evidence of globalization

Globalization has been present since the dawn of modern humans nearly 50,000 years ago in Africa (see Wade 2006). The Roman Empire stretched from Great Britain to the Middle East nearly 2,000 years ago and 500 years ago the age of discoveries led to the expansion of European outreach to the western hemisphere and East Asia. Two distinct periods in more modern times are often cited as intensified phases of globalization—the 20–30 years before World War I and the years since World War II. Both witnessed sharp increases in trade, international migration, and flows of finance, accompanied by rapid changes in technology—electricity, trains, and steamships in the first period, and planes, containers, and telecommunications in the second. While technology was a key factor, policies were also important—such as the reductions in trade and financial barriers. This section reviews some of the key evidence of the most recent period of globalization hinting at what trends can be anticipated over the next 25 years. The section will highlight trends in four broad categories that define globalization—trade in goods and services, international migration, capital flows, and technology and information.

Huge expansion of trade

World trade has exploded since the early 1960s. World exports have grown from just under $1 trillion a year (in 2000 dollars) to nearly $10 trillion a year, annualized growth of some 5.5 percent per year (figure 2.1).[3] They are clearly outpacing global output, which increased at some 3.1 percent per year over the same period. Between 1970 and 2004, the share of exports relative to global output has more than doubled and is now over 25 percent. Throughout the early part of this period the export elasticity (the rate of growth of exports relative to output) was running at about 1.5, but around 1986 the elasticity picked up substantially, peaking at more than 2.5 a decade later. This acceleration came on the heels of the collapse of the Iron Curtain

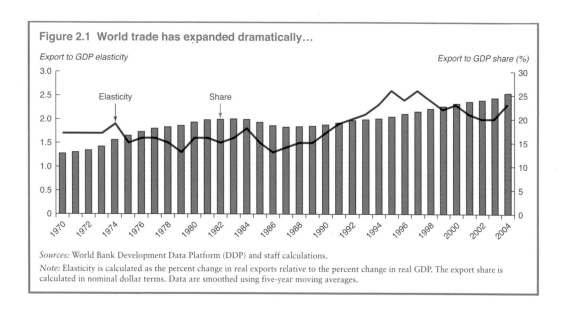

Figure 2.1 World trade has expanded dramatically...

Export to GDP elasticity   *Export to GDP share (%)*

Sources: World Bank Development Data Platform (DDP) and staff calculations.

Note: Elasticity is calculated as the percent change in real exports relative to the percent change in real GDP. The export share is calculated in nominal dollar terms. Data are smoothed using five-year moving averages.

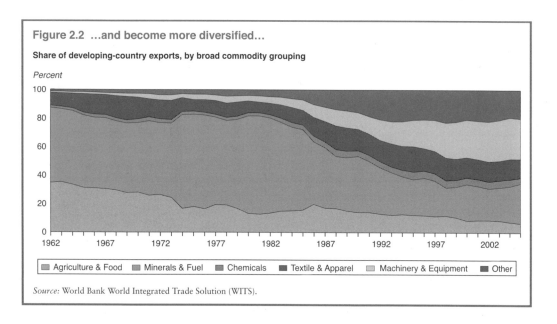

Figure 2.2 ...and become more diversified...

Share of developing-country exports, by broad commodity grouping

Percent

Agriculture & Food   Minerals & Fuel   Chemicals   Textile & Apparel   Machinery & Equipment   Other

Source: World Bank World Integrated Trade Solution (WITS).

and moves by China and India to open their economies and pursue an export-led strategy. Other countries also abandoned inward-looking strategies and saw their exports jump.

A large part of the opening of domestic economies can be attributed to unilateral decisions, as in China and India, but regional and multilateral reductions were also important in promoting global trade. Multilateral negotiations under the guise of the General Agreement on Tariffs and Trade (GATT)—now the World Trade Organization (WTO)—undertook stepwise reductions in trade policies known as rounds, the latest of which, the

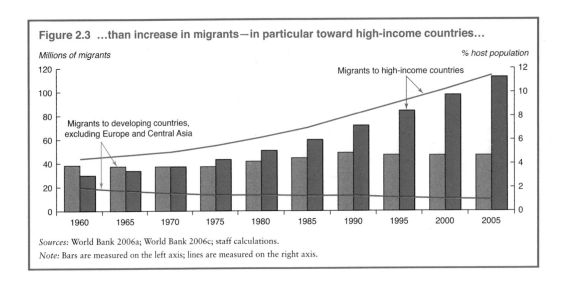

Figure 2.3 ...than increase in migrants—in particular toward high-income countries...

Sources: World Bank 2006a; World Bank 2006c; staff calculations.
Note: Bars are measured on the left axis; lines are measured on the right axis.

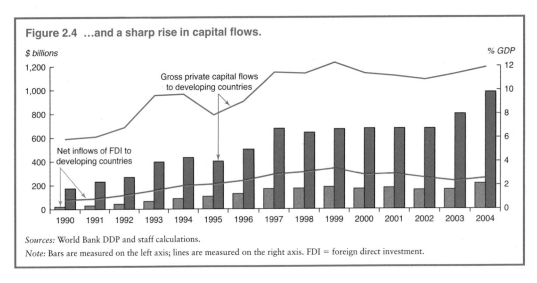

Figure 2.4 ...and a sharp rise in capital flows.

Sources: World Bank DDP and staff calculations.
Note: Bars are measured on the left axis; lines are measured on the right axis. FDI = foreign direct investment.

Doha Development Agenda is the ninth in the series. Though initially largely the realm of developed countries,[4] with the expansion of trade and WTO membership, 149 countries[5] are now involved, perhaps complicating the ability to achieve agreement given the more diverse set of objectives. Since 1990 there has also been an explosion in regional trade agreement notifications, many involving the new transition economies, but also including expansion of the European Union (EU), the North American Free Trade Agreement, and

the Southern Cone Common Market among others, with many others in the pipeline. Though most of these agreements have tended to be trade-creating, they can also divert trade from excluded countries.

Technological breakthroughs—particularly in transportation and communications— emerging business practices, capital flows, and the growth in a skilled workforce have led to an increasing proportion of developing-country exports in manufactured goods that are more traditionally the realm of developed countries

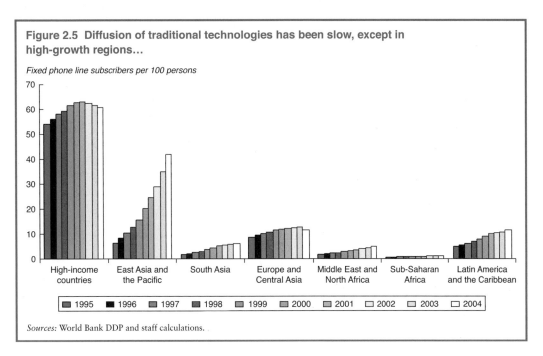

Figure 2.5 Diffusion of traditional technologies has been slow, except in high-growth regions...

Fixed phone line subscribers per 100 persons

Legend: 1995 · 1996 · 1997 · 1998 · 1999 · 2000 · 2001 · 2002 · 2003 · 2004

Sources: World Bank DDP and staff calculations.

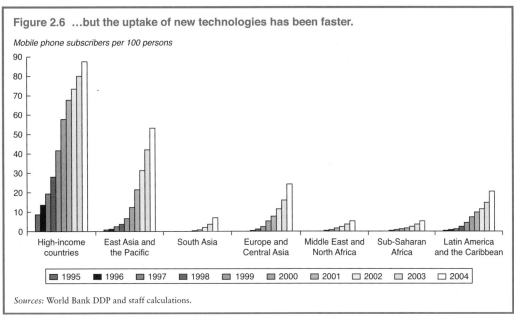

Figure 2.6 ...but the uptake of new technologies has been faster.

Mobile phone subscribers per 100 persons

Legend: 1995 · 1996 · 1997 · 1998 · 1999 · 2000 · 2001 · 2002 · 2003 · 2004

Sources: World Bank DDP and staff calculations.

(figure 2.2). Goods as diverse as car parts, airplanes, semiconductors, and consumer electronics are being sourced in developing countries. For many developing countries this has reduced their dependence on volatile commodities, though in some cases the ease of moving capital has also induced economic volatility, as in apparel manufacturing.

Table 2.1 Services exports rise in line with goods exports

Regions and trade	Levels ($ billions)			Growth rate (percent)		Percentage of GDP		
	1984	1994	2004	1984–94	1994–2004	1984	1994	2004
Exports of services								
World	357.8	978.2	2,009.5	10.6	7.5	3.0	3.7	4.9
High-income countries	303.7	803.9	1,614.2	10.2	7.2	3.3	3.6	4.9
Developing countries	54.1	174.2	395.3	12.4	8.5	2.0	3.8	4.7
East Asia & Pacific	9.1	49.5	115.0	18.5	8.8	1.9	4.7	4.3
South Asia	4.7	9.9	32.3	7.7	12.5	1.8	2.3	3.7
Europe & Central Asia	7.9	47.5	124.6	19.6	10.1	—	5.1	7.0
Middle East & N. Africa	10.7	19.3	36.7	6.1	6.6	—	6.7	6.7
Sub-Saharan Africa	4.5	8.4	20.8	6.5	9.5	2.0	3.0	4.0
Latin America & Caribbean	17.2	39.6	65.8	8.7	5.2	2.5	2.5	3.3
External factor income								
World	330.4	782.4	1,578.3	9.0	7.3	2.8	2.9	3.8
High-income countries	295.2	734.5	1,476.7	9.5	7.2	3.2	3.3	4.5
Developing countries	35.2	47.9	101.5	3.1	7.8	1.3	1.0	1.2
East Asia & Pacific	5.6	15.5	33.7	10.8	8.1	1.2	1.5	1.3
South Asia	0.8	1.3	4.8	4.9	14.0	0.3	0.3	0.5
Europe & Central Asia	1.0	7.3	30.5	21.8	15.3	—	0.8	1.7
Middle East & N. Africa	15.4	7.1	8.1	−7.4	1.3	—	2.4	1.5
Sub-Saharan Africa	1.4	1.9	4.6	3.2	9.3	0.6	0.7	0.9
Latin America & Caribbean	11.1	14.8	19.9	3.0	3.0	1.6	0.9	1.0

Sources: International Financial Statistics (IFS) and staff calculations.
Note: Service exports corresponds to "services credit" from the balance of payments table in IFS (code 78ADDZF). External factor income corresponds to "income credit" from the balance of payments table in IFS (code 78AGDZF). Owing to lack of data, some countries are excluded from regional aggregations. — = not available.

Trade in services has been growing at a pace similar to trade in goods at the global level (table 2.1).[6] Rising from $358 billion in 1984 to $2,000 billion in 2004, the share of services exports in total exports of goods and services has advanced modestly from 16 percent to 17.5 percent. For developing countries in aggregate, services exports have risen from $54 billion in 1984 to nearly $400 billion in 2004, raising its share of GDP from 2 percent to 4.7 percent. The corresponding figure for exports of goods and services is an increase from 19.8 percent of GDP in 1984 to 35.1 percent in 2004 (with no smoothing in the trend). Though South Asia is often mentioned as the main source of the growth in trade in services, the largest contributors to the rise in developing-country service exports over the last two decades have been East Asia and the Pacific and Europe and Central Asia. The latter region has benefited from its opening up to the global economy, its merger with the European Union, and the rapidly rising share of services in its economies.

For developing countries the growth in factor income from abroad has been much less pronounced than the growth in the export of services—and as a share of GDP, it has declined. This is linked to the as yet relatively low level of outbound investments by developing countries. For developed countries, the expansion of foreign income has been on a par with the expansion of service exports driven by rapid investments abroad.

Rapid increase in migration toward high-income countries

A second component of the recent globalization is the rise in international migration, particularly in developed countries. The share of migrants in developed countries (from both high-income and developing countries) has nearly tripled, going from 4.4 percent in 1960 to 11.4 percent in 2005—equivalent to an estimated 112 million persons out of a total number of migrants worldwide of some 190 million (figure 2.3). It is harder to discern the impacts of policies on the level of migration. Much of the South-to-North migration is predicated on the huge income differentials between the two, even taking into account differences in the cost of living. And one would expect that in the absence of (more or less) tight border controls on the movement of people, the number of migrants would increase substantially.[7] Pull factors are also in evidence in developed countries: slowing or declining labor force growth combined with aging and higher education levels is giving rise to labor shortages for certain skill levels and/or in certain sectors. Migration levels in developing countries (excluding the countries of the former Soviet Union) have more or less stayed constant over this time period at about 40–45 million and have declined as a percentage of the population.

More integrated financial and capital markets

The pace of opening of capital markets has been slower than for trade—even among the more homogeneous developed economies. Many countries still maintain restrictions on capital flows but the world has nonetheless seen a huge increase in financial flows both in gross and net terms. Foreign direct investment (FDI), which is particularly attractive for developing countries because it tends to be less volatile than other capital flows and also has other potential externalities such as embodied technology, has risen both globally and in developing countries. From a low initial level of $22 billion in 1990, FDI toward developing countries is currently running at about $200 billion a year, some 2.5 percent of developing-country GDP (figure 2.4). Developing countries currently attract about one-third of total global inward FDI, as FDI into developed countries is running at some $400 billion a year after peaking at over $1,300 billion in 2000 at the end of the dot-com boom. Total private financing of developing countries was nearly $1,000 billion in 2004, over five times the amount in 1990. The aggregate numbers fail to show the wide diversity across developing countries—both in terms of levels (or as shares of GDP) and externalities. For example,

FDI in natural resource sectors does not necessarily have the employment and technological impacts compared with FDI in the electronics sector. A more recent phenomenon has been the increase in outward FDI from developing countries from a low base of about $2.2 billion in 1990 to $41.1 billion in 2004 (World Bank 2006b).

Faster pace of technological take-up and diffusion

Technology has been advancing rapidly—particularly technologies that *shrink* the world, easing the flows of goods, capital, and technology. The improvements in telecommunications are the most striking example. The expansion of computer networking has vastly changed the way large companies organize production and has permitted the introduction of production networks that span the globe. These same networks also open up market opportunities for small firms that are no longer limited to regional markets. Mobile telephony is having the same impact. As the costs of developing mobile networks are much lower than that of traditional fixed-line networks, they have expanded rapidly even in the poorest regions of the world, opening up new market opportunities for once-isolated communities.[8] Though fixed-line telephony continues to be important, at least until wireless technologies mature, its growth has been limited by high fixed costs (figure 2.5) except in the high-growth countries. Mobile technology, by contrast, has taken off (figure 2.6)—perhaps even more sharply than shown by the data, given that the numbers probably vastly understate access since many users are nonsubscribers.

Improvements in transportation technology have also been impressive. The introduction of the container in the 1950s dropped the cost of loading a ship from $5.83 per ton to 15.8 cents, and even more savings came from the vast reduction of time ships spend in port for loading and unloading (see Levinson 2006). The advent of the jumbo jet airplane in the late 1960s led to the rise of cheaper air freight, a key component of the integrated global supply networks. It has enabled farmers in developing countries to export their time-sensitive produce—such as green beans or flowers—to high-income markets. The improvements in transportation and the advent of supply networks and global markets go hand in hand with the improvements in telecommunications and networking.

Looking forward, one would conclude that many of these forces are likely to provide the same impetus to globalization as they have in the past—some with diminishing power, and others perhaps with more. Trade policies have come a long way toward more integrated markets for goods, though tariffs remain high in many developing countries and in some sectors—such as agriculture. Other forms of protection are ever present such as unreasonable product standards or ad hoc safeguard measures. The service sectors have also been largely untouched by the GATT/WTO disciplines, and their reform would likely provide additional impetus to further trade growth. The same could be said for capital flows and the movement of people. However, the greater driver of globalization is likely to be in the technological field, because the telecommunications revolution is still in its infancy. Adoption, though rapid, has still bypassed many, and the technology is evolving—with greater speeds and the broader implementation of wireless broadband expected. And individuals and firms are still learning to adapt to the new technologies and leverage them to open new opportunities and increase productivity.

The world in 2030—the big picture

Preface: assumptions

The central scenario is built up from a number of key driving forces—notably demographic trends, savings, and investment behavior, and the role of technological change, and how these trends interact with globalization (see box 2.1). Some of these forces are, in turn, influenced by

the quality of domestic and international policies. Population is expected to add 1.5 billion people to the planet by 2030, and virtually all of the increase will be in developing countries. Moreover, today's high-income countries and China will become significantly older. Changing demographics weigh heavily on the results influencing the growth of employment, demand trends, and changes in savings and investment behavior (and even productivity).

While demographic trends are fairly predictable, assumptions about productivity growth are subject to a wider band of possibilities. There is no agreement on how to interpret recent productivity growth, let alone how to anticipate future patterns. For example, in the view of Gordon (2000), recent inventions—such as cell phones, the internet, or new drugs—are relatively normal incremental changes to productivity and are unlikely to have the same impact as the new technologies at the beginning of the 20th century—electricity, the internal combustion engine, telephones, radio, television, and indoor plumbing. Other observers, for example David (1990), suggest that it takes time for new discoveries to have their full impacts—either because initial costs are too high, or because there are network externalities, or because it takes time for organizations to change their management practices to fully benefit from the new technologies. Whether one takes a sanguine view of new technologies or not, large parts of the developing world have yet to benefit from "old" technologies.

The macro assumptions on productivity built into the forecast are largely consistent with the estimates of total factor productivity (TFP) growth from the literature (see, for example, Bosworth and Collins 2003). The world saw a period of very rapid TFP growth in the 1960s, followed by a decade of stagnation coinciding with the energy crisis of the 1970s, recovery to an estimated rate of 0.8 percent per year in the 1980s and 1990s, and an acceleration in the 2000s. There have been large variations across regions and time. The central scenario assumes a long-term rate of

Box 2.1 Inside the box—the components of scenario building

The long-term scenarios described in this chapter are based on the World Bank's Linkage model with a dynamic core that is essentially a neoclassical growth model—similar in concept to models used in other recent scenario work (see Goldman Sachs 2003 and PricewaterhouseCoopers 2006, for example). Aggregate growth is predicated on assumptions regarding the growth of the labor force, savings/investment decisions (and therefore capital accumulation), and productivity.

The Linkage model, unlike the aforementioned models, has considerably more structure—see van der Mensbrugghe (2006a) for a detailed description of the model and van der Mensbrugghe (2006b) for a summary description of the model and the assumptions underlying the baseline scenario.

First, it is multisectoral. This allows for more complex productivity dynamics including differentiating productivity growth between agriculture, manufacturing, and services and picking up the changing structure of demand (and therefore output) as growth in incomes leads to a relative shift into manufactures and services.

Second, it is linked multiregionally, allowing for the influence of openness—through trade and finance—on domestic variables such as output and wages. The model is also global, with globally clearing markets for goods and services and balanced financial flows.

Third, the Linkage model has a more diverse set of productive factors, including land and natural resources (in the fossil fuel sectors), and a labor split between unskilled and skilled.

The Linkage model has a 2001 base year and relies on the Global Trade Analysis Project (GTAP) database (release 6.1; see www.gtap.org) to calibrate initial parameters. A scenario is developed by solving for a new equilibrium in each subsequent year through 2030 with the following key assumptions:

The growth in the labor force is driven by demographics—essentially given by the growth of the working-age population. Differentiated growth of skilled versus unskilled workers is partly driven by demographics and partly driven by changes in education rates. As education levels rise (in the younger populations), they eventually drive higher relative growth of skilled workers once they enter the labor force (and older unskilled workers retire).

Savings decisions are partly driven by demographics—rising as youth dependency ratios fall and falling as elderly dependency ratios rise. Investment rates are driven by changes in growth rates (the accelerator mechanism) and differential rates of return to capital. Net foreign savings is the difference between domestic savings and investment.

Productivity is derived by a combination of factors, but is also partially judgmental. First, agricultural productivity is assumed to be factor-neutral and exogenous and is set to estimates from empirical studies (for example Martin and Mitra 1999). Productivity in manufacturing and services is labor-augmenting and a constant wedge is imposed between productivity growth in the two broad sectors with the assumption that productivity growth is higher in manufacturing than in services.

The model assumes that energy efficiency improves autonomously by 1 percent per year in all regions and that international trade costs decline by 1 percent per year.

TFP growth in the range of 1.0–1.4 for the high-income countries, somewhat on the high end of the Bosworth and Collins estimates. The range for developing countries is somewhat wider—between 0.7 and 2.9 toward 2015 and declining slowly thereafter as the positive impacts of rural-to-urban migration fade.

The central scenario is also predicated on only modest changes in the policy environment.

Over the last 25 years, the world has seen a dramatic drop in trade barriers for goods. And although they remain high in some countries and for some sectors (for example, in agriculture), the dismantling of remaining barriers will not have the same impact as in the past. A possible exception: dismantling barriers in services that remain high could produce significant economic gains.

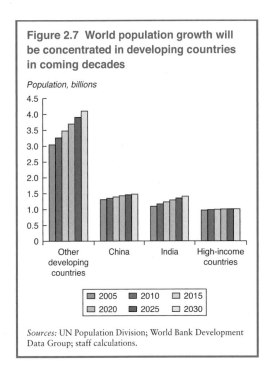

Figure 2.7 World population growth will be concentrated in developing countries in coming decades

Population, billions

Sources: UN Population Division; World Bank Development Data Group; staff calculations.

World population will increase

As noted above, the world will add 1.5 billion persons to its population between 2005 and 2030—going from (about) 6.5 billion to 8 billion (figure 2.7).[9] Roughly 12 percent will be living in high-income countries—down sharply from the 18 percent in 1980 and 14.5 percent in 2005. All but 40 million of this growth in population will occur in developing countries. While this represents a substantial increase in the number of persons—with con-comitant effects on already scarce resources—it also represents a slowing of world popula-tion growth that added 2 billion persons between 1980 and 2005. The global popula-tion growth rate, between 1.7 and 1.8 percent in the 1980s, will slow to 1 percent by 2015 and dip to 0.7 percent toward 2030.

High-income countries would start observ-ing actual population declines—Japan by 2010 and the EU countries soon thereafter. Japan's population under current projections would fall from about 128 million in 2005 to 117 million in 2030. The EU15 would

likewise lose about 10 million persons, falling from 412 million to 402 million. The United States will see a decline in the population growth rate, but fertility is still much higher in the United States than in other high-income countries—owing in part to immigrants' higher fertility. If current trends hold, the U.S. population will climb by 45 million to 345 million in 2030.

The population growth pattern is more highly varied across developing countries. Many of the countries in Europe and Central Asia are already confronted with declining populations—including the Russian Federa-tion, which is losing population and will con-tinue to do so unless trends are reversed—at a rate of about 0.5 percent each year. In the new EU accession countries, population declines average about 0.2–0.3 percent per year through the entire period. At the other end of the spectrum are Sub-Saharan Africa and the Middle East and North Africa, with popula-tion growth rates currently hovering at about 2 percent, declining toward 1.1–1.4 percent per year toward 2030.

The largest contribution to the nearly 1.5 billion increase in developing regions can be attributed to India, representing 320 million additional persons, and to Sub-Saharan Africa excluding Nigeria and South Africa, with a similar increment of 320 million—each contributing 20 percent to the global increase. Despite China's one-child policy and overall aging population, the momentum of the current population will generate 170 million additional Chinese by 2030, another 11 per-cent of the global increase.

The global economy will more than double

It is important to keep in mind, turning to the economic projections, that these are a combi-nation of reasoned quantitative analysis and informed judgment and not predicated on standard statistically based econometric models, as are the short- and medium-term forecasts described in chapter 1. They are intended to highlight certain key aspects of the

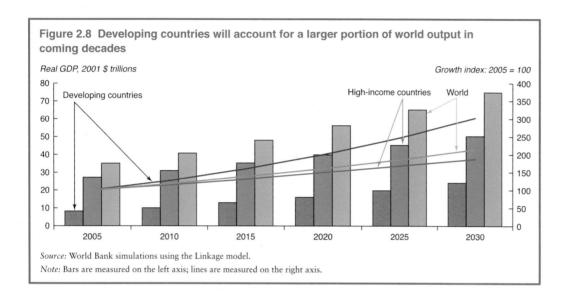

Figure 2.8 Developing countries will account for a larger portion of world output in coming decades

Real GDP, 2001 $ trillions   *Growth index: 2005 = 100*

Source: World Bank simulations using the Linkage model.

Note: Bars are measured on the left axis; lines are measured on the right axis.

baseline scenario that could be robust to a certain number of alternative assumptions—though none that imply highly nonlinear divergence from current trends.

If growth scenarios obtain, the share of output (in real terms) produced by developing countries would shift rather steadily. The global economy would grow from about $35 trillion in 2005 to $75 trillion in 2030, an overall increase of some 2.1 times (figure 2.8).[10] The developing-country share would jump from $8 trillion to $24.3 trillion—effectively tripling its output between 2005 and 2030 and increasing its global share of output from 23 percent to 33 percent.

This represents a modest acceleration of what was observed between 1980 and 2005. The global economy has increased by a factor of 2.1. For high-income countries the projection represents a slight decrease (from 2 to 1.9) but a more significant acceleration for developing countries (from 2.4 to 3.1). Part of this acceleration is due to compositional factors—higher-growth developing countries have higher weights today than back in 1980. However, it is mostly based on the chapter authors' judgment that many developing countries are on an accelerated growth path

as a consequence of the combination of improved initial conditions, better policies, and the still wide gap in productivity—relative to high-income countries. Moreover, developing countries have greater capacity and incentives to adapt new technology as communications technology continues to improve, FDI remains a force in overall development, and education and skill levels improve. If one decomposes the last 25 years in two periods—1980–2000 and 2000–2005—average growth in developing countries jumped from 3.2 percent per year in the first period to 5 percent per year in the second. This recent acceleration has not been shared by all countries—nor is it exclusively a China and India phenomenon.

Perhaps somewhat surprisingly, these differentiated growth rates will have only relatively modest impacts on the ranking of countries/regions based on the volume of output.[11] The rankings of the top six countries/regions would remain identical to those of today led by the United States, the European Union, Japan, China, the newly industrializing economies (NIEs), and Latin America (excluding Brazil and Mexico). India would jump three spots from its current 10th ranking, essentially swapping spots with Canada. Other countries/ regions moving up include the rest of East Asia aggregate, Indonesia, and Iran. Sub-Saharan Africa, with its assumed more modest growth rates, would fall further behind with the rest of Sub-Saharan Africa aggregate losing an additional three spots by 2030.

Looking behind again, one sees that there have been some spectacular jumps in the past 25 years as well as some spectacular declines—most reflected by the fall of the Iron Curtain (table 2.2). The clear winners have been Ireland, Singapore, Sri Lanka, Costa Rica, El Salvador, Equatorial Guinea, and

Table 2.2 Country rankings—1980–2005

Country	1980	2005	Change	Country	1980	2005	Change	Country	1980	2005	Change
United States	1	1	0	Hungary	52	45	7	Jamaica	96	90	6
Japan	2	2	0	Philippines	40	46	−6	Bolivia	98	91	7
Germany	3	3	0	New Zealand	49	47	2	Azerbaijan	80	92	−12
United Kingdom	5	4	1	Algeria	34	48	−14	Ghana	89	93	−4
France	4	5	−1	Nigeria	33	49	−16	Albania	102	94	8
China	10	6	4	Peru	51	50	1	Botswana	117	95	22
Italy	6	7	−1	Romania	37	51	−14	Paraguay	84	96	−12
Canada	8	8	0	Bangladesh	56	52	4	Honduras	97	97	0
Spain	12	9	3	Ukraine	30	53	−23	Ethiopia	83	98	−15
Mexico	13	10	3	Kuwait	50	54	−4	Uganda	103	99	4
Korea, Rep. of	23	11	12	Morocco	60	55	5	Senegal	100	100	0
India	11	12	−1	Vietnam	35	56	−21	Nepal	101	101	0
Brazil	9	13	−4	Kazakhstan	54	57	−3	Gabon	90	102	−12
Australia	14	14	0	Slovak Republic	61	58	3	Mauritius	115	103	12
Netherlands	16	15	1	Croatia	57	59	−2	Madagascar	92	104	−12
Russian Federation	7	16	−9	Slovenia	64	60	4	Namibia	106	105	1
Switzerland	19	17	2	Ecuador	63	61	2	Nicaragua	99	106	−7
Taiwan, China	32	18	14	Oman	73	62	11	Burkina Faso	108	107	1
Sweden	18	19	−1	Guatemala	67	63	4	Mali	111	108	3
Austria	24	20	4	Tunisia	68	64	4	Congo, Rep. of	104	109	−5
Turkey	27	21	6	Syrian Arab Republic	58	65	−7	Georgia	82	110	−28
Saudi Arabia	15	22	−7	Bulgaria	55	66	−11	Benin	113	111	2
Indonesia	20	23	−3	Dominican Republic	69	67	2	Guinea	110	112	−2
Norway	28	24	4	Sri Lanka	86	68	18	Chad	119	113	6
Poland	26	25	1	Sudan	66	69	−3	Armenia	109	114	−5
Denmark	29	26	3	Belarus	62	70	−8	Niger	105	115	−10
Greece	36	27	9	Costa Rica	94	71	23	Kyrgyz Republic	107	116	−9
South Africa	22	28	−6	Lithuania	72	72	0	Malawi	114	117	−3
Argentina	21	29	−8	Kenya	78	73	5	Swaziland	123	118	5
Hong Kong, China	42	30	12	El Salvador	93	74	19	Togo	120	119	1
Finland	31	31	0	Uruguay	70	75	−5	Rwanda	112	120	−8
Ireland	53	32	21	Angola	81	76	5	Central African Republic	122	121	1
Iran, Islamic Rep. Of	17	33	−16	Côte d'Ivoire	71	77	−6	Sierra Leone	116	122	−6
Portugal	45	34	11	Panama	88	78	10	Lesotho	124	123	1
Thailand	38	35	3	Cameroon	76	79	−3	Mauritania	121	124	−3
Israel	48	36	12	Trinidad and Tobago	77	80	−3	Belize	126	125	1
Venezuela, R. B. de	25	37	−12	Yemen, Republic of	79	81	−2	Burundi	118	126	−8
Malaysia	43	38	5	Zimbabwe	74	82	−8	Seychelles	127	127	0
Singapore	59	39	20	Latvia	75	83	−8	Gambia, The	125	128	−3
Colombia	39	40	−1	Bahrain	91	84	7	Guinea-Bissau	128	129	−1
Czech Republic	41	41	0	Equatorial Guinea	129	85	44	Vanuatu	130	130	0
Egypt, Arab Rep. of	46	42	4	Tanzania	65	86	−21				
Pakistan	44	43	1	Iceland	95	87	8				
Chile	47	44	3	Jordan	87	88	−1				
				Estonia	85	89	−4				

Source: World Development Indicators, World Bank.
Note: Based on five-year moving average centered on 1982 and 2003, respectively. Rankings based on GDP in current dollars.

Botswana.[12] More modest, but still substantial improvements include the Republic of Korea, Taiwan (China), Hong Kong (China), Israel, Oman, Panama, Portugal, and Mauritius. There is little obvious commonality across these economies with the exception that none (save Equatorial Guinea) is an oil producer or a transition economy. China's GDP increase has been fast, but it has only moved from 10th place to 6th over the 25 years and India has lost a spot, with both Mexico and Korea jumping over India in the rankings.

Many of the countries, having lost ground in the global ranking, are concentrated among oil producers and transition countries including the Russian Federation, Saudi Arabia, Indonesia, the Islamic Republic of Iran, República Bolivariana de Venezuela, Nigeria, Romania, Bulgaria, Gabon, and Georgia. However, other countries have also fared poorly—for example Brazil, Argentina, and Uruguay in Latin America, and Ethiopia, Tanzania, and Zimbabwe in Sub-Saharan Africa—though it is generally the case that countries that have avoided conflict have managed to maintain their ranking.

Per capita income growth is what matters
Economic size and ranking have their importance, not least in terms of determining power relations, be it at the global, regional, or bilateral level. But from a welfare point of view, what really matters is income per capita, not the overall size of an economy.[13] Using the market dollar exchange rate of an economy provides a biased estimate of individual well-being because prices differ substantially across economies—particularly for nontraded goods such as personal and housing services. For this reason, it is more appropriate to use the PPP exchange rates, which take into account these differences in prices.[14] Even using PPP exchange rates, the speed of convergence between developing- and developed-country incomes would be modest under this scenario. At today's income in PPP terms, the average developing-country resident receives about 16 percent of the average income of high-income countries—$4,800 versus $29,700 (figure 2.9). This ratio would rise to 23 percent in 25 years' time, representing an average developing-country income of $12,200 versus $54,000 for high-income countries.

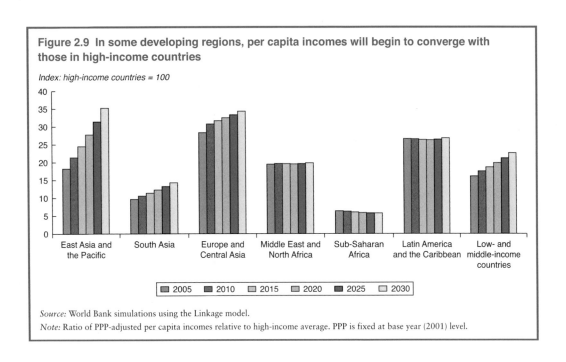

Figure 2.9 In some developing regions, per capita incomes will begin to converge with those in high-income countries

Index: high-income countries = 100

2005 ■ 2010 ■ 2015 ■ 2020 ■ 2025 ■ 2030

Source: World Bank simulations using the Linkage model.
Note: Ratio of PPP-adjusted per capita incomes relative to high-income average. PPP is fixed at base year (2001) level.

There is, perhaps needless to say, great variance across countries. Chinese incomes would rise from 19 percent of the average high-income level to 42 percent, a significant narrowing of the gap and would achieve an average income close to the lower range of today's poorest high-income countries. There would be a further falling behind in Sub-Saharan Africa with its modest per capita growth below the high-income average, and Latin America would see little if any convergence on average. As the previous 25 years have shown, there is plenty of scope for surprises and countries doing significantly better, even compared to countries with similar initial conditions.[15]

The rather modest level of convergence overall nevertheless obscures the fact that market opportunities for both developed and developing countries will increase dramatically as the sheer size of the population of developing countries ensures the growth of a very significant middle and upper class likely to rival the purchasing power of today's high-income consumer (see chapter 3). Thus, notwithstanding the challenge that poverty will continue to hold on the global community, the wider spread of wealth globally will also provide greater means to deal more substantively with poverty and other global concerns such as the environment and health.

The next sections delve more in depth into the underlying assumptions of this central scenario and some of the policy implications that can be derived from them and their potential alternatives.

Demographics are central to the growth scenario

Two significant demographic changes are occurring at the moment. Developed economies have seen a huge decline in fertility rates (well below replacement rate), a stable labor force that will begin to decline, and rapidly aging populations. Developing countries—some earlier than others—are now also seeing significant declines in fertility rates and a substantial reduction in the number of youths relative to those in the labor force. Labor forces are still growing rapidly in most countries owing to the large number of births over the last two decades and most are only seeing modest increases in the share of the elderly in the population because rising life expectancy largely impacts current (and larger) generations rather than past.

For developed economies, the standard economic impacts of slowing population growth and aging suggest that aggregate savings will decline, all else being equal, as aging populations tend to dis-save or consume out of existing assets. This would tend to decrease the amount of savings available for developed countries. The evidence for this dis-saving is mixed and other factors—such as current levels of public and/or international indebtedness—may influence the long-term patterns of savings and investment. On the other hand, lower rates of employment growth could have mixed impacts on investment. Lower labor supply could lessen the need for investment in sectors where labor and capital are close complements.[16] But more intense investment may counteract this effect in sectors where labor and capital are substitutes and labor-saving technology is an option.[17]

Aging populations can have other consequences. Productivity growth could be higher in economies with rapid increases in the number of youth joining the labor force. They can also be associated with changes in consumer behavior with less demand for food and educational services and more demand for leisure and health services (McKibbin 2005; Bryant 2004; Helliwell 2004; Tyers and Shi 2005). There could also be fiscal implications as promises to earlier generations in terms of social welfare benefits prove hard to finance with a lower tax base. This eventually may involve a combination of lower benefits and delay of retirement age or other forms of higher labor-force participation rates by the elderly.

For developing countries, some of these impacts are reversed. With a lower proportion of youth to care for—including provisions for housing, education, and nourishment—more can be saved and invested, particularly because many countries still have a low proportion of elderly. To the extent that available savings from developed countries decline, the higher savings in developing countries would tend to offset the decline.

Starting with employment, developed-country employment growth, though positive through 2010 at about 1.2 million new jobs per year, becomes negative thereafter, with an average loss of about 700,000 jobs between 2010 and 2015, jumping to an annual average loss of over 3.2 million between 2025 and 2030 (figure 2.10).[18] This latter number represents a decline of about 1 percent per year. Among other things, this negative employment growth implies—through standard growth accounting—that combined capital accumulation and productivity will have to accelerate to compensate if aggregate growth of 2–3 percent per year is to be maintained. The start of the decline in the labor force varies across countries, already (potentially) observable in Japan, beginning in the European Union shortly after 2010, and delayed in the United States (and Australia and New Zealand) until sometime

between 2020 and 2025—somewhat later than even for the NIEs of East Asia.

Labor force growth is still rapid in developing countries—though on a declining trend throughout the period. Currently, developing countries need to increase employment by nearly 50 million jobs per year to keep up with working-age population growth under the proviso of no change to the labor force participation rate including females. This latter assumption may be dubious in light of the fact that fertility is declining rapidly in developing countries. The largest needs are in the largest countries, with China and India needing to create 8–10 million jobs each year. This may be easier in these rapidly growing economies. Countries in Sub-Saharan Africa also need to create close to 10 million jobs each year. With their lower economic growth rates and relatively small urban populations, the task appears to be much harder.[19]

The trends for China also show the impacts of its decades-long population policies limiting births. In a relatively near future, employment growth will decline precipitously

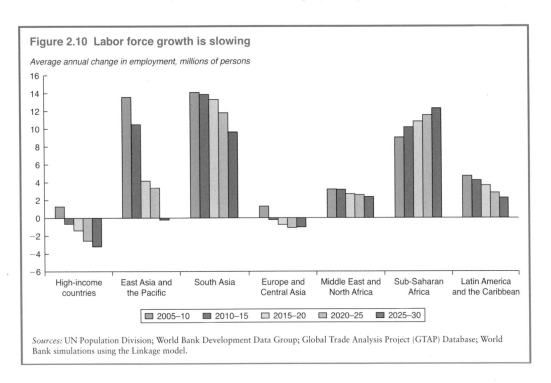

Figure 2.10 Labor force growth is slowing

Average annual change in employment, millions of persons

Legend: ■ 2005–10 ■ 2010–15 □ 2015–20 □ 2020–25 ■ 2025–30

Sources: UN Population Division; World Bank Development Data Group; Global Trade Analysis Project (GTAP) Database; World Bank simulations using the Linkage model.

from over 5 million between 2010 and 2015 to under 500,000 between 2015 and 2025 and will turn negative thereafter. The only other region affected by negative employment growth is Europe and Central Asia, whose population is more similar in structure to the European Union than to the average developing country.

In summary, employment growth initially will provide significant stimulus to economic growth, but its share will decline rapidly in most developing regions as the current generation of youth join the workforce and leave behind a smaller pool of potential workers as fertility continues to fall.

The demographic projections for youths and the elderly are distinctly different in nature mainly because the future elderly are all alive today and thus the projection is based on changes to mortality rates that tend to be easier to gauge than changes to fertility rates. In fact, the UN population forecasts—the basis of the World Bank's forecasts—are predicated on all countries converging toward population replacement levels of fertility by 2050. This implies an *increase* in fertility in many high-income countries, where fertility has dropped to between 1 and 1.5 births per woman.[20]

Over the longer term, the increase in developed-country fertility would lead to a slight rise in the share of the population aged 15 and below, and even an absolute rise, sometime after 2020 (figure 2.11).

The growth in the number of youths in developing countries will stay more or less constant on average over the entire time horizon—though again highly variegated across regions, with large declines in East Asia and the Pacific and Europe and Central Asia offset by positive if declining growth rates in Sub-Saharan Africa and to a lesser extent South Asia. But even in Sub-Saharan Africa, the assumption of replacement-level fertility will lead to a sharp decline in births. Between 2005 and 2030, the share of youths in Sub-Saharan Africa will drop from 44 percent to 35 percent. Despite this leveling, the pressure to educate (and provide health services) for the young in Sub-Saharan Africa will be a challenge in a region that is significantly off-track in terms of achieving the Millennium Development Goals

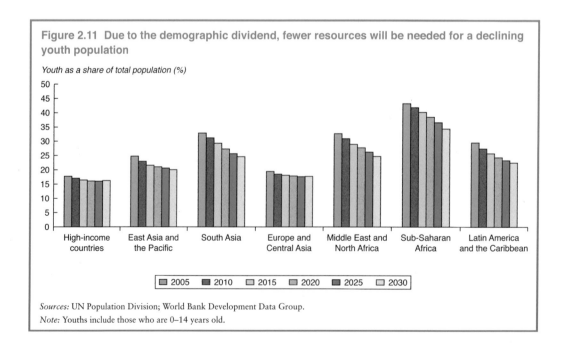

Figure 2.11 Due to the demographic dividend, fewer resources will be needed for a declining youth population

Youth as a share of total population (%)

Legend: 2005, 2010, 2015, 2020, 2025, 2030

Regions: High-income countries, East Asia and the Pacific, South Asia, Europe and Central Asia, Middle East and North Africa, Sub-Saharan Africa, Latin America and the Caribbean

Sources: UN Population Division; World Bank Development Data Group.

Note: Youths include those who are 0–14 years old.

(MDGs) by 2015. The number of young people in Sub-Saharan Africa will jump by 100 million from 300 million currently, so it is not simply a question of building new classrooms and training new teachers for today's population, but also taking into account the bulge in the student-age population as one looks forward.

Potentially, the resources to take care of the youth will improve as the number of workers grows more rapidly than the number of youths in developing countries. The dependency ratio—defined as the number of youths per 100 workers—will drop pretty steadily between 2005 and 2030, starting at a level of 60 and falling to 47. Even with the sharp drop in the youth dependency ratio in developing countries, they will still have an average ratio considerably higher than the average in high-income countries centered at around 35.[21] These ratios will reach developed-country levels in East Asia and the Pacific and in Europe and Central Asia—pretty rapidly in both cases—by about 2015. Both Middle East and North Africa and Sub-Saharan Africa stand out as having particularly high youth dependency rates—85 and 93 (per 100 workers), respectively, well above the average for

developing countries. These ratios will drop, but even in 2030 will remain at 60 or above.

The number of elderly will more or less double over the next 25 years—from 464 million in 2005 to about 910 million in 2030. By and large, future population aging is a developed-country phenomenon—though only one in three elderly currently lives in developed countries and another one in three lives in China or India. The number of elderly per 100 workers in developed countries would rise from 30 to 53 between 2005 and 2030 and reach 63 in Japan and 59 in the EU (figure 2.12). Even in the United States the rate could nearly double from today's low of 23 to 44 in 2030. This will undoubtedly necessitate forceful policy changes because existing unfunded promises to future elderly would require unprecedented taxes on workers.

For developing countries, aging populations (as defined by the number of elderly per 100 workers) will rise only slowly from current levels through about 2020, but will start accelerating modestly afterwards to reach a level of nearly 19 starting from 12 in 2005. This is still well below the developed-country average of 30 today and differs widely across regions.

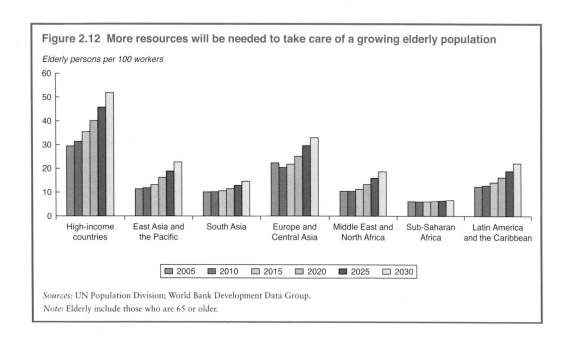

Figure 2.12 More resources will be needed to take care of a growing elderly population

Elderly persons per 100 workers

Legend: 2005, 2010, 2015, 2020, 2025, 2030

Sources: UN Population Division; World Bank Development Data Group.

Note: Elderly include those who are 65 or older.

China will see a sharper rise in its elderly dependency rate, moving from 12 currently to 25 by 2030. This could be contrasted with India, which has a level similar to China's at 11, but rising to only 16 by 2030. As mentioned earlier, population-wise Europe and Central Asia is more similar to high-income regions and the elderly dependency ratio will hit 34 by 2030. What moderates this to some extent in Europe and Central Asia is the inclusion of Turkey with its relatively young and large population and, more unfortunately, the precipitous decline in life expectancy in some parts of Europe and Central Asia.

These demographic trends provide a significant opportunity for many developing countries[22] that will be able to devote less resources to their youth and that do not yet have to devote significant resources to their elderly—although they would be well advised to avoid making some of the choices that developed countries have made regarding long-term commitments to their elderly without adequately making provisions for them.

The four channels of globalization

What follows is a discussion of the four key channels of globalization and how they interact with the development process—trade in goods and services, movement of persons, financial flows, and technological diffusion.

Trade integration will accelerate

The trade dimension of globalization has perhaps been the most prominent, especially with the emergence of Asia and the transition economies over the last two decades. Growth in trade has outpaced growth in output by a factor of two or more and the causes behind this phenomenon are in place to sustain it over the next two decades.

Income growth, changing comparative advantage, and the push toward greater openness—the impasse in the Doha Round negotiations notwithstanding—will continue to lead to expanding global trade over the next two decades. Though import tariffs have

dropped dramatically since 1980, they still remain stubbornly high in some sectors, for example in agriculture and services, or in some countries. Protection can also take other forms, for example antidumping, questionable standards, or variable levies (as bound tariffs are typically well above applied tariffs). Progress in opening markets has stalled at the multilateral level, but countries continue to pursue liberalization either unilaterally or through bilateral and regional agreements.

While the standard theory of trade has focused on comparative advantage, new trade theory places much more emphasis on the role of specialization. Specialization is manifested in two ways. The first is consumers' desire for greater varieties of the same categories of goods. Whereas 25 years ago consumers had a relatively modest selection of automobiles or fashion, today's range of consumer goods is huge. This love of variety has provided producers from a diverse set of countries with opportunities to export. A second form of specialization is represented by production networks that allow for the breaking up of the production process across multiple firms and/or countries. The growth in production networks has been predicated on many technological advances—both physical, as in telecommunications and transport, and management processes, such as supply chain logistics. There is little evidence that these factors will subside anytime soon.

Under the central scenario, the level of exports would more than triple—from about $9 trillion in 2005 to over $27 trillion in 2030—with a concomitant rise in the world export-to-output ratio, jumping to 34 percent from 25 percent currently. For developing countries exports will increase from about $3 trillion to over $12 trillion, reflecting in part these countries' greater output growth. These baseline numbers are predicated on the assumption of no change to current trade policies.[23] Under a broad reform scenario whereby all countries reduce tariffs on merchandise goods (and domestic agricultural protection) by three-quarters, exports by developing countries would increase by an additional $2 trillion in 2030, a jump of some 18 percent over the baseline.

The push and pull factors driving international migration will persist

International migration has risen substantially recently—though the lack of reliable data, particularly of irregular migration, makes it difficult to assess the actual number of migrants in either developed or developing countries. Current estimates are that 11.4 percent of developed countries' population are foreign-born, up from 6.2 percent in 1980. South-South migration is also an important phenomenon, but data prove even less reliable.

While developing countries on average will see improvements in living standards relative to high-income countries, the forces underlying South-to-North migration will continue to have a strong impact. First, there is the existing, considerable wage gap (even taking into consideration differences in purchasing power) that will shrink, but will still be substantial well into the future. Second, the combination of existing migrant stocks (and the push to reunite family and friends) with potential reductions in migration costs will provide ongoing impetus for South-to-North migration. Third, the slowing growth of the workforce in developed countries and the aging of populations will be a pull factor in increasing migration over the next two decades.

However, unlike the trade in goods and services, or the flow of capital, migration is subject to considerable regulation and control and is also fraught with many additional considerations. Sending countries are concerned with the social and family aspects of outward migration, or in some cases with brain drain. The receiving countries may also be concerned with the social implications of migration and the economic and fiscal consequences, particularly for those whose populations compete directly with the migrants.

Notwithstanding these legitimate concerns, in a global context, the economic impacts of increasing South-to-North migration can be highly beneficial. Any form of economic restriction on the exchange of goods and services has an economic cost and migration is no different. *Global Economic Prospects 2006* (World Bank 2006a) explored in depth the main impacts of such migration, illustrating in particular that the greatest beneficiaries are the migrants themselves, though through remittances, the sending countries could also gain substantially. The aggregate impacts for the receiving countries are also on balance positive, though they could have negative distributional consequences.

This chapter's central scenario uses the underlying UN methodology and projections for the growth in country population and makes no additional assumptions as regards international migration. Though migration can make a significant impact for the migrants themselves, in the context of a 25-year scenario, international migration is unlikely to have large macroeconomic impacts save perhaps for a handful of smaller economies or countries that receive high levels of remittances. The United Nations forecasts the net number of migrants to developed countries to increase by 98 million between 2005 and 2050, or about 2.2 million annually. This is expected to more or less offset the net natural population decrease in developed countries (that is, the excess of deaths over births). For developing countries, this represents only 4 percent of total incremental population between 2005 and 2050 (and thus a small fraction of the total population) (see UN 2004).

Financial integration will intensify

Savings, investment, and finance. The global financial system is likely to change dramatically over the course of the next 25 years, as technological innovations and even greater integration of markets expand the reach of global financial intermediaries. Some of these changes are impossible to anticipate. For example, it is not clear whether the future communications technologies will favor a continued concentration of financial intermediation, or encourage the growth of global banks and other financial institutions in a wide range of markets, or lead to even greater decentralization as smaller investments are required to obtain the information necessary to carry out financial transactions. Other changes can be partially anticipated. For example, as developing countries take up a greater share of global output, it is likely that their importance in financial markets will continue to grow. Some decline is already apparent in the dominance of the dollar as a currency of lending and reserves (World Bank 2006b), but whether currencies from developing countries will play a major role in global financial markets is not yet apparent.

One major issue facing developing countries over the next quarter-century is the impact of demographic trends on the countries' access to external savings. The rise in old-age dependency ratios in industrial countries, and in some developing countries, is likely to be associated with a decline in saving, a rise in interest rates, and a fall in their current account surplus. All else being equal, the elderly tend to save less or even dis-save, as they live off of savings earned during their working years. While forecasts of saving rates are uncertain, and estimations of the relationship between aging and saving rates vary widely, the prospect of reduced global saving over the coming decades needs to be considered seriously.

The coming savings decline. The life-cycle theory of consumption argues that saving rates are low during young adulthood to provide for children, rise as individuals save for retirement, and then fall as retirees live off of their accumulated assets. This theory is subject to significant qualifications, as individuals also save to provide a bequest for their children and to maintain a stock of wealth to deal with adverse shocks. Saving rates also are influenced by a host of macroeconomic factors, including growth, interest rates, inflation, borrowing constraints, fiscal policy, pension systems, and income distribution (Loayza, Schmidt-Hebbel, and Servén 2000). Econometric estimates have provided mixed support for the view that savings behavior is governed by life-cycle considerations.[24] On balance, some decline in savings can be expected as elderly dependency ratios increase.

This simple theory of individual behavior, in conjunction with demographic trends set off by the baby boom after World War II and the impressive increases in longevity in the developing world, has dramatic implications for the global economy. For Europe, Japan, and East Asia, which have relatively high saving rates and supply a large share of global financial flows, the rise in dependency ratios should lead to a decline in savings.[25] By contrast, the very low saving rates in Sub-Saharan Africa may be at least partially explained by the region's very high youth dependency ratios. Saving rates should rise as these young people move into the workforce, boosting investment and growth.

The decline in saving rates is not expected to follow a smooth trend over the next 25 years. In industrial countries, saving rates should rise in the near future, as the bulk of the baby boom generation remains in the workforce during peak saving years. However, over the next 20 years this generation will retire, and saving rates will go down. Russia and some of the other countries of the former Soviet Union are likely to see a decline in the labor force, and thus savings, owing to rising elderly dependency ratios shortly after the industrial countries, followed closely by China and some other parts of East Asia. Latin America and South Asia may see some effect of rising elderly dependency by the end of the forecast period. By contrast, Sub-Saharan Africa and the Middle East and North Africa have relatively young populations and should see increasing labor force participation and savings through 2030. Overall, the forecast drop in global saving is quite substantial, from 21.6 percent of income in the first half decade of this century to 19.9 percent by 2030.

Demographic influences also imply a decline in investment demand, as fewer workers are available for each unit of investment.[26] Other aspects of aging may boost investment demand. Aging may spur investments in human capital to compensate for reduced numbers of workers (Fougère and Mérette 1997). The decline in the labor force is likely to lead to higher wages, thus increasing investments that save on labor, either in productive processes or in the supply of services at the household level. Similarly, aging may accelerate technical progress by increasing incentives to innovate. Cutler and others (1990) estimate that a decline of 1 percentage point in labor force growth in 29 countries for 1960–85 was associated with a 0.5 percentage point increase in TFP growth. On the other hand, older workers may be less innovative, reducing technical progress (Börsch-Supan 1996).

On balance, it is likely that investment will decline in regions where elderly dependency ratios are rising, but not by as much as savings, leading to a decline in these countries' current account surplus (or a rise in their deficit), along with a rise in global interest rates. This is roughly consistent with findings in Helliwell (2004), where half the impact of demographic change was matched by a corresponding change in investment, and half showed up in the current account. Estimates of reduced form relationships between demographic ratios and current account balances (Bryant 2004), cross-country time-series analysis (Lührmann 2003), and forecasting models based on estimations from historical relationships (IMF 2004; Turner and others 1998; Higgins 1998) find that countries with dependency ratios that are rising relative to other countries' tend to experience a weakening of current account balances.[27]

Implications for developing countries' access to finance. According to this chapter's simulations, the high-income countries' current account surplus is likely to deteriorate by $800 billion by 2030, or 1.7 percent of GDP. The decline in capital flows to developing countries and the rise in interest rates on developing countries' loans may be greater than anticipated by this demographic model. Developing countries are likely to

remain relatively risky investments. If risk aversion rises with age, the aging of the rich countries will imply a greater premium for risk, and thus less willingness to lend to developing countries. Higher risk premia could result either because older individuals control a greater share of investment funds, or because the share of pensions and other institutional investors in financial systems increases.[28] In the United States, the number of Americans aged 65 and over will double between 2000 and 2030, so the asset holdings of the elderly are likely to grow substantially compared with total holdings (Bellante and Green 2004).

It is likely that risk aversion does rise with age. Older individuals have less time to make up any shortfall in savings owing to the high volatility of investment returns. In the standard models of portfolio choice, the only factor that explains age-related differences in portfolio allocation is differences in risk aversion (Poterba and Samwick 1997). Bodie, Merton, and Samuelson (1992) show that older individuals will place a smaller share of their portfolio in risky assets than will younger individuals if the latter can vary their supply of labor to offset volatility in asset returns. Kimball (1993) argues that facing increasing risks in general, for example higher medical risks, should make individuals less willing to bear other risks, for example financial risks. Samuelson (1989) concludes that, assuming that one must ensure a minimum level of wealth (to ensure subsistence) at retirement, younger individuals will be more willing to take risks than older.

Despite this theoretical support, empirical estimates of the relationship between age and risk aversion are inconclusive (Ameriks and Zeldes 2004).[29] Measuring whether aging is associated with a shift to less risky assets is fraught with difficulty because it is hard to distinguish the impact on portfolio allocation of age, of the person's date of birth (different age cohorts may behave differently), and of the date of observation.[30] Moreover, the data on household allocation, even in the United

States, are incomplete and subject to measurement error.

One way that developing countries could adjust to account for increased risk aversion in financial markets is a greater use of securitization, particularly of future receivables, such as export revenues, remittance receipts, and diversified payment rights (DPRs). Securitization or structured finance techniques in developing countries are designed to enhance the credit ratings of debt issued by borrowers, typically to an investment grade status. This can allow sub–investment grade borrowers to pierce the sovereign "rating ceiling," which often constrains the access of subsovereign entities in developing countries to international capital markets (Ketkar and Ratha 2001). Securitization usually results in reduced spreads and longer maturities for emerging market debt issues, compared to conventional or unstructured debt. While traditional items such as oil and gas and mining receivables were among the first to be securitized, other assets (such as remittances and DPRs) have increasingly taken their place in recent years (figure 2.13).

Fundamentally, however, developing countries will need more than innovative financing techniques to deal with the coming decline in savings in high-income countries. They will need to improve creditworthiness through sound fiscal and monetary policies, maintenance of an appropriate exchange rate, open trade policies, and institutional reform to improve the efficiency of investment. Relatively youthful countries in Sub-Saharan Africa and the Middle East and North Africa can benefit from the coming rise in savings in their economies, but only if an appropriate investment climate provides secure financial instruments for keeping savings, and efficiently allocates saving to productive investment. As capital becomes scarcer in the global economy, many developing countries will have the opportunity to improve financial returns and diversification through capital outflows, while low-income countries in particular could benefit from South-South flows. South-South capital flows have risen greatly over the past decade (World Bank 2006b), and demographic trends will provide a further impetus over the next quarter-century. In short, policy reform and a strengthening of the institutional environment should enable developing countries to maintain their access to the savings required for growth in the face of a decline in external finance from industrial countries and a rise in global interest rates.

The transition to the medium term. Expectations of the decline in industrial countries' savings over the medium term may have important implications for short-term instability in financial markets. The sustainability of the U.S. current account deficit is an important vulnerability. As outlined in previous editions of *Global Economic Prospects*, there is a danger that investors will lose confidence in the ability of the United States to finance continued, large deficits, leading to a sharp decline in external finance and thus some combination of large increases in interest rates and a sharp depreciation of the dollar. Anticipated demographic trends would exacerbate the shortfall between the existing level of the U.S. current account deficit and what foreigners are willing to finance.

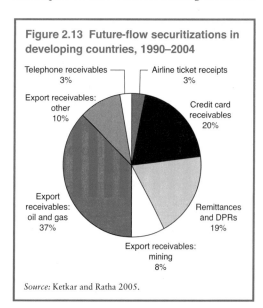

Figure 2.13 Future-flow securitizations in developing countries, 1990–2004

Telephone receivables 3%
Airline ticket receipts 3%
Export receivables: other 10%
Credit card receivables 20%
Export receivables: oil and gas 37%
Remittances and DPRs 19%
Export receivables: mining 8%

Source: Ketkar and Ratha 2005.

The basic issue is that the baby boom generation in the United States is now passing through what should be its period of highest saving—if baby boomers are to ensure that they have adequate financial resources to sustain themselves through retirement. While high immigration rates (relative to those in other industrial countries) should continue to support labor force growth for the next decade, the U.S. labor force is forecast to slow to 0.5 percent from 2005 to 2015 (compared with 1.3 percent from 1995 to 2005) and should actually decline beginning about 2020. At the same time, U.S. personal saving rates are at their lowest point since the government began compiling consistent statistics in 1959.[31] If saving rates do not rise in the near term, the country will be in a very poor position to face rising dependency ratios, a declining labor force, and hence an impetus for further declines in savings.

More generally, unfunded pension liabilities combined with anticipated demographic trends pose a considerable challenge to industrial-country policy makers that could imply slow growth, economic instability, or both. Industrial-country governments may impose higher taxes to cover unfunded pension costs, eroding incentives to work and invest. Alternatively, governments may accommodate the conflicting demands of pensioners and current workers through monetary expansion, leading to inflation and a more pronounced economic cycle. In any event, an inability to appropriately deal with the challenges posed by the demographic transition would have serious consequences for the global economy.

Technological diffusion: productivity, information, and knowledge

It has long been recognized in the economic literature that higher incomes are produced in the long run primarily through productivity growth rather than factor accumulation. With declining labor forces in some countries and declining labor force growth in all, productivity will play a more prominent role in maintaining economic growth over the next 25 years.

Trade, FDI, foreign travel and education, and improvements in mass communication have all played a significant role in the past 25 years to enhance productivity in many parts of the world—and a reinforcement of these trends is likely to continue.

More than ever before, all countries have access to a large share of the world's most advanced technology through improvements in communications technology and access to the World Wide Web.[32] The capacity to harness these technologies has enabled countries such as China and Thailand to quickly advance up the technology ladder and evolve from exporting natural resource– and/or low-skilled, labor-based goods toward exporting advance technology–laden goods such as microprocessors and flat panel displays. Given the greater availability of information and technology, what will differentiate countries is their ability to adopt these technologies—the skill level of their workforce, the appropriate capital and infrastructure, openness to trade and FDI, and more generally the investment climate.

Some technologies actually allow firms and even individuals to overcome these obstacles. Mobile telephony and access to the Internet have the potential to transform and raise information sharing to unprecedented levels, particularly for the poorest and most isolated in the global economy. For example, Sub-Saharan Africa has long lagged most developing countries in telecommunications infrastructure. Mobile telephony penetration has been impressive (figure 2.6)—and as noted above, the number of subscribers most likely largely understates the actual access because small-scale mobile service firms have made service available to a much broader share of the population through the selling of access to small time slices of mobile phone service.

A significant portion of productivity growth can be captured by technology embodied in imported inputs and capital, or through learning by doing or imitating. At the same time the larger and more diverse developing economies have built considerable, if yet infant capacity in research and development. But one particular challenge for the global community will be to improve the research and development potential for underfunded regions and sectors—for example to jumpstart a green revolution in Sub-Saharan Africa or in medical research to alleviate the scourge of tropical diseases.[33]

What will happen if growth is slower—or faster—in the next 25 years?

History has shown that past trends are not immutable over time. In fact, the only thing certain about the future is that surprises will occur. However, even if growth rates turn out to be faster or slower than in the central scenario, the demographic and globalization-related strains in the global economy identified in that scenario are likely to persist—if in somewhat different form. If developing countries grow by only by 1.5–2 percent per capita over the next 25 years, a glum scenario from any point of view, globalization-related problems would remain—including the issues examined in subsequent chapters, such as income distribution, labor market adjustments, and the environment. Slower growth is likely to heighten all of these problems, as countries

would have fewer resources to tackle them and be more reluctant to compromise in undertaking multilateral action. Faster growth would likely ease distributional concerns and labor market adjustments, but increase pressures on the global environment. The bright side of faster growth for the environment is that an accelerated pace of technological changes and investments in capital stock means that abatement technologies can be adopted sooner and at lower costs than with slower growth.

A slow-growth scenario

The last quarter-century has shown a diversity of growth trends across regions, but trends have been less volatile in the global aggregates. It is hard to identify in the global aggregates well-known systemic crises such as the Latin America debt crisis, the fall of the Berlin Wall, or the more recent Asian financial crisis and its aftermath—with the one notable exception of the energy crisis of the 1970s. Figures 2.14a–c show the evolution of long-term per capita growth rates over the period 1970–2005. The growth rates reflect the 10-year period average growth rate for each year. That is, the 1970 number reflects the average annual growth rate between 1960

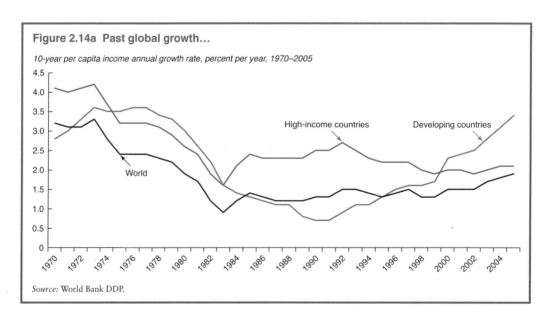

Figure 2.14a Past global growth...

10-year per capita income annual growth rate, percent per year, 1970–2005

Source: World Bank DDP.

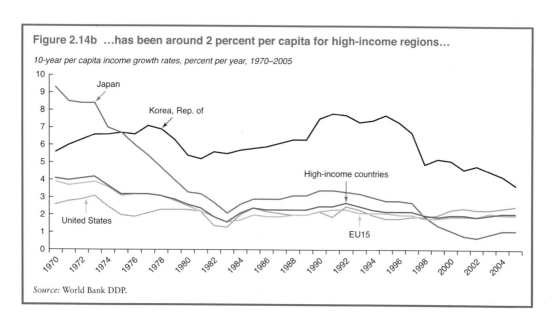

Figure 2.14b ...has been around 2 percent per capita for high-income regions...

10-year per capita income growth rates, percent per year, 1970–2005

Source: World Bank DDP.

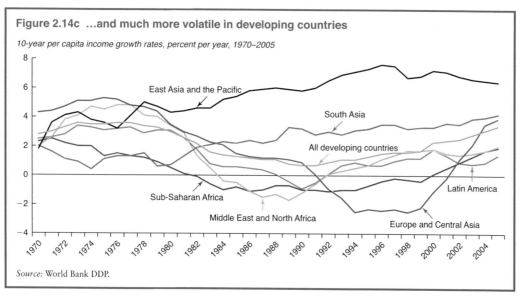

Figure 2.14c ...and much more volatile in developing countries

10-year per capita income growth rates, percent per year, 1970–2005

Source: World Bank DDP.

and 1970 in per capita terms. By 2005, the growth rate for developing countries had accelerated to 3.4 percent.

If instead of the 3.1 percent growth in per capita incomes assumed for developing countries in the central scenario, developing countries were to grow at their average for the entire 25-year period of 1.9 percent (with world growth a meager 1.4 percent), their incomes would be about 25 percent lower per capita. This translates into a reduction of GDP in 2030 by some $5.5 trillion, nearly $800 per person. This would be disappointing, and it underscores the importance of competent collective global economic management—and well-conceived domestic policies.

Still, it would take a sharp set of shocks to depress growth rates to this level. And only if these shocks were to occur in tandem, in more than one region, and with some adverse policy feedbacks would rates likely be depressed substantially below this level. Even then, the reversal in the growth and global integration process worldwide would likely be relatively short-lived. One reason is that one sees much greater stability on average for the three major economies of the world—Japan, the European Union (EU15), and the United States (figure 2.14b). Together, they make up more than two-thirds of the global economy. The European Union, and even more so Japan, benefited after the end of World War II from catching up to the United States and rebuilding after the devastation of the war. The oil crisis of the 1970s made a dent in the long-term growth rate in the early 1980s, but after a period of adjustment, long-term growth was fairly steady throughout much of the remaining period. The exception is Japan, which had a long period of adjustment during the 1990s, perhaps in part related to its changing demographics—occurring earlier than elsewhere. Korea, which in 1980 was not yet considered a high-income country, continued to show the process of catch-up that is only now beginning to show signs of fading. The figure suggests that it would take a really major event to shove the high-income countries off their relatively steady rate of 2 percent growth. The early energy crisis was such an event for a few years, but the long-term stagnation in Japan has not had the same impact.

It is always possible that nonlinear disturbances may cause a break in trends. The downside risks are also potentially considerable. As history has shown, countries could backtrack on their commitment to openness. Failure to address the negative consequences of a more integrated global economy could generate domestic pressures to reverse the process of opening. International tensions might degenerate into tit-for-tat tariff escalation or competitive devaluations. This was certainly an important factor in driving the world into recession in the 1930s. The world is probably more integrated today than in the 1930s, with many more actors having a much greater stake in an open global economy. But in many countries, domestic pressures to reverse the trends toward greater openness are ever present and one can never be too complacent about the strength of existing international institutions.

A key downside risk for high-income countries may come from the transition from a regime of steady economic growth and relatively stable labor force to one with a declining labor force and a rising and dependent population of elderly. The long stagnation of Japan through the 1990s and early part of this decade may be an indication of the pressures high-income countries will face in the next decades. The pressures are already being felt in Europe and the United States as economic policy makers attempt to deal with the impending "transfer" crisis—the benefits promised to aging baby boomers will translate into ever-higher tax rates on ever-smaller workforces unless benefits are modified. The way out will most likely involve a package of steps, in order to minimize the overall costs, but there is no guarantee that these steps will be politically acceptable.

The history of the 20th century, if not earlier, has also shown the danger to the global well-being from the competition for ever-scarcer resources, for example energy or minerals. The overall outlook for resources, at least through 2030, suggests the ability to cope with a growing global economy. Smoothly functioning markets should be able to allocate resources and/or provide the right signals for developing and supplying alternatives. Nonetheless, interference with markets that lead to substantial market disturbances could lead to a rise in international tensions and pressures to use military force. Over the last 50 years, conflicts that have arisen have been relatively contained, but in a changing global environment where economic and political objectives do not necessarily align, the chance for miscalculations could lead to broader-based conflict with significant global implications (see box 2.2).

Box 2.2 Challenge of geopolitical shifts for long-term economic forecasts: lessons of history

The economy does not exist in a vacuum; it is affected in myriad ways by the political, historical, and social context in which economic agents act, and history shows that to ignore this geopolitical context can lead the economic forecaster awry. For example, at the beginning of the 20th century the prevailing mood in Europe and its offshoots (such as the United States) was one of optimism and confidence. Per capita growth in Europe had accelerated to an unprecedented 1.5 percent between 1896 and 1913 on the heel of 1.1 percent growth between 1820 and 1896 coming after three centuries of near-zero growth. This growth was sustained by a relatively peaceful geopolitical environment thanks to the *Pax Britannica* and a stable balance of power in Europe, rapid technological change brought about by the first (steam) and second (electricity) industrial revolutions, and policy changes that enhanced openness, such as Britain's decision to reduce protectionism. However, this rapid economic growth was accompanied by important political, social, ideological, and military changes, and by 1913 there was a growing sense that war was somehow inevitable.

Based on the historical growth of the 30 years to 1900 and using standard econometric estimates, one would have predicted a fairly optimistic GDP trend for the "G-5" (France, Germany, Japan, the United Kingdom, and the United States) for the first half of the 20th century. The box figure shows the central prediction and the upper and lower bounds. The prediction is calculated by assuming yearly shocks similar in nature to those observed between 1870 and 1899 and implicitly on the strength of economic dynamics generated by continued globalization and technological progress. With the geopolitical shocks of the early 20th century, however, economic development followed a very different path. In fact, by 1949, actual GDP (of the G-5) was almost $300 billion (in 1990 international dollars) below the *lower-bound* prediction, an amount equivalent to 13 percent of actual output, highlighting the substantial and persistent effects of adverse geopolitical events.

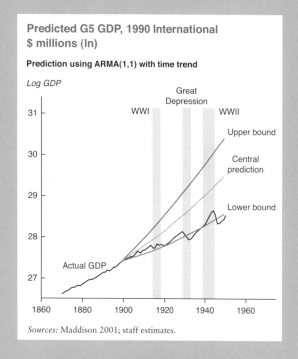

Predicted G5 GDP, 1990 International $ millions (ln)

Prediction using ARMA(1,1) with time trend

Sources: Maddison 2001; staff estimates.

By 1913 the political environment had deteriorated and led to outbreaks of conflict that ultimately escalated into World War I. In its aftermath, the Great Depression arose from a severe real economic shock that was exacerbated and propagated worldwide owing to poor economic management, an unprepared financial system, and weak institutions. In the long run, however, the forces pushing worldwide economic integration forward dominated the adverse impact of political shocks and globalization recovered powerfully after World War II. Policy was decisive in facilitating postwar resurgence: to keep "history at bay" in the words of a noted historian, domestic and international institutions were built that have allowed globalization to flourish in an environment of relative global peace.

Source: Fardoust and Goldberg 2006.

The ability of the planet to carry a growing population with rapidly growing demand for goods and services may be put to a severe test as the world moves forward. And even if catastrophes are largely avoided in the years to 2030, there is growing evidence that action needs to be taken soon, if not immediately, to avoid catastrophe in some future not far away. Rising incomes provide an opportunity—and the desire—to deal with many environmental issues, but this is no guarantee that the right decisions will be taken. Major changes in the environment, such as higher-than-predicted temperatures and/or dramatic changes in weather patterns could seriously impact regional economies, if not the global economy, with lower productivity, or worse yet, sickness and deaths.

Deviations from the central scenario are more likely to be in the form of extended periods of very rapid growth in some countries and regions and extended periods of stagnation in others, such as those witnessed over the past 25 years. A cataclysmic event that affects the entire globe for an extended period has a low probability—though from a geopolitical point of view, the world is likely in a period of transition. The end of the Cold War has shifted the world's major stress point and was, to a large extent, a conflict among the industrial countries—even if it had global spin-offs. New tensions are more likely to arise between the traditional industrial powers and developing countries—those that are rapidly rising and will ask for an increased voice in global discussions and decision making and those from failed states and/or regions. The already extensive integration of many countries in a global economy raises the stakes for all, but also provides an incentive to find a resolution through peaceful methods rather than through violence.

What if the world grows faster?

The global economy is benefiting from another period of sustained and broad-based growth. Among reasons are improved macroeconomic conditions (such as less inflation and inflationary expectations), more sustainable

debt levels (at least for developing countries on average), more diversified economies with less reliance on volatile commodities, a much greater role for services (which tend to be less volatile), much improved production management with lower inventories (which tended to be a major factor in past business cycles), and better macroeconomic management, particularly monetary policy.

The past 25 years have had numerous setbacks afflicting growth in the developing countries. Four of the six regions have suffered from very long bouts of stagnant or even negative growth—Sub-Saharan Africa, the Middle East and North Africa, Latin America, and Europe and Central Asia. They each had specific reasons for these periods of depressed growth ranging from Latin America's debt crisis in the 1980s, the Middle East and North Africa's (and, to a lesser extent, Africa's) energy decline, and Europe and Central Asia's emergence from its transition toward market-based economies. Nonetheless, growth has been much improved overall since 1998, in almost all regions, significant crises notwithstanding, and the decade-long run to 2005 produced increases per capita of some 4.6 percent annually.

Therefore the upside potential is even higher for developing countries, not only for technological and policy reasons, but also because the current momentum in the global economy remains strong. Developing-country growth could exceed 3 percent in 2020 and be down to 2.2 percent by 2030 in the central scenario (figure 2.15).

The upside potential for the high-income countries, however, is much more muted. This scenario therefore implies greater income convergence between developing countries and developed countries. It would also imply much greater weight for developing countries in the global economy. Instead of rising to 37 percent from an initial share of 21 percent in 2001, the developing-country share in global output would be 43 percent. More remarkably, China's share would climb to 15 percent, almost on a par with Europe, from its share of 3.7 percent in 2001, whereas the share for the

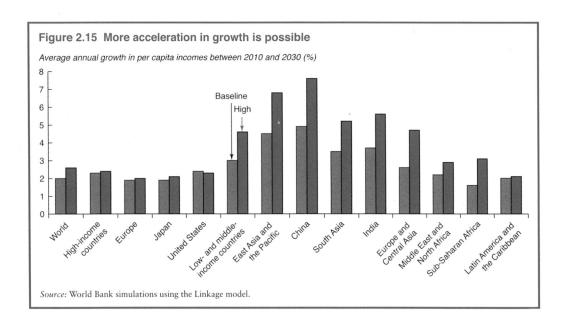

Figure 2.15 More acceleration in growth is possible

Average annual growth in per capita incomes between 2010 and 2030 (%)

Source: World Bank simulations using the Linkage model.

United States would drop to less than 25 percent from an initial position of 32 percent.

At the global level, the difference in the two scenarios—the central and the high-growth scenario—translates into an additional $11 trillion in 2030, of which $10 trillion is additional income for the developing countries—that is, an overall increase of 44 percent. Thus, much is at stake. This difference in outcome is about the same as one would have calculated in 1980 using the previous 10-year growth to predict where developing countries would be in 2005.

A number of discrete policy changes can have significant impacts on long-term growth even if they do not individually imply large deviations from baseline growth rates—particularly as seen from a regional or global level. The aforementioned trade liberalization scenario that is limited to merchandise goods only would raise the average developing-country growth rate by 0.2 percentage points and as high as 0.5 percentage points for some regions. Cumulatively over a 25-year period, this additional growth would end up as significantly higher incomes for many. This illustrates the importance of making progress in the current round of multilateral negotiations known as the Doha Development Agenda—without even describing the considerable distributional impacts of removing protection in the most distorted sectors, such as agriculture, could have in many developing countries.[34]

There are many other choices facing policy makers—most going well beyond the ability of this chapter's analytical framework to capture, such as improving institutions and the investment climate, deepening infrastructure, and implementing policies to achieve or surpass the MDGs and make for a healthier and more productive labor force. Cumulatively, making the right policy choices could dramatically change the growth prospects for a large number of countries. There are a number of countries that have demonstrated the ability to achieve very high growth rates for very long periods even with very different initial conditions in terms of endowments—human and natural—and institutions. In the same vein, getting "everything" right may not necessarily lead to the kind of high growth rates that many countries in East Asia have been able to generate.

The potential nonlinearities could also surprise on the upside. This chapter may be seriously underestimating the potential for further technological change because the world is still at the dawn of the information age, the biotechnology revolution, and other innovations. The chapter also assumes a rather benign policy environment even though barriers to trade in some instances, for example agriculture and services, are still prohibitively high, and many countries can still make vast improvements in domestic policies that could improve the investment climate and lead to capital deepening. Cumulatively some of these changes could have the same impact as that witnessed in East Asian economies starting with Japan in the 1950s and 1960s, followed by the newly industrializing economies, and now more recently by China.

Challenges of the coming globalization

The discussion suggests that an abrupt reversal in current trends—particularly toward a global economic collapse—has a very low probability. The central scenario—and any reasonable upward or downward deviation around it—will generate mostly positive consequences, but not exclusively. Globalization and growth will have uneven impacts leading to structural change, job losses in some sectors and regions, and the risk of some being left behind. And virtually any growth scenario will put stress on natural resources in the absence of corrective action.

Income distribution and jobs

As mentioned, incomes rise rapidly in developing countries—increasing an average 3.6 percent per capita across all regions, with the fastest growth in East and South Asia.[35] This is some 1 to 1.2 points more than income growth in developed countries, so there is some overall convergence in incomes—with some important exceptions, for example Sub-Saharan Africa and Latin America.

The distributional gains across households will largely reflect household endowments—of capital, land, and skills—and changes to the underlying returns to these endowments. The

returns to endowments could also be influenced by sectoral changes such that a migrant moving from rural to urban areas and from a low-wage country to high-wage country may benefit from higher wages even given the same intrinsic endowment (that is, skill level), albeit perhaps with a correction in welfare due to changes in prices.

The central scenario includes labor market segmentation between agricultural and nonagricultural sectors (for unskilled labor alone). The segmentation is only partial because agricultural workers seek higher-paying jobs in urban areas. All else equal, this would tend to raise wages in rural areas and cap wage rises in urban areas (compared with a no-migration scenario). The scenario suggests that the rural exodus could be a significant factor in the years ahead with the share of agricultural workers dropping from about 51 percent currently to less than 35 percent in 2030. Owing to population increase, this leads to only a small decrease in the agricultural labor force, but to an increase of over 1 billion in urban workers. The outward movement of agricultural workers is highest in East Asia and the Pacific and leads to a decline in the urban wage premium.

Another critical dimension in determining distributional outcomes is the change in the so-called skill premium, that is, the ratio of skilled wages relative to unskilled wages. According to the estimates (and definitions) of the authors of this study, the share of skilled workers is approximately 32 percent in developed countries and less than 10 percent in developing countries. The scenario assumes an acceleration of skilled workers relative to unskilled workers. Despite the acceleration in numbers, the skill premium tends to increase in most regions under this scenario. This reflects the assumption that skilled labor is a complement to capital, so demand for it increases more rapidly than supply. The skill premium increases most rapidly in those countries with a high investment rate. A second factor is the relative glut of unskilled workers as the rural exodus—largely an unskilled phenomenon—continues. A third factor is the relatively higher concentration of skilled workers in high-income elastic sectors, notably services.

In summary, the increase in value added for all developing countries can be decomposed into volume and price effects and further differentiated by factor of production. The average annual increase is 4.0 percent over the entire period. There is a rotation in value added toward skilled workers, their total share increasing from 11 percent to 17 percent, largely taken from capital's share that declines to 47 percent from 59 percent in 2005. Thirty percent of the increase is determined by the increase in unskilled wages and 15 percent by the increase in skilled wages (figure 2.16). The former is more important because of the relative weight of unskilled workers in total value added. Combined, wage increases account for 44 percent of the total increase in value added. The next-largest segment is the increase in the capital stock, representing 44 percent of the growth in value added (with changes in the return to capital not a factor). The results suggest a modest improvement for workers in developing countries over 25 years relative to owners of capital, but with a somewhat better outcome for skilled workers.

Under the baseline scenario, the poverty MDG is reached in 2015 at the global level, with the headcount index falling to 11.8 percent

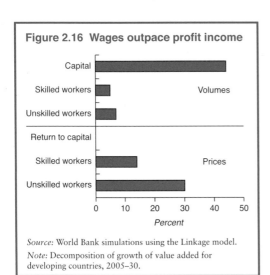

Figure 2.16 Wages outpace profit income

Source: World Bank simulations using the Linkage model.
Note: Decomposition of growth of value added for developing countries, 2005–30.

in 2015 from 20.2 percent in 2003 (table 2.3). The MDG target is just under 14 percent.[36] The poverty MDG is met broadly in all regions with the glaring exception of Sub-Saharan Africa, which will miss by a wide margin. By 2030, the percent of poor living on $1 a day or less will be near 8 percent of the developing-country population, or roughly 550 million persons.[37] Even with the longer term horizon, it is unlikely that the 2015 poverty MDG will be met in Sub-Saharan Africa without an acceleration in growth and more targeted interventions.

The global environment will come under increasing stress

While incomes, inequality, and poverty are at the heart of the debate on globalization and its impacts, energy and more specifically environmental impacts are lurking not far behind. Though the energy issue had been somewhat relegated to a less prominent position during most of the 1990s and early 2000s, the recent run-up in fossil fuel prices and the more alarming evidence of global warming have returned energy and environment to the front pages.

With world growth in the central scenario running at about 3 percent per year on average, primary energy demand (coal, oil, and natural gas) runs at about 2 percent per year. Under standard assumptions, this would not generate any significant tension on energy markets, with prices rising at about 1.4 percent per year in real terms from base year levels. Demand for natural gas would tend to outpace demand for oil and coal as policies and technology tend to favor this relatively cleaner fuel. Renewable and nuclear energy would tend to see somewhat higher growth rates (see chapter 5), but from a low base and therefore making only a modest impact. To accelerate their adaptation requires a more significant push from policies to increase investment in these technologies and taxes on conventional fuels to induce greater substitution.

Stagnant or declining production in high-income countries and high growth in some developing countries would lead to some (perhaps dramatic) changes in net trade in fossil

Table 2.3 Regional breakdown of poverty in developing countries

| | Millions of persons living on | | | | | | | |
| | less than $1 per day | | | | less than $2 per day | | | |
Region	1990	2003	2015	2030	1990	2003	2015	2030
East Asia and the Pacific	472	213	57	18	1,116	745	317	148
China	375	179	50	16	825	531	229	108
Rest of East Asia and the Pacific	97	34	7	2	292	213	88	40
Europe and Central Asia	2	9	5	3	23	71	40	26
Latin America and the Caribbean	49	49	38	30	125	134	118	103
Middle East and North Africa	6	5	3	1	51	62	45	31
South Asia	462	472	273	159	958	1,131	1,017	902
Sub-Saharan Africa	227	320	345	337	382	530	613	653
Low- and middle-income countries	1218	1,068	721	547	2,654	2,671	2,150	1,863
Excluding China	844	889	671	531	1,829	2,140	1,921	1,755

| | Percent of the population living on | | | | | | | |
| | less than $1 per day | | | | less than $2 per day | | | |
Region	1990	2003	2015	2030	1990	2003	2015	2030
East Asia and the Pacific	29.6	11.5	2.8	0.8	69.9	40.2	15.5	6.7
China	33.0	13.9	3.6	1.1	72.6	41.2	16.5	7.3
Rest of East Asia and the Pacific	21.1	6.0	1.1	0.2	63.2	37.7	13.5	5.4
Europe and Central Asia	0.5	1.9	1.0	0.6	4.9	15.0	8.4	5.5
Latin America and the Caribbean	11.3	9.1	6.1	4.1	28.4	24.9	18.8	14.2
Middle East and North Africa	2.3	1.7	0.7	0.2	21.4	21.0	12.3	6.5
South Asia	41.3	33.2	16.2	8.1	85.5	79.5	60.2	46.0
Sub-Saharan Africa	44.6	45.0	37.4	29.9	75.0	74.5	66.5	58.0
Low- and middle-income countries	27.9	20.2	11.8	7.8	60.8	50.5	35.1	26.7
Excluding China	26.1	22.2	14.2	9.7	56.6	53.5	40.6	31.9

Source: World Bank.

fuels. The high-income countries may be subject to an increase in their energy imbalance amounting to some $400 billion in 2030 (in 2001 dollars), more than a doubling from $175 billion in 2001. China's small deficit could balloon to over $100 billion and India's to $50 billion. The positive counterparts on a regional basis would be the Middle East and North Africa, Sub-Saharan Africa, Russia, and Latin America. Dutch-disease-type effects combined with the political economy of natural resource–rich countries may make it difficult for some to diversify their economies and prepare for a post-energy future.

Relatively benign economic impacts as regards energy do not imply that the negative externalities associated with continued dependence on carbon-based fossil fuels will not lead to severe environmental consequences—if not immediately, at some point in the future. There is mounting evidence that the

impacts of rising greenhouse gas concentrations are accelerating—at least in some parts of the world, notably at the two poles. Even accelerated penetration of clean energy is likely to leave the world largely fossil fuel dependent—at least over the next two decades—thus technologies need to be developed that limit the damage from burning conventional fuels, such as carbon sequestration. Such technologies combined with policies to accelerate the use of renewable fuels and improve energy efficiency would form the basis of a package to deal more forcefully with greenhouse gas emissions. These are developed further in chapter 5.

These three problems will require policy responses

The purpose of this chapter has been to outline a plausible evolution of the global economy and to highlight some of the key findings from the forward-looking exercise. Irrespective of whether growth rates exceed or fall short of the central scenario, it has exposed several problems that require further analysis and policy response. Three of the most important problems—income distribution, tensions in labor markets, and environmental risks that require multilateral response—are the subjects of the next three chapters.

Notes

1. Measured as the difference in the number of poor in 2002 using the 1990 poverty incidence (headcount) and the actual number of poor (at the $1/day poverty line).

2. *World Development Indicators 2006*, table 2.19.

3. Unless otherwise stated, historical growth rates are calculated using a log-linear regression growth model.

4. The first five rounds, concluding with the Dillon Round in 1961, involved 13–38 countries at most.

5. As of December 11, 2005 (www.wto.org).

6. The comparisons with goods trade are not necessarily straightforward. First, there are no price indexes for trade in services, so they are measured only in current dollar terms. Second, it is more difficult to evaluate trade in services, so their level is likely to be underestimated.

7. There is recent evidence that migration from the new EU member countries is higher than analysts had anticipated. See John Kay, "How the Migration Estimates Turned Out So Wrong," *Financial Times,* September 5, 2006.

8. Anecdotal evidence is provided in Sharon LaFraniere, "Cellphones Catapult Rural Africa to 21st Century," *New York Times,* August 25, 2005; Rodrique Ngowi, "Africa's Cellphone Explosion Changes Economics, Society," *Associated Press,* October 16, 2005; and Kevin Sullivan, "For India's Traditional Fisherman, Cellphones Deliver a Sea Change," *Washington Post,* October 15, 2006.

9. To avoid repetition, unless stated otherwise, all incremental values represent changes between 2005 and 2030—either absolute levels or average annual compound rate changes.

10. All prices are at 2001 levels—the base year of the scenario. Volume growth will therefore reflect 2001 weights. Prices and values reflect changes with respect to the model numéraire, which is a price index of manufactured exports from the high-income countries—similar in concept to the World Bank's manufactured

unit value (MUV) index. This index is set to 1 in the base and all subsequent years. Thus future values, for example of GDP, do not integrate the normal secular increase in prices that are generated by changes in money supply. Technically the price of manufactured exports of high-income countries is fixed and only changes in relative prices matter. Say for example that world GDP is 100 in 2001 and 200 in 2030 in real terms, that is, the volume of output has doubled. Say that relative to the numéraire, the price of GDP is unchanged so that the value is also 200. If instead there were a steady increase in nominal inflation, say prices would have increased by an average of 2.5 percent per year, the price of GDP would have more or less doubled between 2001 and 2030 and nominal GDP would be 400, not 200. There would of course be no change in volume growth, and assuming super-neutrality, all relative prices would also be identical to assuming zero nominal inflation.

11. The rankings refer to the model-based aggregation, not at the actual country level.

12. To attenuate the problems with exchange rate movements, the rankings are based on a five-year moving average of dollar-based GDP centered on 1982 and 2003.

13. Here welfare is equated with income per capita, but of course the authors recognize that there are many other variables that affect individual well-being—such as health, family and friends, and so on.

14. One such commonly used index is the so-called Big Mac index popularized by the *Economist.* This index compares the cost of purchasing a Big Mac in a variety of cities across the world. While McDonald's prides itself on selling a well-recognized and largely homogeneous product across the world, the raw inputs in a Big Mac—perhaps priced the same everywhere if one assumes that they are perfectly traded on world markets—only represent a small portion of the cost of the final product. A large portion of the Big Mac will be composed of the wages paid to local workers and managers and the rent on land and buildings. These are likely to be much lower in many developing countries and hence represent an approximation of the PPP exchange rate. Thus if a Big Mac sells for an average of $4 in the United States but $1 in China, the PPP exchange rate would be 4. When this calculation is scaled up, if China's GDP is evaluated at 8 trillion renminbi and converted to U.S. dollars at a rate of 8 renminbi per $1, its GDP in dollar terms (at the market exchange rate) is $1 trillion. Using a PPP exchange rate of 4, the Chinese economy would then evaluate to $4 trillion. However, this chapter argues that this conversion is largely valid to make intercountry welfare comparisons and not for making judgments about the relative size of the respective economies.

15. There is recent theoretical and empirical work on what makes countries grow that could provide more practical implications for policy makers than the widely discussed cross-country panel regressions. Both of these strands rely on complementarities across policies and other development-related necessities such as infrastructure needs. In the theoretical literature this has been referred to as the O-ring theory of growth and comes from the analogy with the U.S. space shuttle disaster. In that disaster, it was a simple and cheap O-ring that failed. So despite the billions of parts and scientific know-how that goes into putting the shuttle in space, the failure of any part, no matter how simple or inexpensive, is enough to bring it down. In growth theory, the same can be applied. A country can have, say, 9 out of 10 growth-related necessities absolutely perfect, but if the 10th is a failure, there will be no take-off because of the complementarities across these necessities. Recent empirical work by Hausman, Rodrik, and Velasco (2004) has used so-called growth diagnostic tools to assist in finding the bottlenecks to growth and providing a road map for the appropriate sequencing of policies to overcome the bottlenecks.

16. For example, fewer office workers could reduce the need for office space, computers, furniture, and the like.

17. Car manufacturing in Japan is much less labor intensive than in other countries owing to the scarcity (and hence the price of) labor. Agriculture in the United States could become more mechanized in the absence of abundant cheap labor ("The Worker Next Door" by Barry Chiswick, *New York Times*, June 3, 2006).

18. These numbers are based purely on the growth rate of the working-age population, defined as the population aged between 15 and 65. In effect it currently assumes that labor force participation rates are zero for the rest of the population and that the participation rates for the 15–65 group are fixed. Further, it makes no explicit assumption regarding migration, though one could infer that the proportion of migrants as a share of the population remains constant.

19. Much of the recent turnaround in Sub-Saharan Africa is also largely based on increased global demand for natural resources—whose labor intensity in most cases is relatively low, save for agriculture.

20. The standard replacement rate, that is, the rate of fertility that would keep population at a steady-state level is 2.1 births per female, to take into account average mortality rates and other factors.

21. Of course, this represents a relatively narrow definition of dependency because an increasing number of youths pursue education well beyond high school and often with parental support.

22. Several additional points are worth highlighting regarding the demographic scenario. Though most of the macroeconomic literature refers to the youth and elderly dependency ratios, it could also be true that there are macroeconomic dimensions to the gross dependency ratio, that is, the ratio of all nonworkers to workers. Countries that have had high births in the recent past and that have relatively low labor force participation rates will tend to have higher total dependency ratios, all else being equal. Sub-Saharan Africa, for example, has relatively greater declines in the total dependency ratio than the Middle East and North Africa despite its more rapid population growth because the labor force participation rate is higher. In fact, on this score, Sub-Saharan Africa has a lower dependency ratio than Latin America, which has lower workforce participation and a more rapidly aging population. Altering assumptions on labor force participation—for example a rise in female and/or elderly participation—could affect these total dependency ratios.

23. The baseline does track changes in policies between the base year of 2001 and 2005, notably China's commitments following its accession to the WTO, EU expansion, and the removal of the textile and apparel quotas.

24. The literature on empirical studies of the life-cycle theory is voluminous. Studies of macroeconomic data in industrial countries have found significant relationships between dependency ratios and saving rates (see for example Masson and Tryon 1990; Meredith 1995; IMF 2004; Higgins 1998; Masson, Bayoumi, and Samiei 1998; Lee and Kim 2005). By contrast, household survey evidence typically finds only weak, or even positive effects, of dependency ratios on savings (Turner and others 1998). The difference is likely due to weaknesses in the survey data (for example, the surveys often do not include pension data), the failure to adequately assess the disproportionate impact of the wealthy on aggregate savings, differences in age cohort behavior, and the failure to consider interactions among households, firms, and government.

25. This would reverse the trend of past decades. Bloom and Canning (2004) estimate that one-third of the East Asian economic miracle may be accounted for by a demographically induced rise in savings and investment. Higgins and Williamson (1996) find that much of the rise in Asian saving rates since the 1960s is due to a decline in youth dependency ratios.

26. On the other hand, Börsch-Supan, Ludwig, and Winter (2001) claim that the elasticity of substitution between capital and labor is close to one in industrial countries, meaning that production processes can be modified easily to substitute labor for capital, which would limit the impact of demographic change on investment.

27. OECD (2005) notes that the model-based simulations typically assume that labor is immobile, that capital is perfectly mobile, and that investors have

perfect foresight. Allowing for immigration, capital account restrictions, and risk aversion would reduce the magnitude of capital flow shifts in response to aging.

28. The share of institutions, defined as pension funds, insurance corporations, and mutual funds in household portfolios in OECD countries has risen from 17 percent in 1970 to 38 percent in 2003 (OECD 2005). World Bank (1997) shows that regulations also limit the share of investments by institutional investors in foreign assets.

29. Morin and Suarez (1983) and Bakshi and Chen (1994) find evidence that risk aversion rises with age; Riley and Chow (1992) and Halek and Eisenhauer (2001) find that risk aversion declines with age until 65, but then increases; while Bellante and Saba (1986) and Jianakoplos and Bernasek (1998) find that risk aversion falls with age. Bellante and Green (2004) find that risk aversion tends to increase with age, for any given level of wealth.

30. For example, Poterba and Samwick (1997) find significant differences in asset ownership of different birth cohorts. Older households today are more likely to hold relatively risky stock, and less likely to hold tax-exempt bonds, than younger households. But this says nothing about how the current, older-generation attitudes will change as they age.

31. Considerable controversy exists concerning the appropriate measure of personal savings in the United States, the determinants of the steady decline in saving rates, and the extent to which low saving represents household dependence on the rise in housing assets or reliance on pensions. Whatever the actual level of saving, there is little doubt that appropriately measured, it has fallen significantly over the past two decades.

32. Not all technologies are freely available, of course. Patents and other forms of intellectual property protection imply that still significant portions of technological transfers will come through joint ventures with firms holding the rights to those technologies.

33. The philanthropic efforts of the Bill and Melinda Gates Foundation and others provide some reason for optimism that progress can be made in some of these areas.

34. Significantly more detail on the potential impacts of various Doha scenarios is available in Anderson and Martin (2006).

35. Per capita growth is somewhat higher when measured at PPP exchange rates owing to different weights—notably for China.

36. The 2015 forecast represents some changes from last year's poverty forecast published in *Global Economic Prospects 2006*. The first notable difference is the change in the base year for the forecast—now 2003 instead of 2002. Despite the more recent year, both the number and percentage of poor (at the $1-a-day level) is higher in the base year, respectively 1,068 and 20.2 percent compared with 1,011 and 19.3 percent. (A printing error appeared in last year's report regarding the 2002 numbers for the $1-a-day poverty indicator.) Principally this is due to three factors. (1) Population figures have been revised. (2) The new estimates for the base year incorporate 38 new surveys covering the 2003/04 period. Many of the new surveys include large countries such as Argentina, Brazil, Mexico, and the República Bolivariana de Venezuela in Latin America; Pakistan in South Asia; and Nigeria in Sub-Saharan Africa. (3) Adjustments to a common base year incorporate the latest information on price inflation and growth in private consumption. These same factors also impact the forecast to 2015, since the new surveys will be associated with new estimates of the poverty-to-growth elasticity and the revised population forecasts will impact the estimate of the absolute number of poor. One additional factor has been a revision to the Chinese estimate of the poverty elasticity with respect to changes in the income distribution (as measured by the Gini coefficient). The estimate of this elasticity has been revised upward so that more poverty is associated with a rise in inequality. While for most countries, the 2015 forecast assumes distribution neutrality, in the case of China, both the rural and urban Gini coefficient is assumed to deteriorate by 10 percent. Thus, a rise in this elasticity leads to a worsening of poverty, all else remaining constant, though counteracted, nonetheless, by relatively high income growth.

37. The 2030 poverty forecast does not use the same methodology as the poverty forecast for 2015 and instead is based on a straight poverty and growth elasticity approach. The 2015 forecast uses all of the available household information at the country level combined with a country-specific forecast of per capita consumption growth. The 2030 forecast uses the elasticity approach at the regional level. It combines the implicit growth elasticities from the 2003/2015 poverty forecast with the regional per capita growth rate between 2015 and 2030 as anticipated in the central scenario. The projection is meant to be broadly indicative of potential improvements and to highlight regional differences.

References

Ameriks, John, and Stephen P. Zeldes. 2004. "How Do Household Portfolio Shares Vary with Age." Working Paper, Columbia Business School, New York, NY.

Anderson, Kym, and Will Martin, eds. 2006. *Agricultural Trade Reform and the Doha Development Agenda*. Washington, DC: Palgrave Macmillan and the World Bank.

Bakshi, Gurdip, and Zhiwu Chen. 1994. "Baby Boom, Population Aging and Capital Markets." *Journal of Business* 67 (2): 165–202.

Bellante, Don, and Carole A. Green. 2004. "Relative Risk Aversion among the Elderly." *Review of Financial Economics* 13: 269–81.

Bellante, Don, and Richard P. Saba. 1986. "Human Capital and Life-Cycle Effects on Risk Aversion." *Journal of Financial Research* 9 (1): 41–51.

Bernanke, Ben S. 2006. Remarks made at the Federal Reserve Bank of Kansas City's Thirtieth Annual Economic Symposium, Jackson Hole, WY, August 25.

Bloom, David E., and David Canning. 2004. "Global Demographic Change: Dimensions and Economic Significance." In *Global Demographic Change: Economic Impacts and Policy Challenges,* proceedings of a symposium, pp. 9–56, sponsored by the Federal Reserve Bank of Kansas City, Jackson Hole, Wyoming, August 26–28, 2004.

Bodie, Zvi, Robert C. Merton, and William F. Samuelson. 1992. "Labor Supply Flexibility and Portfolio Choice in a Life Cycle Model." *Journal of Economic Dynamics and Control* 16: 427–49.

Börsch-Supan, Axel. 1996. "The Impact of Population Ageing on Savings, Investment and Growth in OECD Area." In *Future Global Capital Shortages: Real Threat or Pure Fiction?* Paris: Organisation for Economic Co-operation and Development.

Börsch-Supan, Axel, Alexander Ludwig, and Joachim Winter. 2001. "Aging and International Capital Flows." NBER Working Paper No. 8553, National Bureau of Economic Research, Cambridge, MA.

Bosworth, Barry P., and Susan M. Collins. 2003. "The Empirics of Growth: An Update." *Brookings Paper on Economic Activity* 2: 113–206.

Bryant, Ralph C. 2004. "Cross-Border Macroeconomic Implications of Demographic Change." In *Global Demographic Change: Economic Impacts and Policy Challenges,* proceedings of a symposium pp. 9–56, sponsored by the Federal Reserve Bank of Kansas City, Jackson Hole, Wyoming, August 26–28, 2004.

Cutler, David M., James M. Poterba, Louise M. Sheiner, Lawrence H. Summers, and George A. Akerlof. 1990. "An Aging Society: Opportunity or Challenge?" *Brookings Papers on Economic Activity* 1: 1–73.

David, Paul A. 1990. "The Dynamo and the Computer: An Historical Perspective on the Modern Productivity Paradox." *The American Economic Review* 80 (2) (May): 355–62.

Fardoust, Shahrokh, and Jonathan E. Goldberg. 2006. "Predicting the Future, Looking into the 'Rearview Mirror.'" World Bank, Washington, DC, August.

Fougère, Maxine, and Marcel Mérette. 1997. "Population Aging and Economic Growth in Seven OECD Countries." *Economic Modeling* 16: 411–27.

Goldman Sachs. 2003. "Dreaming with BRICs: The Path to 2050." *Global Economics Paper* 99 (October).

Gordon, Robert J. 2000. "Does the 'New Economy' Measure Up to the Great Inventions of the Past?" *Journal of Economic Perspectives* 14 (4) (Fall): 49–74.

Halek, Martin, and Joseph G. Eisenhauer. 2001. "Demography of Risk Aversion." *Journal of Risk and Insurance* 68 (1): 1–24.

Hausman, Ricardo, Dani Rodrik, and Andrés Velasco. 2004. "Growth Diagnostics." Kennedy School of Government, Harvard University, Cambridge, MA.

Helliwell, John F. 2004. "Demographic Changes and International Factor Mobility." NBER Working Paper No. 10945, National Bureau of Economic Research, Cambridge, MA.

Higgins, Matthew. 1998. "Demography, National Savings, and International Capital Flows." *International Economic Review* 39 (2): 343–69.

Higgins, Matthew, and Jeffrey G. Williamson. 1996. "Asian Demography and Foreign Capital Dependence." NBER Working Paper No. 5560, National Bureau of Economic Research, Cambridge, MA.

IMF. 2004. *World Economic Outlook.* Washington, DC: International Monetary Fund.

Jianakoplos, Nancy Ammon, and Alexandra Bernasek. 1998. "Are Women More Risk-Averse?" *Economic Inquiry* 36: 620–30.

Ketkar, Suhas, and Dilip Ratha. 2001. "Development Financing during a Crisis: Securitization of Future Receivables." Policy Research Working Paper No. 2582, World Bank, Washington, DC.

———. 2005. "Recent Advances in Future-Flow Securitization." *The Financier* 11/12: 1–14.

Kimball, Miles S. 1993. "Standard Risk Aversion." *Econometrica* 61 (May): 589–611.

Lee, Jong–Wha, and Soyoung Kim. 2005. "Global Implications of Demographic Changes." Korea University. Paper prepared for the keynote speech at the International Symposium on Aging Problems in Northeast Asia, August 25–26, Fudan University, China.

Levinson, Marc. 2006. *The Box: How the Shipping Container Made the World Smaller and the World Economy Bigger.* Princeton, NJ: Princeton University Press.

Loayza, Norman, Klaus Schmidt-Hebbel, and Luis Servén. 2000. "Saving in Developing Countries:

An Overview." *The World Bank Economic Review* 14 (3): 391–414.

Lührmann, Melanie. 2003. "Demographic Change, Foresight and International Capital Flows." *MEA Discussion Paper* 38-03, Mannheim Research Institute for the Economics of Aging (MEA), Universität Mannheim, Germany.

Maddison, Angus. 2001. *The World Economy: A Millennial Perspective.* Paris: Development Centre Studies, OECD.

Martin, Will, and Devashish Mitra. 1999. "Productivity Growth and Convergence in Agriculture and Manufacturing." World Bank Policy Research Working Paper No. 2171, Washington, DC. August.

Masson, Paul, Tamim Bayoumi, and Hossein Samiei. 1998. "International Evidence on the Determinants of Private Saving." *World Bank Economic Review* 12 (3): 483–501.

Masson, Paul, and Ralph W. Tryon. 1990. "Macroeconomic Effects of Projected Population Aging in Industrial Countries." *IMF Staff Papers* 37 (September): 453–85.

McKibbin, Warwick J. 2005. "The Global Macroeconomic Consequences of a Demographic Transition." Centre for Applied Macroeconomic Analysis, Australian National University, August.

Meredith, Guy. 1995. "Demographic Change and Household Saving in Japan." In "Saving Behavior and the Asset Price Bubble in Japan," IMF Occasional Paper No. 124, International Monetary Fund, Washington, DC.

Morin, Roger A., and Antonio Fernandez Suarez. 1983. "Risk Aversion Revisited." *The Journal of Finance* 38 (4): 1201–16.

OECD. 2005. *Financial Market Trends: Ageing and Pension System Reform, Implications for Financial Markets and Economic Policies,* Vol. 2005, Supplement 1. Paris: Organisation for Economic Co-operation and Development.

Poterba, James M., and Andrew A. Samwick. 1997. "Household Portfolio Allocation over the Life Cycle." NBER Working Paper 6185, National Bureau of Economic Research, Cambridge, MA.

PricewaterhouseCoopers. 2006. "The World in 2050: How Big Will the Emerging Economies Get and How Can the OECD Compete?" March.

Riley, William B., and K. Victor Chow. 1992. "Asset Allocation and Individual Risk Aversion." *Financial Analysis Journal* 48 (6): 32–37.

Samuelson, Paul A. 1989. "A Case At Last for Age-Phased Reduction in Equity." *Proceedings of the National Academy of Sciences* (November): 9048–51.

Turner, David, Claude Giorno, Alain De Serres, Ann Vourc'h, and Pete Richardson. 1998. "The Macroeconomic Implications of Ageing in a Global Context." Economic Department Working Papers No. 193, Organisation for Economic Co-operation and Development, Paris.

Tyers, Rod, and Qun Shi. 2005. "Global Demographic Change, Labour Force Growth and Economic Performance." Faculty of Economics and Commerce, Australian National University, June.

UN (United Nations). 2004. *World Population Prospects: The 2004 Revision.* New York: Department of Economic and Social Affairs, Population Division. Available at www.un.org/esa/population/publications/WPP2004/2004EnglishES.pdf.

van der Mensbrugghe, Dominique. 2006a. "Linkage Technical Reference Document: Version 6.0." World Bank, Washington, DC.

———. 2006b. "Scenario Building through 2030 with the Linkage Model." World Bank, Washington, DC.

Wade, Nicholas. 2006. *Before the Dawn: Recovering the Lost History of Our Ancestors.* New York: Penguin.

World Bank. 1997. *Private Capital Flows to Developing Countries: The Road to Financial Integration.* New York: Oxford University Press.

———. 2006a. *Global Economic Prospects: Economic Implications of Remittances and Migration.* Washington, DC: World Bank.

———. 2006b. *Global Development Finance.* Washington, DC: World Bank.

———. 2006c. "South-South Migration and Remittances." World Bank, Washington, DC.

3

Income Distribution, Inequality, and Those Left Behind

Over the past 20 years, the global distribution of income has undergone significant structural shifts. While aggregate measures of global inequality have changed little between the 1980s and today, the relative positions of countries and the welfare of millions of the world's citizens have experienced much more dramatic transformations. The sustained high growth rates of China and India (and to a lesser extent, those of other Asian nations) lifted millions out of poverty, while the stagnation in many African countries caused them to fall behind. In comparing the world income distribution in 1980 with that in 2002, one study notes that the poorest country in 2002 had a lower income per capita than the poorest country in 1980 (Bourguignon, Levin, and Rosenblatt 2004). The same is true for the entire bottom 6 percent of the world income distribution. Are these trends likely to continue in the future? Who will be the poor and the rich of 2030 under the global scenarios developed in the previous chapter?

Average incomes of people in developing countries are expected in chapter 2's baseline scenario to converge slowly toward levels in high-income countries. But for households in particular countries and particular social groups, improvements in living standards over the coming decades are likely to be much more dramatic than those suggested by the averages—and other households are likely to benefit less than average. This chapter explores future trends in income distribution to identify households positioned to benefit most and least, and suggests policy interventions to help spread the benefits of the anticipated growth over the next several decades. Building on the demographic and educational trends described in the previous chapter, it explores whether incomes are likely to become more equal across and within countries. It also examines the role of globalization in producing these outcomes, through the lens of microanalysis at the household level (see box 3.1; see also Bussolo and others [forthcoming], available at www.worldbank.org/prospects/gep2007, for methodological details).

Findings for any specific country or region should be taken with a grain of salt. First, microsimulation techniques used here mimic markets' adjustments and agents' responses only imperfectly. Furthermore, potentially large measurement errors and comparability issues affect the income and consumption data used in the microsimulation model. Second, the focus on income (or consumption) inequality deals with inequality of *outcomes* and not inequality of *opportunities*. This is because it is less difficult to measure income inequality than to measure inequality of opportunities.

For details on the methods used to project the world income distribution in 2030 please visit www.worldbank.org/prospects/gep2007.

Box 3.1   Changes in demographic structure, occupational choices, and factor rewards determine the authors' hypothetical 2030 world income distribution

This chapter's forward-looking exercise is based on methodologies developed in recent literature, including Bourguignon and Pereira da Silva (2003); Ferreira and Leite (2003, 2004); Chen and Ravallion (2003); and Bussolo, Lay, and van der Mensbrugghe (2006). The objective of the exercise is to create a hypothetical income distribution for all countries of the world in 2030. The starting point is global income distribution in 2000, assembled using data from household surveys for 84 countries and data on income groups (usually vintiles) for the remaining countries (see this book's Web site for a full detailed list). The hypothetical 2030 distribution is then obtained by applying three main exogenous changes to the initial distribution: (a) demographic changes, including aging and shifts in the skill composition of the population; (b) shifts in the sectoral composition of employment; and (c) economic growth, including changes in relative wages across skills and sectors.

In reality these changes take place simultaneously, but in this chapter's simplified framework they are accommodated in a sequential fashion. In the first step, total population in each country is expanded until it reaches the World Bank's projections for 2030. The structure of the population is also changed; for example, as fertility rates decrease and life expectancy increases, older age cohorts will become larger in many countries. To accommodate these changes in the surveys data, larger weights have been assigned to older people than have been assigned to younger individuals. In the next step, workers move from traditional agricultural sectors to more dynamic industrial and service sectors, and new incomes are estimated for these movers. Finally, consistent with an overall growth rate of real income per capita, changes in labor remuneration by skill level and sector are

applied to each worker in the sample depending on their education and sector of employment. The number of workers changing sectoral occupation and the differential growth rates in wage rewards used to "shock" the study's micro-data are consistent with the results of the global computable general equilibrium (CGE) model described in the previous chapter. (Note that the outcomes of the CGE model are also influenced by the same demographic changes described above.)

The sequential changes described above reshape national income distribution under a set of strong assumptions. In particular, income inequality within population subgroups formed by age, skills, and sector of employment is assumed to be constant over the period. Moreover, data limitations affect estimates of the initial inequality and its evolution. In particular, consumption data are not available for all countries' surveys, so, to get a global picture, the study had to include countries for which only income data were available. Consumption expenditure is a more reliable welfare measure than income, and its distribution is normally more equal than the distribution of income. Finally, measurement errors implicit in purchasing power parity (PPP) exchange rates, which have been used to convert local currency units, also affect comparability across countries.

The resulting income distribution should thus not be seen as a *forecast* of what the future distribution might look like; instead it should be interpreted as the result of an exercise that captures the *ceteris paribus* distributional effect of demographic, sectoral, and economic changes. Although the results of this exercise provide a good starting point for debating potential policy trade-offs, they should not be used as the basis for detailed policy blueprints.

Note: For details see www.worldbank.org/prospects/gep2007.

Therefore policy conclusions based on income inequality scenarios in this chapter should be considered with caution. For example, some degree of inequality can be the

reflection of efficient incentive structures, even though excessive levels of inequality are often associated with market distortions and protection of vested interests. Moreover, the redistribution of opportunities has to include "deep" institutional reform often accompanied or "financed" by some redistribution of outcomes. These concerns notwithstanding, individuals' economic status can shape the opportunities they have to improve their situation (World Bank 2005), so income levels are often correlated with access to better education and health, which in turn are key determinants of future earnings. To reiterate a central message of the 2006 *World Development Report* (World Bank 2005: 10), "equity-enhancing redistributions can often be efficiency-increasing."

With these limitations in mind, the chapter's exploration of the distributional effects of future scenarios in the global economy raises some broad policy issues. It highlights five key messages:

- For a large number of people in developing countries, the convergence to Organisation for Economic co-operation and Development (OECD) income levels will come much faster than the average numbers suggest. In 2030, 16.1 percent of the world population will belong to what can be called a "global middle class," up from 7.6 percent in 2000. That is, in 2030 more than a billion people in developing countries will buy cars, engage in international tourism, demand world-class products, and require international standards for higher education. Compare that with only 400 million people in developing countries who had access to these kinds of living standards in 2000. Assuming faster income convergence in a scenario where developing countries continue for the next 25 years the sustained pace of growth in recent years, the share of the global middle class in the world population will rise even further, to 19.4 percent. This large middle class will create rapidly growing markets for international products and services—and become a new force in domestic politics.
- Poverty will decline worldwide, but the remaining poor are likely to be more concentrated in Sub-Saharan Africa. At present, almost half of the poorest tenth of the world's people live in South Asia; by 2030 this could be reduced to just one-fifth. By contrast, Africa, now home to one-third of the world's poorest people, may see its share double by 2030. The likelihood of this outcome is high, even if favorable developments in Africa continue.
- In a given growth context, individuals will realize most of their income gains by moving from one social group to another. The income gains that people achieve by migrating out of agriculture into manufacturing and services or by attaining higher skill levels surpass by far the gradual increases of those who do not move. Consequently, and conditional on higher sustainable growth rates, policies that reduce restrictions to mobility across sectors and that provide broader access to education are key to spreading the benefits of growth.
- Although general indicators of global income distribution will probably change little, growth will generate pressure toward increasing inequality *within* a number of developing countries, calling for policy interventions to offset these forces. Trade integration, a key aspect of globalization and important for efficiency, does not seem to systematically increase inequality. As average incomes rise, the number of poor will shrink and the tax base will grow, making effective assistance easier to provide and social safety nets a viable remedy for increasing inequality.
- Although investing in education may not by itself be enough to spur growth, improved access to education at any given level of growth can limit the rise in income inequality and reduce poverty by facilitating the movement of poor people from low-paying jobs in agriculture to higher-paying jobs in industry and services.

The global distribution of income

Assessment of past inequality trends is contentious

Assessing what has happened to global income distribution in the last two decades—and what will happen in the next 25 years—presents challenges. Part of the difficulty lies with choosing an appropriate measure of inequality. The literature identifies three main approaches to measuring income inequality, all of which have strengths, but each of which measures a slightly different thing.[1]

- *Intercountry inequality* is a concept favored by macroeconomists. It measures relative movements of per capita incomes across countries and gives each country an equal weight in the world distribution (that is, population size does not matter). This literature tends to conclude that in the last two decades, income distribution has become more unequal.

- *International inequality* takes into account the relative sizes of countries (that is, results are population-weighted). Its proponents (such as Theil and Seale 1994) point out that failing to use population weights will cause, for example, the fast growth of China to be exactly offset by the anemic growth rates of Malawi or Honduras, even though the number of Chinese citizens who experienced improvements in their incomes far exceeds the populations of either of the other two countries.[2] The broad consensus in this literature is that income inequality has decreased, although this finding is mostly driven by the fast growth in China and India.[3]

- *Global inequality*, which compares individual incomes regardless of country of citizenship, is a fairly recent concept (Milanovic 2002). It takes into account within-country inequality, which is ignored by the international inequality approach, where each individual is deemed to earn the country's average income. To a large extent, fast growth in the large emerging economies tends to offset the increases in inequality within countries; therefore by this measure, global inequality has remained roughly constant since the late 1980s.

Even though these three methodologies can yield quite different pictures of past and future trends, and none is clearly preferable to the others (Ravallion 2004), it is worth elaborating on some general trends.[4]

Intercountry measurements of inequality suggest that the last five decades of development have done little to bring the average incomes of developing countries closer to those of OECD countries. For example, Quah (1996, 1997) finds "emerging twin peaks" in the global distribution, supporting the argument that the relative distance between the top and the bottom of the global income distribution has increased since the 1950s. More generally, Pritchett (1997) has concluded that a "big time" divergence in incomes occurred between 1870 and 1990, evidenced by a doubling of the gap between the per capita incomes of the rich and poor countries.[5] Underlying this general pattern is a large degree of variation in individual country performance, with growth peaks and valleys across various regional groupings and time periods. However, the overall trend is of an increasing distance between countries in different income brackets, although Pritchett (1997) also shows evidence of convergence at the top of the distribution (that is, among the group of today's high-income countries).

Once different weights are assigned to countries based on their population (using the international inequality approach), the global income distribution appears to have improved. For example, Bourguignon, Levin, and Rosenblatt (2004) demonstrate a decrease in world income inequality between 1980 and 2002, as long as the relevant inequality measures are not too sensitive to the distance of mean income from the bottom.[6] A similar decrease is observed by Atkinson and Brandolini (2004).[7] However, these approaches do not take into account inequality *within* countries (see box 3.2 for the importance of accounting for within-country distributional changes),

Box 3.2 Aggregate economic performance: distribution matters

In measuring social welfare, economists have struggled to provide simple statistics that reflect changes in both aggregate income (that is, the gross national product—GNP) and distribution. This box presents a graphic approach—the growth incidence curve (GIC)—that, by jointly measuring size and distribution effects, provides an intuitive evaluation of welfare changes.

The basic idea behind the GIC was already present more than 30 years ago in a well-known study entitled "Redistribution with Growth." In this study, Chenery and others (1974) proposed to use the weighted sum of the growth of all income groups as a summary measure for changes in social welfare. In a typical developing country the top two quintiles—the richest 40 percent of the population—would normally account for about three-quarters of total GNP. Therefore the GNP growth rate, the most commonly used index of performance, measures the income growth of the richer minority and "is not much affected by what happens to the income of the remaining 60 percent of the population" (Chenery and others 1974: 40). The trends observed in aggregate economic performance will differ according to the weights associated to the various income groups. Chenery and others (1974) found that when using GNP growth rates, where the weights are income shares of the initial distribution,

Brazil, Mexico, Panama, and República Bolivariana de Venezuela showed strong positive growth. However, because of their worsening income distributions, when equal weights (0.2 for each quintile) or poverty weights (0.6 for the poorer 40 percent, 0.3 for the next 40 percent, and 0.1 for the richest quintile) are used, these countries display much lower welfare increases. Conversely, countries enjoying improving income distribution during the 1960s and 1970s, such as Colombia, El Salvador, Sri Lanka, and Taiwan (China), scored better when their performance was measured with indicators that gave more weight to poorer individuals.

This weighting idea underlies the GIC, originally proposed by Ravallion and Chen (2003). The GIC is a graphical representation of the growth rate in income or consumption at each percentile of the distribution. It can summarize the distributional effects of income growth by plotting the cumulative share of the population (the x-axis) against the income growth rate of the nth percentile of the distribution (the y-axis) when the population percentiles are ranked in ascending order of income. Ravallion and Chen (2003) show that a measure of pro-poor growth can be obtained by integrating under the GIC. However, a simple comparison of the growth rate of the poorest percentiles against the mean

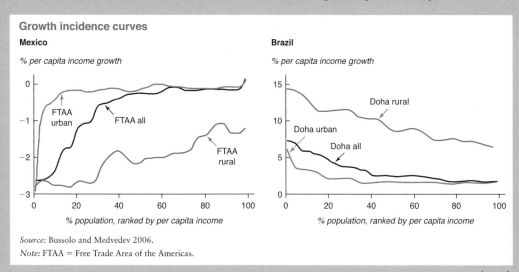

Growth incidence curves

Mexico

% per capita income growth

Brazil

% per capita income growth

% population, ranked by per capita income

Source: Bussolo and Medvedev 2006.

Note: FTAA = Free Trade Area of the Americas.

(continued)

Box 3.2 *(continued)*

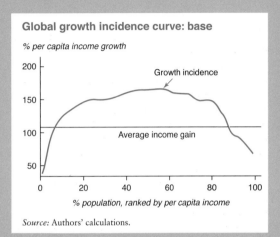

Global growth incidence curve: base

% per capita income growth

Growth incidence

Average income gain

% population, ranked by per capita income

Source: Authors' calculations.

growth rate of the entire distribution already demonstrates whether income growth is biased for or against the poor. For example, consider the effects of trade liberalization on the income distributions of Mexico and Brazil (obtained from Bussolo and Medvedev 2006). While both reforms (the Free Trade Area for the Americas in Mexico and the Doha Round in Brazil) produced similar gains in

aggregate gross domestic product (GDP), poor Mexicans gained much less than poor Brazilians. In other words, the GIC for Mexico shows that trade reform can be somewhat regressive, whereas strong progressivity is observed for Brazil. This implies that focusing exclusively on changes in macro variables cannot convey the full amount of information needed to evaluate different policy alternatives.

Now consider the global GIC in the microsimulation here, obtained by comparing the initial situation in 2000 with a final distribution in 2030. It shows that for 81 percent of the world's population, per capita income will rise faster than the global average.

The growth incidence curve shows that the pattern of expected growth is not clearly pro-poor, since the poorest 2 percent of households gain less than half of the global average. Instead, future changes in the global economy are likely to particularly benefit the households in the third, fourth, and fifth world income deciles. Although these changes do not favor the extremely poor (because the benefits are not concentrated at the bottom of the income distribution), the poor and the middle class, taken together, benefit much more than the rich.

which has been steadily increasing since the late 1980s (World Bank 2005). Nonetheless, the extent to which increases in inequality within countries have offset the decreases in inequality between them is a hotly debated subject.[8] Therefore the overall direction of change in global inequality since the 1980s is not clear.[9]

Bourguignon, Levin, and Rosenblatt (2004) offer a "mobility" argument to reconcile the seemingly divergent strands of the literature on intercountry and international inequality. Most of the improvement in global income distribution since the mid-1980s has been driven by increases in the incomes of millions of people in East and South Asia. So the individuals at the bottom of the income distribution today are not the same as the poor of 20 years ago. Therefore, "those who insist upon equal-weights inequality and corresponding worsening of the distribution have in mind the implicit

mobility argument. For them, the fact that some world citizens lost (for example, in Sub-Saharan Africa or the Former Soviet Union) is not necessarily compensated by the fact that others, initially poorer, in China or India have gained. The initial income position matters and the social cost of falling incomes is not compensated by the social gain of increasing incomes, even if these changes take place in the same income range" (Bourguignon, Levin, and Rosenblatt 2004: 21).

Using the global inequality approach (which takes into account within-country inequality), Milanovic and Yitzhaki (2002) proposed disaggregating world income distribution into three categories irrespective of country of citizenship—the poor, the middle class, and the rich, where the middle class is defined as individuals earning an income falling between the per capita income of Brazil and the per capita income of Italy. They then showed that, in 1993, the resulting middle-class group accounted for 8 percent of global population and 12 percent of global income, and that income differences between the rich, the poor, and the middle class captured 90 percent of inequality between countries and almost 70 percent of total global inequality.[10]

The next section turns to the future and uses the concept of global inequality and three global classes to identify the characteristics of those whose fortunes are likely to improve— the new global middle class—and of those who risk falling behind.

The future: an emerging global middle class

While the global middle class' share in the population remained largely the same from 1993 to 2000, its income share rose from 12 percent to 14 percent (table 3.1). By 2030, the size of this group is projected to surpass one billion, making it the fastest-growing segment of the world's population.[11] Meanwhile its income share will remain largely unchanged, indicating that inequality between countries is falling. Today 56 percent of the members of the middle class reside in developing countries; in 2030 this share should reach 92 percent.[12]

The results of table 3.1 are based on an absolute definition of the "global middle class": the per capita income thresholds are approximately equal to $4,000 and $17,000 (in 2000 international dollars) and remain the same in 2030.[13] Since an average middle-class family from a developing country has 4.3 household members, these income boundaries imply annual household earnings of $16,800 to $72,000 in PPP terms. This absolute definition implies that today (as of 2000) many of the *relatively* rich in developing countries are in the global middle class, while the vast majority of the absolutely rich (per capita incomes above $17,000) live in OECD countries. Since the study projections contain only positive growth rates for all countries in the world, there is some "natural" expansion in the absolute size of the middle class. However, since these growth rates represent growth in *real* incomes, it is not appropriate to eliminate this "natural" expansion by setting higher thresholds for 2030 relative to the thresholds of 2000.[14] The study's definition of the global middle class is based on real purchasing power, which remains constant throughout the model horizon and is therefore equally relevant in 2000 and 2030.[15]

Table 3.1 The global middle class is growing, its composition changing

Percentage shares

	1993		2000		2030	
	Pop.	Income	Pop.	Income	Pop.	Income
Poor (per capita income below the average of Brazil)	76	29	82.0	28.7	63.0	17.0
Middle class (per capita income between Brazil and Italy)	8	12	7.6	13.8	16.1	14.0
High-income country nationals			3.4	6.8	1.2	1.0
Low- and middle-income country nationals, of which:			4.2	7.0	14.9	12.9
East Asia and the Pacific			1.3	2.0	7.3	6.4
Eastern Europe and Central Asia			0.8	1.3	2.2	1.9
Latin America and the Caribbean			1.5	2.7	2.6	2.2
Middle East and North Africa			0.4	0.6	0.8	0.7
South Asia			0.1	0.1	1.6	1.3
Sub-Saharan Africa			0.2	0.3	0.5	0.4
Rich (per capita income at or above the average of Italy)	16	58	10.5	57.5	20.9	69.0
Total	100	100	100.0	100.0	100.0	100.0

Source: Authors' calculations.
Note: Totals may not sum to 100 because of rounding. Estimates for 1993 are from Milanovic (2002).
Thresholds of Brazil and Italy are annual per capita incomes (2000 PPP) of US$3,914 and US$16,746.

There are several reasons behind the dramatic increase projected in the size of the middle class and the major shift in composition in favor of the low- and middle-income countries. Faster population growth in the developing world is responsible for some of the change in the composition. Thus regions with population growth above the world average (for example, South Asia and Sub-Saharan Africa) will increase their share in the global middle class. The main determinant of joining the middle class ranks, however, is not population growth but income growth. Although East Asia's population grows more slowly than the world average, this region is projected to increase its share of residents in the global middle class by a factor of five, compared with a doubling for Africa. The difference is due to the fact that annual per capita income growth in Asia is forecast to be more than twice the growth in Sub-Saharan Africa, easily offsetting the decline in the former's population share.

Another determinant of the changing composition of the middle class is the (unequal) shape of the initial income distribution by region. South Asia, which could see a dramatic increase (87-fold) in the share of its residents in the global middle class, is currently the least unequal region in the world. This means that the benefits of its projected per capita growth of 3.9 percent per year (roughly equal to that of East Asia) are distributed across the population much more equally than in other regions. Sub-Saharan Africa, by contrast, has an initial inequality level that is twice as high. Therefore the same amount of growth would be much less effective at moving large numbers of people up the ladder of income distribution.

Most developing-country members of today's (as of 2000) global middle class earn incomes far above the averages of their own countries of residence. In other words, being classified as middle class at the global level is equivalent to being at the top of the distribution in many low-income countries. For example, as of 2000, 165 million (out of the total 231 million) developing-country citizens in the global middle class are in the top 20 per-cent of earners within their own countries. By contrast, only 10 percent of global middle-class members occupy the lower seven deciles of their national income distributions. Thus, for many nations, the correspondence between the global middle class and the within-country middle class is quite low.

The situation will change quite dramatically by 2030. A full 42 percent of developing-country members of the global middle class will be earning incomes in the seventh decile or lower at the national level. Consider the example of China, where 56 million people belonged to the global middle class in 2000—each of them earning more than 90 percent of all Chinese citizens. By 2030, there will be 361 million Chinese in the global middle class, and their earnings will range from the sixth to the ninth decile of the Chinese national income distribution.[16] They will no longer be among the richest Chinese citizens but will probably be considered upper middle class. Another example is Brazil, a country that grows one-third as fast as China in per capita terms. Even with slower growth, the number of Brazilians in the global middle class will expand by more than one-third by 2030. The compositional change is also important. In 2000, the Brazilians in the global middle class were split evenly across the eighth and ninth income deciles of their national distribution. By 2030, 75 percent of the members of the global middle class will earn the incomes of the sixth and seventh deciles in Brazil, and no member of that class will earn more than 80 percent of the country's population.

Consistent with these data, by 2030 the middle class, together with the rich, will account for a larger share of the population in a greater number of countries. In 2000, the middle class and the rich exceeded 40 percent of the population in just six developing countries, and these countries were home to 0.7 percent of the population of the developing world. By 2030, the middle class and the rich will exceed 40 percent of population in 30 countries, and these countries will account for 36 percent of the world's developing-country population. Therefore, although the

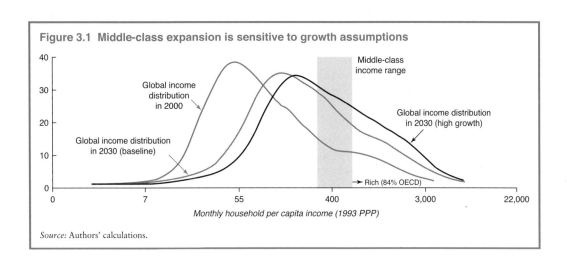

Figure 3.1 Middle-class expansion is sensitive to growth assumptions

Global income
distribution
in 2000

Global income distribution
in 2030 (baseline)

Middle-class
income range

Global income distribution
in 2030 (high growth)

Rich (84% OECD)

Monthly household per capita income (1993 PPP)

Source: Authors' calculations.

ability of the global middle class (together with the rich) to influence policy in many low- and middle-income countries is initially limited by its small size, this group is likely to become a much stronger political force at both the global and national levels by 2030. The increase in developing-country nationals in the global middle class may also strengthen developing countries in the global policy arena.

It is important to emphasize that the projected expansion in the global middle class is not a formal forecast. Alternative assumptions about income and population growth, as well as effects of policy interventions, can have a significant impact on the estimates of table 3.1. Figure 3.1 illustrates some of these possibilities by plotting the income distribution of the world in 2000 and in 2030 under different growth assumptions.[17] The size of the global middle class is represented by the area under the distribution curve between the two middle-class boundaries. Faster growth shifts the peak of the distribution closer to the middle-class threshold, although even the optimistic scenario here—which increases growth to 1.6 percent above the baseline growth rates—falls short of moving the thickest part of the distribution into middle-class territory. Still, under the high-growth scenario the global population share of the middle class rises to 19.4 percent,

allowing an additional 235 million people to gain access to middle-class standards of living.

In addition to growth assumptions, policy intervention at the global and national levels—such as trade liberalization—can also affect the rate of middle-class expansion. The effects of policy reforms are considered in the policy section at the end of this chapter.

The growth of the global middle class may have far-reaching consequences

The ascent of hundreds of millions of developing-country nationals into the global middle class will produce a large group of people in the developing world who can afford, and will demand access to, the standards of living that were previously reserved mainly for the residents of high-income countries. This has two major implications: the demand for international goods and services will rise, and pressures for policies that favor global integration will increase.

Goods and services. Much of the effect of the middle-class expansion on the world economy will be realized through a changing demand for goods. The fact that the middle class will be growing twice as fast as the overall population implies that multinational enterprises will be able to market their products to a much larger audience in 2030 than they do today.

Furthermore, the rules of this new global marketplace will be increasingly determined by the tastes and preferences of the developing world, particularly the desires of consumers in East and South Asia. Therefore, while most of the world's purchasing power will continue to be concentrated in the OECD countries, the global economic influence of those countries will vastly diminish. By 2030 marketing to the developing world will be a much more important strategy for multinationals than it is today.

The rise of the global middle class will also affect demand for services. For example, given the strong correlation between education levels and income, the growing middle class is likely to demand more and better education. The share of the global middle class in developing countries with less than a secondary school certificate is projected to decline from 47 percent in 2000 to 38 percent in 2030. This is roughly comparable to the mean education levels among rich individuals in 2000, when 32 percent of the working-age population had not completed secondary school. Furthermore, by 2030 the likelihood of completing at least primary school will be virtually the same for the rich and the middle class.[18] The increased emphasis on education among the middle class will help establish the foundations for continued growth in the developing countries, as rising educational attainments and growing demand for schooling deepen the human capital stocks across the developing world.

Demand for health services is also likely to rise with the growth in the global middle class. The ability to afford better care is a major determinant of health outcomes: the World Bank (2005) estimates that eliminating within-country differences in infant health would prevent 3.1 million infant deaths in developing countries—more than three-quarters of the total reduction that could be achieved by lowering mortality to the OECD averages. However, the increasing demand for education and health is likely to put pressure on the budgets of developing-country governments and will require heightened policy attention in the future.

The rise of the global middle class is also likely to increase the demand for international tourism services. Already in 2004, 20 percent of all outbound tourism came from East and South Asia, with an additional 6 percent from Africa and the Middle East (World Tourism Organization 2006). By 2020 the overall number of tourist arrivals is expected to double to 1.5 billion, with a growing share coming from developing regions (figure 3.2).

Integration policies. A significantly larger global middle class composed mainly of developing-country nationals will exert a stronger influence on international and domestic policy making. As shown above, by 2030 these middle-class members will constitute a significant share of their home country populations, allowing them to have a greater say in the policy process.

Some evidence points to a correlation between rising incomes and a shift in demand toward more globalization-supportive policies. Recent literature has found that pro-trade preferences are significantly correlated with an individual's skill level and the relative abundance of skilled labor in a given country (Scheve and Slaughter 1998; O'Rourke 2003). These results link pro-trade attitudes to the predictions of the Stolper-Samuelson trade theorem, which states that wage rates for skilled workers rise (relative to the returns of other factors) in skill-abundant countries as international trade increases. Mayda and Rodrik (2005) confirm these findings, while showing that individuals' relative economic and social status is highly correlated with pro-globalization preferences. Therefore, not only will the new global middle class possess the means to purchase products previously targeted mainly toward consumers in the OECD countries, but their demand for these products is likely to become a major driver of calls for further openness.

The literature on the political economy of trade policy proposes that the direction of policy is determined by the preferences of the median voter (Mayer 1984).[19] Today the median voter in most developing countries is

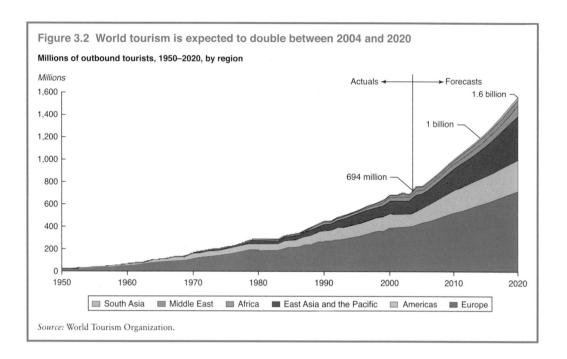

Figure 3.2 World tourism is expected to double between 2004 and 2020

Millions of outbound tourists, 1950–2020, by region

Source: World Tourism Organization.

unlikely to be a member of the middle class, which may help explain why some studies find a negative relationship between pro-market policies of the incumbent party and its performance at the ballot box (Olivera and Lora 2005). However, the near-tripling of the global middle class by 2030 increases the likelihood that the median voter in many countries will have a pro-openness stance.

These changes are likely to have an impact not only on the domestic policy arena (for example, increased pressure for unilateral lowering of tariffs) but also on negotiations in multilateral forums such as the World Trade Organization (WTO). Countries with a rapidly growing middle class could emerge as strong proponents of improved dialogue and faster progress on multilateral liberalization of trade in goods and services.

However, as calls to remove trade restraints become stronger in some countries, they may turn weaker in others. Liberalization of trade may also lead to an antiglobalization backlash from lower-income citizens of industrial countries, who will experience increased wage and

employment competition from developing-country nationals entering the global middle class. Therefore understanding and managing the effects of globalization on within-country distribution of income are likely to become more important in the future; this point will be revisited later in this chapter.

Other policy goals—among them improved transparency, intensified anticorruption efforts, and demand for a more open society and cleaner environment—are also likely to move to the forefront of the policy agenda with the expansion in the size of the middle class. Although most of these issues are usually more easily addressed by domestic policy, multilateral efforts can assist the progress. For example, Bonaglia, Braga de Macedo, and Bussolo (2001) found a strong link between increased trade openness and lower corruption in a large sample of countries between 1980 and 1998. Other challenges, such as improving the quality of the environment, require at least as much cooperation on the multilateral front as they do in domestic policy circles. (See chapter 5 for a discussion of these issues.)

Africa may fall behind

Even though a rising share of the global population will have access to living standards currently reserved mainly for OECD nationals, more than half the world in 2030 will continue to earn less than middle-class incomes. Although the share of people whose living standards fall below those of the middle class will decline from 82 percent in 2000 to 66.5 percent in 2030, those left behind are likely to become increasingly concentrated in Sub-Saharan Africa, revealing geographic polarization in the lower ranges of the global income distribution. By 2030 Sub-Saharan Africa alone could be home to almost 55 percent of the poorest decile of the world income distribution—an 80 percent increase from its initial share in 2000 (figure 3.3). In other words, in 25 years the likelihood that a random person in the bottom decile will live in Africa may increase twofold, indicating a significant deterioration of relative living standards in Sub-Saharan Africa compared to other regions. [20]

There are three main factors driving Africa's decline: high initial income inequality, relatively high population growth, and the lowest per capita income growth among developing-country regions. The second and third reasons imply that more and more Africans are falling behind the rest of the world, while the first compounds the problem by limiting the ability of the poor to enjoy the growth benefits equally. Similar mechanisms operate in Latin America, which also is expected to increase its share in the bottom decile. Slower growth of income per capita relative to other regions means that the share of Latin America in the bottom decile could rise by 50 percent in 2030—a much slower increase than that of Sub-Saharan Africa, but significant nonetheless. This underscores the universal importance of growth and growth-oriented policies, which are equally relevant for low- and middle-income regions.

The bleak outlook for Sub-Saharan Africa (and to a lesser extent Latin America) is not foreordained or immutable. Policies that raise growth rates, both international and domestic, as well as policies aiming at efficiency-enhancing redistributions, can lead to different outcomes. Consider the third column of figure 3.3, which represents the high-growth scenario described in chapter 2. In this scenario, Sub-Saharan Africa performs slightly better because it experiences a larger-than-average increase in per capita growth. By contrast, Latin America falls further behind. It is important to keep in mind that figure 3.3 summarizes a relative measure of performance and that everyone's living standards improve under high growth relative to the baseline. However, the important point is that while growth is effective in raising living standards, closing the income gap with wealthier countries requires faster-than-average growth—which is successfully achieved in South Asia but not in Sub-Saharan Africa, even under this chapter's optimistic growth scenario. Similarly, maintaining one's relative standard of

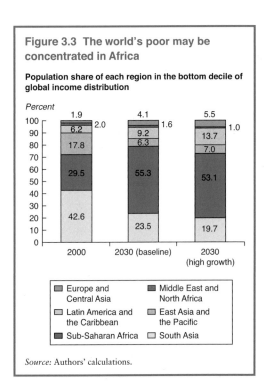

Figure 3.3 The world's poor may be concentrated in Africa

Population share of each region in the bottom decile of global income distribution

Percent

Legend:
- Europe and Central Asia
- Latin America and the Caribbean
- Sub-Saharan Africa
- Middle East and North Africa
- East Asia and the Pacific
- South Asia

Source: Authors' calculations.

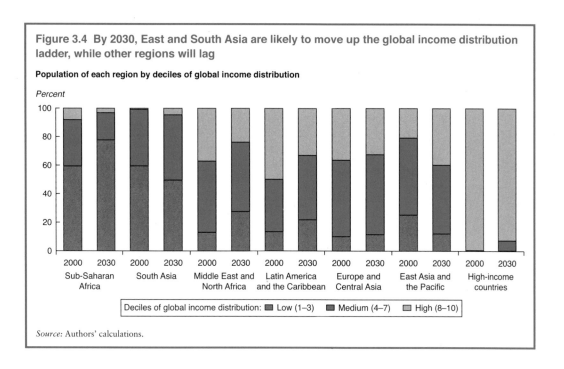

Figure 3.4 By 2030, East and South Asia are likely to move up the global income distribution ladder, while other regions will lag

Population of each region by deciles of global income distribution

Percent

living is also conditional on growing at least as fast as the global average.

The relative stagnation in Africa and Latin America is not limited to the poorest 10 percent of the world. Virtually all Africans are at risk of underperforming their counterparts from other regions. For example, in 2000, 59 percent of the population of Sub-Saharan Africa and 25 percent of the population of East Asia were in the bottom third of the world income distribution (figure 3.4). By 2030, more than three-quarters of the population of Sub-Saharan Africa is likely to be among the world's poorest, while only 16 percent of East Asia's residents will remain in the bottom third. This contrasting performance is largely a function of the difference in per capita income growth rates. South Asia will continue to be the largest group in the three bottom deciles in 2030 owing to the very high initial poverty rates. But its citizens are moving up through the ranks of the global distribution at a fast pace owing to high per capita growth and, unlike in the initial situation,

most of South Asia's poor will earn incomes in the second and third deciles in 2030. The growth effect is exactly the opposite in Sub-Saharan Africa, where an average African is 30 percent more likely to be in the three bottom deciles in 2030 than in 2000.

Moving away from geographic regions, it is possible to identify alternative typologies of countries whose citizens could fail to improve or even lose their position in the world income distribution. One group includes low- and middle-income energy exporters, defined as countries whose exports of oil or natural gas exceed 20 percent of their total value of exports.[21] In 2000 citizens of energy-exporting countries made up 15 percent of the first (bottom) decile of the global income distribution. By 2030, the population share of energy exporters in the poorest decile could rise to 27 percent. Similarly, agricultural exporters may fall behind by 2030.[22] While in 2000 their citizens accounted for just one-tenth of the poorest global decile, that share could rise to 23 percent in 30 years. Although everyone in the above countries will be better off in 2030 than they are today in absolute terms, these developments imply a large deterioration in the *relative* living standards of a large share of the population.[23]

The outlook for Sub-Saharan Africa underlines the importance of international efforts to reduce poverty. International development policy is already focused on the problems facing Sub-Saharan Africa, but still more attention is needed. One avenue for improving the lot of countries left behind will be the increased demand for multilateral trade liberalization. Another mechanism of global income redistribution that has the potential to help the poor is represented by international aid. (These two global policies are discussed in more detail in the final section of the chapter.)

Within-country inequality and poverty reduction

The moderately sanguine conclusions about the expansion of the middle-class population and the increasing access of developing-country residents to living standards currently reserved to OECD nationals are only one part of the global income-distribution story. Changes in the distribution of income *within countries* are no less important. Worsening inequality can mute the positive effects of growth on poverty reduction in both the short and long run, increase the risk of social alienation of people at the bottom of the income distribution, and perhaps produce counterproductive backlashes against further integration with the global economy.

On balance, past trends of inequality are mixed

When one looks backward, clear trends of rising or falling inequality are difficult to identify, but recent evidence casts doubt on the view of unchanging inequality. Some empirical studies concerned with the intertemporal evolution of inequality and its possible determinants have found that income inequality within countries shows no time trend. Li, Squire, and Zou (1998), using the Gini coefficients for 47 developing and developed countries covering the period 1974–94, found no significant time trend. Bruno, Ravallion, and Squire (1998) found very few countries that had recorded discernible long-term changes in inequality in either direction.

More recently, however, this view of constant income inequality has been challenged by some new evidence. Focusing on the OECD countries between the 1970s and 1995, Osberg (2003) concluded that inequality changed relatively little in Canada, Sweden, and Germany, but that income distribution in the United Kingdom and the United States saw substantial increases in polarization.[24] Similar conclusions were reached by Atkinson (2003).

In the developing world, inequality has generally increased in many, if not most, countries since 1980, even though a sizable minority of countries have exhibited the opposite trends toward greater equality. In East Asia, inequality has increased significantly over the last several decades—and more so during the recent period of high growth in China and Vietnam than in the earlier years of growth of the East Asian "tigers" (World Bank 2005). However, Ravallion and Chen (2004) caution against drawing a causal relationship between growth and inequality in China, since inequality increased fastest during periods of slow growth. In South Asian countries, the evolution of inequality in India is difficult to ascertain owing to data problems, but other countries in the region experienced very large increases in inequality during the 1990s (World Bank 2005). For the countries of Latin America, de Ferranti and others (2004) show that inequality increased almost uniformly during the 1980s (a period of volatile and low growth coupled with high inflation), but that in the 1990s (a period of improved macroeconomic stability) the deterioration was less pronounced and limited to approximately half the countries in the region.

Is trade a cause of changes in inequality?

One potential determinant of inequality is the increasing integration of developing countries into the global economy, which, while raising overall incomes, may also increase the return to more mobile factors of production such as capital and highly skilled workers. But the impact of trade (one channel of globalization) on income inequality shows no consistent pattern. Another source of the past decade's increase in inequality could be increases in the premium for skills generated by technological change. The effects of trade are difficult to isolate from technological diffusion and foreign investment, and the combination may raise the relative wages of skilled workers and widen the distribution of income (for more details see the "Policy Implications" section below and chapter 4).

Demography and social mobility affect equality and poverty

Another determinant of inequality is demographic change. The aging of the world's population may increase inequality, as older workers often earn higher salaries (Deaton and Paxson 1997) and inequality tends to be higher among older age cohorts (Jenkins 1995; Mookherjee and Shorroks 1982).[25] The mixed rise in inequality in developing countries has been accompanied by a fall in poverty, largely driven by high growth rates in East and South Asia. Nevertheless, rising inequality will hamper further poverty reduction, particularly in Africa, where poverty is rising and inequality remains high. This section and the next one assume circumstances of healthy growth in the modern sectors, which give rise to new jobs in industry and services. The role that intersectoral mobility can play in reducing poverty is then considered, as well as how policies can help the *poor* move between occupations and take advantage of the new opportunities offered by growth.

Moving from low-paying jobs in agriculture, where poverty rates are often high, to higher-paying jobs in industry or services is a major avenue for individuals looking to escape poverty. The size of the migration-related reduction of poverty depends on the initial poverty rate in agriculture, and the income differential between households whose heads are employed in agriculture and those whose heads are employed in nonagricultural activities. For all developing countries in the sample, the headcount poverty ratio falls by 2 percentage points (calculated as an unweighted average) when 10 percent of the agricultural population moves to industry or services. In Sub-Saharan Africa, where agricultural households account for 75 percent of national poverty and agriculture-related incomes are only 47 percent of incomes earned in the other sectors of the economy, the equivalent reduction in poverty is 4 percent. This reduction could be larger, but not all migrants are poor, and not all of the poor who migrate escape poverty.[26]

Although migration does not lead to a large reduction in poverty at the national level, the improvement in welfare of individuals migrating from agriculture can be quite large. Even for impoverished migrants who fail to escape poverty, an increase in income from migration can reduce the poverty gap. Other long-term effects can also be attributable to the migration process. By reducing the labor supply in the agricultural sector, wages of nonmovers in this sector tend to rise, exerting a direct positive impact on relatively poor households.

Education facilitates mobility

To help the poor take advantage of new growth opportunities, governments can implement measures ranging from expanding relevant infrastructure to increasing poor people's access to credit and insurance. This section focuses on how *education* can improve the pro-poor effects of the described employment shift out of agriculture.[27] To the extent that the poor lack access to education, intersectoral migration may be limited. The unequal access to education in many developing countries is documented in World Bank (2005) and works cited therein. Among the relevant findings: family members of households headed by women and of rural households have marked disadvantages in attaining higher levels of education. Additionally, parents' initial wealth and education greatly influence their children's educational achievements and their expected earnings, thereby contributing to future income inequalities. For many countries, the correlation between the education level of the head of the household and the average level of education of the other members of the household was observed to be very high. The average value for this correlation in the developing-country sample is almost 0.4.

The influence of education on the poverty-reducing impact of intersectoral migration is illustrated in figure 3.5 for a sample of developing countries. For the majority of these

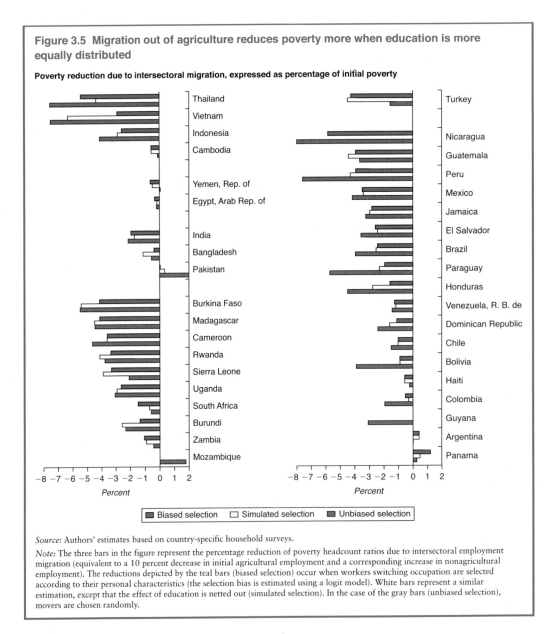

Figure 3.5 Migration out of agriculture reduces poverty more when education is more equally distributed

Poverty reduction due to intersectoral migration, expressed as percentage of initial poverty

Source: Authors' estimates based on country-specific household surveys.

Note: The three bars in the figure represent the percentage reduction of poverty headcount ratios due to intersectoral employment migration (equivalent to a 10 percent decrease in initial agricultural employment and a corresponding increase in nonagricultural employment). The reductions depicted by the teal bars (biased selection) occur when workers switching occupation are selected according to their personal characteristics (the selection bias is estimated using a logit model). White bars represent a similar estimation, except that the effect of education is netted out (simulated selection). In the case of the gray bars (unbiased selection), movers are chosen randomly.

countries, heads of households who are more educated, younger, and already in urban areas are more likely to migrate from agriculture—and less likely to be poor.[28] Thus poverty reduction through intersectoral mobility is limited, reflecting a phenomenon known as biased selection, represented by the teal bars of the figure.[29] By contrast, if heads of households were randomly selected to move out of agriculture, poverty reduction would be greater, as a larger share of the poor would move (shown in the gray bars of the figure).

One way the government could improve the poverty-reducing impact of intersectoral mobility would be to increase access to education. Consider this thought experiment. If every individual initially employed in agriculture were given the same level of education, poverty reduction would rise closer to the random selection case (referred to as "simulated selection" and represented by the white bars of figure 3.5). For example, in Burkina Faso, a migration out of agriculture of 10 percent of those employed in agriculture reduces poverty by 5.5 percent in the best-case scenario, that is, when the poor and nonpoor have the same chances of moving. Poverty decreases by a smaller amount, 4 percent, when movers are selected according to their characteristics and the nonpoor have a greater chance to move. If Burkinabe policy makers were able to grant the same education level to all citizens employed in agriculture, the intersectoral migration considered here would approach the outcome of the best-case scenario: poverty reduction would be 5.4 percent.

It is important to reiterate that complementary policies are necessary to exploit fully the poverty-reducing impact of expanding access to education. As already said, in many countries a poor investment climate limits the ability of the economy to absorb newly educated workers. Improvements in economic policies and institutions are often critical to encouraging the higher investment required to employ graduates. And care must be taken to maintain quality standards. Raising access to education means providing the trained teachers, infrastructure, and materials required for a useful educational experience, not just enrolling everyone in school.

By 2030, inequality within countries may rise, leaving the unskilled poor farther behind

More than two-thirds of low- and middle-income countries in the study sample, comprising 86 percent of the population in the developing world, are projected to experience a rise in inequality by 2030. For some countries the increase is quite significant (figure 3.6).

Rising inequality is worrisome because there is an inverse relationship between inequality and poverty reduction.[30] Even if growth is distribution-neutral (that is, if the incomes of the poor rise by the same amount as average incomes), inequality can still hamper the ability of growth to reduce poverty. This point is illustrated in the left panel of figure 3.7, which plots the relationship between the partial (neutral) poverty elasticity of growth and the Gini coefficient for a sample of 84 developing countries (see also World Bank 2005). This elasticity has been calculated by simulating a counterfactual income distribution, where the income of each person in a given country rises by 1 percent, and calculating the resulting percentage change in the poverty headcount. The results show that there is a robust positive relationship between the level of initial income inequality and the absolute value of the poverty elasticity. At low levels of income inequality, a 1 percent increase in per capita growth generates a more-than-proportional change in the poverty headcount. However, as inequality rises to the high levels of Lesotho or Haiti, the ability of growth to reduce poverty approaches zero. A similar relationship is observed for the total elasticity of growth (the right panel of figure 3.7), which is calculated using observed income growth rates and therefore allows inequality to vary within the sample period. These results show that, while growth is the major vehicle of lifting individuals out of poverty (see Dollar and Kraay 2002), it is

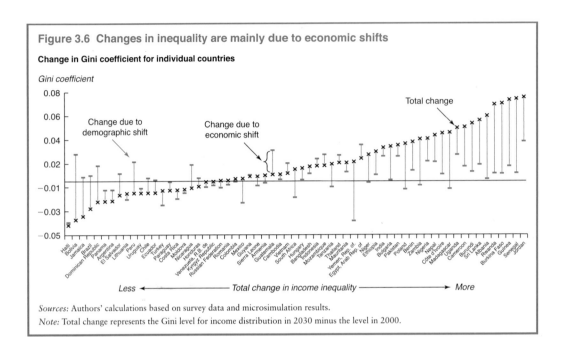

Figure 3.6 Changes in inequality are mainly due to economic shifts

Change in Gini coefficient for individual countries

Sources: Authors' calculations based on survey data and microsimulation results.
Note: Total change represents the Gini level for income distribution in 2030 minus the level in 2000.

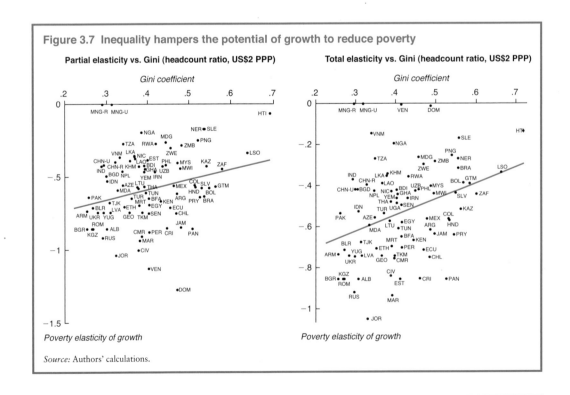

Figure 3.7 Inequality hampers the potential of growth to reduce poverty

Source: Authors' calculations.

more likely to be pro-poor when initial inequality is low.

Figure 3.7 thus demonstrates the long-term benefits of reducing income inequality: in addition to a contemporaneous reduction in poverty that may be expected from lowering inequality, policies that promote a more equal distribution of income are likely to enable the economy to realize greater poverty reduction from future growth. The projected rise in inequality would imply that in 2030 poverty elasticities will be lower and, with more unequal income distribution in 2030, countries will need higher growth rates than they need today to achieve a given reduction in poverty. If higher growth rates cannot be achieved, the countries will need more active redistribution policies.

Within-country inequality in 2030: two main drivers

In each country, income distribution is affected by two sets of factors: shifts in the *demographic structure* of the population, in terms of aging and education attainment, and changes in *rewards for individuals' characteristics*, such as their education level, experience, sector of employment, and so on. Although in the real world these demographic and economic shocks occur simultaneously and jointly determine inequality changes, this analysis applies each of them sequentially and decomposes the total change into various components.

This study's view of the demographic structure of the world in 2030 is based on the World Bank's population projections by age group and a simple model of human capital accumulation that assumes a continuation of the educational trends observed over the 1980–2000 period. Controlling for other factors, both the level and dispersion (inequality) of household income tend to increase with the age and education of the household head.[31] Therefore as the population shares of groups with more income inequality rise, one may expect to see higher inequality.[32] However, as shown by teal tick marks in figure 3.6, there is no clear pattern in changes in inequality driven by demographic forces. One explanation

is that countries with relatively large public sectors and relatively high education levels (such as countries in Eastern Europe and the Commonwealth of Independent States) tend to have more egalitarian distribution of income among skilled workers, possibly because their governments and other bureaucracies have more compressed wage structures. Hence, changes in the demographic structure work to *reduce* income inequality. By contrast, many countries in Latin America and Sub-Saharan Africa experience an increase in inequality as the shares of older and more skilled workers rise, since wage dispersion within these groups tends to be high.

Although aging and the accumulation of human capital imply important changes in the demographic structure of many countries, the overall effect of demographic changes on inequality varies within a narrow band (figure 3.6). On the other hand, widening gaps in factor rewards, and particularly in the premium paid for higher skills, tend to produce larger changes in inequality and generally determine the overall direction of the effect. This is shown in figure 3.6, where for large changes in inequality, the distance between the black and teal marks—that is, the change in inequality attributable to changes in economic factors—increases, a sign that economic factors are the most important determinant for the final level of inequality.[33]

The initial skill premia and the pattern of growth experienced by each country determine the consequences for inequality of the economic factors. Those consequences are obtained by applying the changes in the factor rewards of the model in chapter 2 to the income sources of individual households. For example, countries in Latin America are characterized by high initial income inequality and relatively slow growth rates. This implies a slower transition to a service-oriented economy and lower rates of capital deepening—both of which dampen the growth of the wages of skilled workers, whose labor is a complement to capital and is highly demanded in the service sectors.

Since initial wage gaps are high—the per capita income of a household headed by an unskilled worker in Brazil is only 27 percent of that of a household headed by a skilled worker—and growth is relatively unskilled-intensive, unskilled wages rise faster than skilled incomes and inequality tends to fall (figure 3.6).[34] The reduction in inequality is compounded by the diminishing rural-urban wage differentials in countries with a comparative advantage in agriculture, which tends to be relatively unskilled-intensive. For example, farm workers in Brazil—a country with one of the largest decreases in the Gini coefficient—earned 40 percent of the average manufacturing wage in 2000 but will likely earn more than 72 percent of the average industrial wage in 2030.

By contrast, countries in East and South Asia will experience increasing inequality, driven by low initial skill premia and high per capita growth rates. Faster income growth generates more demand for skill-intensive products and requires higher rates of investment, both of which increase the returns to skilled labor. For example, one of the largest increases in inequality in the sample is observed in India—a country with low initial

inequality (the incomes of unskilled-headed households are 52 percent of the skilled-headed incomes) and an average per capita growth of more than 4 percent, which leads to a substantial rise in the skill premium. The rise in inequality is somewhat mitigated by convergence between farm and nonfarm incomes, but this effect is quite small because growth is concentrated in the nonagriculture sectors.

In sum, changes in income inequality over the next 30 years are likely to be driven mainly by changes in the rewards for individual characteristics and investment in education—rather than globalization in isolation. Countries with low initial inequality and fast growth are likely to experience a worsening distribution of income, while countries with slower growth rates and greater initial inequality in income are likely to see inequality fall. The results therefore illustrate a "convergence" of income distributions across countries, which can be interpreted as a manifestation of the Kuznets hypothesis or as a consequence of the globalization-induced equalization of factor prices.

It must be borne in mind that these trends are driven by the assumptions of the baseline scenario and are far from inevitable. Figure 3.8

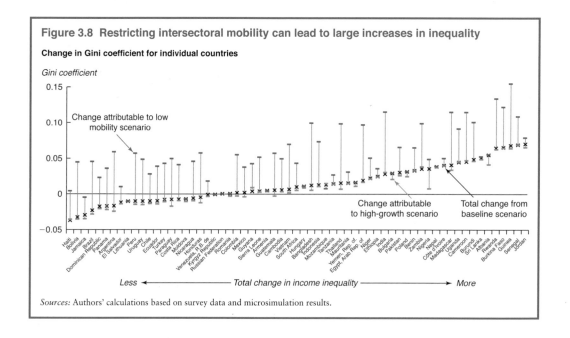

Figure 3.8 Restricting intersectoral mobility can lead to large increases in inequality

Change in Gini coefficient for individual countries

Sources: Authors' calculations based on survey data and microsimulation results.

illustrates the inequality consequences of two alternative scenarios: the high-growth scenario introduced earlier (gray marks) and a low-labor-mobility scenario (teal marks), where unskilled workers are not allowed to move from farm to nonfarm activities. By increasing rural incomes, the high-growth scenario reduces within-country inequality, although the overall magnitude of the changes is not very large. On the other hand, limiting the intersectoral mobility of workers markedly increases income inequality for the majority of countries. For example, India experiences an 11-point increase in the Gini coefficient, which makes its level of income inequality approximately the same as that of República Bolivariana de Venezuela.

The inability of workers to take up jobs in the urban sector counteracts the natural processes of growth and urbanization, applying upward pressure on nonfarm wages while depressing earnings in agriculture. Even in such countries as Brazil, which has a comparative advantage in agriculture, labor-market rigidities in the low-mobility scenario result in a significant increase in inequality. Because distortions can have severe effects on inequality, policy makers must be careful not to erect barriers to labor mobility.[35] On the other hand, as is argued below, public intervention can counteract the tendencies toward rising inequality by creating new opportunities that benefit low-income groups.

Who is left behind: the face of the poor in 2030. As is true today, in 2030 most people in the lowest income decile will be without primary school education, will work in agricultural sectors, and will live in rural areas. Lack of education appears to be the single most important characteristic common to people at the bottom of the distribution. Completing primary education reduces the probability of being in the lowest income decile in every developing country in the forecast. However, the magnitude of this effect varies dramatically across countries. Consider, for example, the cases of Rahmane and Ali, two

young men who live in rural areas of Senegal and Yemen, respectively. Rahmane and Ali have not completed primary education, work in agriculture, and belong to families whose per capita income is in the poorest decile. After completing his primary education, Rahmane's probability of remaining in poverty would be reduced by more than 13 percentage points. This is explained, to a great extent, by the 40 percent increase in his income produced by completing his primary school education. Ali's efforts to combine his hard work in the field with elementary studies will not be met with as great a reward. Once he gets his primary school degree, his probability of escaping poverty will fall by less than 1 percentage point, because his income will increase only 6 percent.

This example illustrates the large variation in the welfare effects of education among different countries in different geographical regions. In Europe and Central Asia, for example, completing primary school reduces the probability of being in the lowest income decile by 11 percentage points and increases income by less than 3 percent (table 3.2). By contrast, in Sub-Saharan Africa, completing primary education reduces the probability of being in the lowest income decile by 7.2 percentage points and increases income by more than a third. Even among countries in the same region, there is heterogeneity. For example, in the Middle East and North Africa, as mentioned, a Yemeni who obtains a primary education is only slightly less likely to end up in the lowest income decile (a difference in probability of less than 1 percentage point), whereas Egyptians with a primary education improve their chances of escaping the bottom decile by more than 10 percentage points. Nevertheless, there is a strong negative correlation within all regions between the returns to education and the marginal effect of primary school education on the probability of being in the lowest decile: where the return to education is high, the probability of remaining poor is low.

Additional variables, such as the number of elders in the household and the gender and

Table 3.2 Where the return to education is high, its poverty-reducing impact is also high

Poverty and income effects due to completing primary education (regional averages)

Region	Marginal effect on probability of being in the lowest decile	Marginal effect on returns to primary schooling	Within-region correlation between effect of primary school completion on poverty and return to primary schooling
Sub-Saharan Africa	−0.072	0.340	−0.674
East Asia and the Pacific	−0.079	0.242	−0.733
Europe and Central Asia	−0.111	0.264	−0.743
Latin America and the Caribbean	−0.066	0.431	−0.464
Middle East and North Africa	−0.056	0.229	−0.996
South Asia	−0.068	0.257	−0.946

Source: Authors' estimates based on country-specific household surveys.
Note: For each country, the income of a head of household and the probability of the head of household being in the bottom income decile depend on individual and household-specific characteristics—among them education, age, gender, and sector of employment. As simple averages for all the countries within the six developing regions, the first two columns represent the marginal effect of completing primary school on the probability of being in the bottom decile and on income, respectively.

Table 3.3 Some factors affect the probability of being in the lowest income decile more than others—and the differences are changing over time

Poverty effects of specific characteristics (developing-country averages)

Factor	Marginal effects on probability of being in the lowest decile (2000)	Marginal effects on probability of being in the lowest decile (2030)	Difference (2000–30)
Primary school	−0.066	−0.081	0.016
Secondary school	−0.110	−0.100	−0.011
Gender (women = 1)	0.020	0.017	0.006
Age	0.002	0.002	0.000
Age squared	0.000	0.000	0.000
Number of elderly in the household	0.021	0.020	0.003
Industry effects			
Mining	−0.028	0.011	−0.038
Manufacturing	−0.066	−0.013	−0.054
Public services	−0.066	0.008	−0.071
Construction	−0.060	−0.007	−0.057
Retail, Hotels	−0.076	−0.025	−0.051
Transport communications	−0.065	−0.023	−0.050
Finance services	−0.065	−0.014	−0.047
Other services	−0.067	−0.018	−0.052
Others not well specified	−0.011	0.020	−0.026

Source: Authors' estimates based on country-specific household surveys and microsimulation results.
Note: For each country, the probability (estimated with a probit model) of the head of household being in the bottom income decile depends on individual and household-specific characteristics—among them education, age, gender, and sector of employment. As simple averages for all the developing countries, the first two columns represent the marginal effect of each independent variable estimated at the initial and final years, respectively. For each country, the difference between the marginal effects between the two years has been calculated for each factor and the factor's average across all countries is shown in the last column.

the sector of employment of its head, among others, affect the likelihood of being poor (table 3.3). Everything else being equal, households headed by a woman are more likely (by 2 percentage points) to be in the lowest income decile than are households headed by a man. A similar difference is observed between workers in agricultural sectors and those in nonagricultural sectors. Working in the former increases the probability of being in the lowest income decile by 5 percentage points.

The correlations between poverty and individual characteristics change over the forecast period. Owing to a slightly increasing skill premium, completing primary education reduces the probability of a person being in the lowest income decile by 6.6 percentage points in 2000; it could reduce that probability by 8.1 percentage points by 2030. Hence lack of education is likely to become a more important determinant of who is left behind in the next 25 years. By contrast, the gender of the head of household will become less important. As just noted, in 2000, households whose head was a woman were 2 percentage points more likely to be found in the lowest income decile than were male-headed households. That difference could shrink to 1.7 percentage points in 2030. Finally, as agricultural incomes approach those generated in other sectors,[36] disparities in the probability of poverty of workers in the agricultural sector and those in other industries may be less in 2030 than they were in 2000.

Policy implications

These forecasts of growth, demographic shifts, and trends in inequality point to significant challenges—and opportunities. Developing countries' growing participation in the global middle class will represent a substantial improvement in welfare for hundreds of millions of people, increase the weight of developing countries in the global economy and in international policy, and possibly even increase support for open economic policies that could further improve growth rates. While poverty will fall quite sharply, hundreds of millions of people, concentrated in Africa, will continue to live on less than $1 a day. Demographic shifts, coupled with unequal access to both wealth and services, are likely to increase inequality within countries, thus further hampering the potential for overall growth to reduce poverty. Policy can help lessen the effects of these tendencies.

Global policies: is development assistance a useful instrument to reduce inequality?
The improving fortunes of the developing world raise the question of whether official development assistance (ODA) is still necessary. It is—for the following reasons.

Aid flows can have a significant impact on the global distribution of income when they raise the incomes of the poorest countries. To be sure, aid has to be well invested and relatively free of corruption to be fully effective. Bourguignon, Levin, and Rosenblatt (2006) show that as long as aid is distributed equally—that is, it does not change the national income distribution—in recipient countries, its effect can be particularly beneficial to the poor: 41 percent of all aid accrues to the bottom decile of the global income distribution and another 25 percent to the second decile.[37] Furthermore, empirical evidence demonstrates that aid can lead to additional growth in the recipient countries, although some studies reach the opposite conclusion (Easterly, Levine, and Roodman 2004), and others show that aid can enhance growth only in the presence of good institutional characteristics (Burnside and Dollar 2000; Collier and Dollar 2002).

To illustrate the potential effect of aid on incomes by region, consider a simple exercise that adopts the same methodology that Bourguignon, Levin, and Rosenblatt (2006) used to estimate the global redistribution effects of aid flows. This chapter calculates growth rates without aid using the empirical relationship between annual income growth and ODA estimated by Collier and Dollar (2002).[38] It is further assumed that the share of aid in developing countries' GDP does not change between 2000 and 2030, that institutional quality[39] remains constant, and that aid is distributed equally *within* recipient countries.[40] By removing all aid, the forecast growth rate for Sub-Saharan Africa would fall by more than 0.5 percentage points a year, or almost one-third of projected per capita income growth. By contrast, the complete cessation of aid flows would have small effects on growth in East Asia and Latin America.

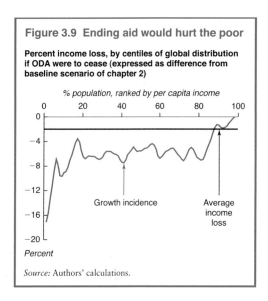

Figure 3.9 Ending aid would hurt the poor

Percent income loss, by centiles of global distribution if ODA were to cease (expressed as difference from baseline scenario of chapter 2)

% population, ranked by per capita income

Source: Authors' calculations.

Figure 3.9 extends this approach to the full set of countries in the microsimulation model.[41] For the world as a whole, per capita income gains are 2 percent lower than in the baseline. Distributional effects are much more pronounced, with 87 percent of the world experiencing greater-than-average losses, although no one ends worse off in 2030 than they were in 2000. The bottom 1 percent of the income distribution experiences an income loss of 17 percent relative to the baseline. Expressed positively, the poorest 1 percent will see their incomes rise by 37 percent between 2000 and 2030 if aid levels remain unchanged, versus a 20 percent real income gain if their countries receive no aid.

These results are only illustrative. The exercise assumes that the allocation of aid and the effectiveness of aid in promoting growth follow their historical patterns. The growth penalty of aid removal is thus constant through the forecast period—and such fast-growing countries as China and India appear to be penalized for not receiving developmental assistance, even though they may require significantly less of it by 2030. In reality, improvements in the allocation of aid to the poorest countries and to countries with good policies could boost aid effectiveness and

enable larger reductions in poverty than those anticipated in this study's forecasts. On the other hand, efforts to reduce poverty could be hampered by conflict, macroeconomic instability, or high levels of corruption that afflict many of the poorest countries.[42]

A final limitation of the approach followed here is that it does not consider the general equilibrium effects of removing aid. In fact, the different without-aid growth rates may have implications for global trade (among other effects) and thus may affect relative prices of goods and factors: these second-order effects are not considered here. However, even with these limitations, the conclusion that aid can be powerfully pro-poor, combined with the worsening outlook for Sub-Saharan Africa in the baseline, underscores the importance of focusing the aid flows on Africa and improving its effectiveness.

Global policies: further liberalization of trade stands to benefit everyone

The lowering of trade barriers around the world would benefit all segments of the world population, including the poor. Previous estimates showed that full multilateral trade reform could lift roughly 100 million people out of extreme poverty (defined as living on less than $2 a day)—see Anderson, Martin, and van der Mensbrugghe (2006). Increased preference for free trade, combined with greater visibility of the plight of the poor, may help implement the global reforms that can be effective in elevating the living standards of the poor.

Unfortunately, as illustrated by the impasse in the multilateral Doha negotiations, the progress toward freer trade is currently stymied and will take a major effort among the rich and poor countries together to realize even its limited progress.

This section illustrates the potential effects of a successful global trade reform by implementing a scenario with a 75 percent cut in tariffs and domestic support in all countries by 2025,[43] thus projecting into the future the liberalization trend of the past few decades. The resulting income gains, which include the

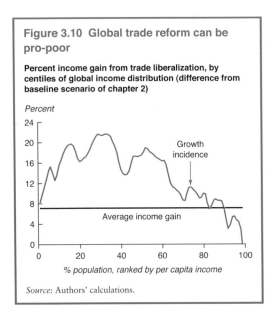

Figure 3.10 Global trade reform can be pro-poor

Percent income gain from trade liberalization, by centiles of global income distribution (difference from baseline scenario of chapter 2)

Source: Authors' calculations.

positive effects of increased trade openness on productivity, are quite modest: average per capita income (in PPP terms) in the final year rises by 7 percent relative to the baseline. The distributional consequences of trade reform are summarized in figure 3.10, which for each centile of the global distribution shows the income gains experienced over and above the baseline improvements in income.[44] Despite the modest overall gain, trade reform is decidedly pro-poor in the sample because the poorest households experience income gains above the global average. Furthermore, the bottom 30 percent gain slightly more than the four middle deciles, and more than twice the increase in incomes experienced by the top 30 percent of the world.[45] In absolute terms, these income gains translate into a 13 percent increase in the size of the global middle class and reduce the number of people earning less than middle-class incomes by 231 million relative to the baseline.

Domestic policies: powerful instruments to attain mutually reinforcing growth and equity objectives

Well-designed domestic policies are likely to be the most powerful instruments to reduce both inequality and poverty in any specific country. Such policies need not interfere with sustainable long-term growth. In fact, as clearly shown by World Bank (2005: 10), the "dichotomy between policies for growth and policies specifically aimed at equity is false," and governments should be able to design equity-enhancing policies that can also increase efficiency. Even so, potential trade-offs may arise. Raising direct taxes to excessive levels to finance social services, such as education, targeted to the poor may create disincentives and even curb investment. However, in the long run, once access to education has become more equitable, a larger share of the population will be educated; growth should also be higher. These long-term benefits of redistribution should be considered when assessing trade-offs between equity and efficiency.

In addition, specific policies that may boost growth, such as trade liberalization, may in some cases negatively affect the poor. In many cases, the solution consists of designing complementary policies that mitigate the adverse poverty consequences of reform rather than abandoning or modifying the pro-growth policy, either of which may have even worse consequences for equity. In the trade-liberalization example, mitigation policies may range from investing in access roads to improve access by the poor to markets, to setting up or improving safety nets, and to better labor-market policies and institutions.

The design and successful implementation of a development strategy that positively reinforces growth and equity objectives is highly country-specific. It will depend, among other things, on countries' initial conditions in terms of equity, institutions, and economic structures. Yet from recent literature, and through one's consideration of the scenarios described in this and the previous chapters, some policy lessons emerge that may be relevant for a large number of countries.

A first lesson can be inferred by observing that with increasing incomes and the expansion of the middle class, governments should be able to collect larger revenues and thus gain fiscal space for redistributive spending. Furthermore, the composition of tax sources also changes with a shift toward more direct taxes and fewer indirect taxes. Unfortunately the distributional impact of such a shift cannot be tested directly on this study's household survey data, which do not report tax payments, but the available literature is not overly optimistic. For example, ex post studies for Chile, a country with one of the most effective tax systems in Latin America, estimated that in 1996 the after-tax Gini coefficient was 0.496—slightly *higher* than the before-tax index of 0.488.[46] Lopez and others (2006) show that income inequality in European countries is barely affected by taxes and social security contributions, indicating that the overall distributional effect of taxation is almost equivalent to that of a proportional (flat-rate) tax. The same study also shows that redistribution takes place mainly through transfers rather than through taxes: in most European countries transfers seem to be almost equally distributed across the population, thus contributing to a substantial reduction in income inequality before tax and transfers.

This evidence suggests that although taxation can be redistributive, at least in principle, transfers and expenditures (for education, for example) may be governments' preferred levers of redistribution. This chapter has emphasized the critical role that education can play in reducing poverty. Improving access to education can reduce poverty both by increasing individual productivity and by facilitating the movement of poor people from low-paying jobs in agriculture to higher-paying jobs in industry and services. Even more important, public spending on education (as well as on health and other human capacity), when targeted toward the poor, can produce a double dividend, reducing poverty in the short run and increasing the chances for poor children to access formal jobs and thus break free from the intergenerational poverty trap. Empirical evidence of the double advantages of targeted education programs has been emphasized by other studies. Morley and Coady (2003) state

that "a good deal of the *success* of these programs stems from their system of targeting [...] On average 71 percent of conditional [for education] cash transfer program benefits go to the bottom 40 per cent of families." Evidence on the educational impact of these programs is sparser, and given their relative recent implementation, very little is known about the long-term earnings benefits accruing to the recipients. However, the existing evidence is strongly positive: most reviewed programs have achieved their objectives of increasing enrollment rates among their targeted population.[47]

Increasing educational levels must be accompanied by a strong investment climate to ensure productive jobs for the newly educated, and the quality of education needs to be maintained. The shift from agriculture should be undertaken within a wider context of improving agricultural productivity and expanding opportunities in modern sectors, not through policies that discriminate against agriculture. Labor-market policies are important in aiding worker adjustment and enhancing mobility, but too often such policies end up raising the cost of hiring labor and push workers into informal sectors or unemployment. World Bank (2005) emphasizes the role of labor unions in improving worker conditions, but cautions that product markets must be competitive to prevent the unions from commanding rents at the expense of consumers. Success stories include unionizing landless export agriculture workers in northeastern Brazil, which resulted not only in better worker protections but also enhanced productivity and quality of output.

Government intervention is another mechanism for improving working conditions. Cambodia was able to significantly limit labor abuse in the textiles sector through a monitoring program designed to improve labor standards in exchange for higher U.S. import quotas. The Slovak Republic lowered employment taxes and increased labor-market flexibility through concentrated efforts by a reform-minded government seeking to join the European Union.

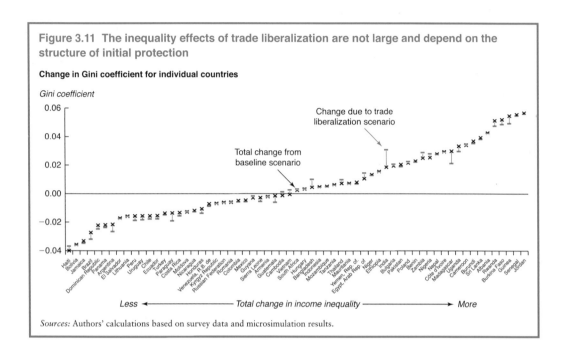

Figure 3.11 The inequality effects of trade liberalization are not large and depend on the structure of initial protection

Change in Gini coefficient for individual countries

Sources: Authors' calculations based on survey data and microsimulation results.

Domestic policy reforms can also strongly influence the final effects on inequality and poverty of multilateral trade reforms. As shown above, multilateral trade liberalization has a discernible impact on global income distribution; however, the "pure" trade policy effect on within-country inequality does not seem to be very large (figure 3.11). Within-country inequality will change according to the initial pattern of protection, the evolution of global prices, and the sectoral and factor-specific productivity impacts (see Winters, McCulloch, and McKay 2004 and Bussolo and Round 2005). For example, in a scenario where global trade barriers are eliminated and international prices for agricultural goods increase, Brazil, which currently protects skill- (and capital-) intensive industries more than it does agriculture, will likely experience a reduction of within-country inequality. Conversely, India or Mexico, countries with tariff structures that protect unskilled workers (especially in agriculture), will probably have to face pressure toward increasing inequality. Because they assume that other factors will remain equal, these have been labeled "pure" trade effects. Clearly,

well-designed additional policy interventions, especially those that improve education and infrastructure and address other "behind the border" investment climate reforms, can militate against the inequality changes that may result from trade liberalization.

Such policies are likely to play an increasingly important role in the future, not least because the coming globalization will include two new challenges—the integration of large emerging economies such as China and India, and the global sourcing of services. While the above scenario explores the impact of reductions in tariffs on goods, the global sourcing of services, enabled by new advances in technology, is leading to an increasing number of services-related tasks—and increasingly higher-skilled tasks—being undertaken in developing countries. This will bring new implications for wage distribution along the skill spectrum, and most likely change the inequality results shown in figure 3.11. The implications of this combination of technological advance and trade integration for workers in developing and developed countries are discussed in more detail in chapter 4.

Notes

1. In this discussion the authors have adopted the naming conventions of World Bank (2005). Milanovic (2005) refers to the following different measurements as inequality concepts 1, 2, and 3.

2. Bourguignon, Levin, and Rosenblatt (2004) point out that using the intercountry concept may represent an implicit welfare judgment, whereby the rising incomes of more populous countries cannot offset the losses of smaller countries when their incomes are falling.

3. The influence of China and India is so large that omitting these two countries would reverse the conclusion: international inequality excluding China and India has increased in the past two decades (World Bank 2005).

4. It should also be noted that measurement of inequality is sensitive to both the precise indicators used to measure it and the time horizon chosen.

5. The ratio of per capita incomes of the richest and poorest country in the sample has grown by a factor of more than five.

6. Bourguignon, Levin, and Rosenblatt (2004) show that it is possible to produce rising inequality statistics if, for example, the sensitivity of the Atkinson inequality index to deviations from mean income at the bottom of the distribution is set sufficiently high (over five).

7. Atkinson and Brandolini (2004) use the Gini coefficient, the Theil index, and mean logarithmic deviation to show that income inequality declined between 1970 and 2000.

8. Bourguignon and Morrison (2002) argue that inequality between countries has been responsible for most of the time-series variation in global inequality. See also Milanovic (2002), who shows that in 1993, inequality between countries accounted for three-quarters of global inequality.

9. Some of the studies examining global inequality have relied on parameterized Lorenz curves to add the within-country dimension to the analysis: see for example, Sala-i-Martin (2002a, 2002b), and Bhalla (2002). Others, such as Milanovic (2002) and World Bank (2005), have built up the global distribution from household surveys.

10. The between-group decomposition is accomplished by giving each person within the group that group's average income. As a result, differences between the average incomes of the rich, the poor, and the middle class account for 68 percent of total world inequality. On the other hand, if every person in the world is assigned the average income of his or her country of residence, income differences between countries account for 76 percent of global inequality. Thus, income differentials between the rich, the poor, and the middle class are responsible for the bulk of global variation in incomes.

11. The size of the middle class doubles between 2000 and 2030. In comparison, the number of the rich increases by 75 percent and the number of the poor decreases by 19 percent.

12. The number of developing-country citizens in the global middle class increases 3.25 times between 2000 and 2030. The share of low- and middle-income country nationals among the rich rises even faster (4.7 times), but their influence in this group is likely to be moderate, as OECD citizens will still constitute one-half of the category.

13. Note that this is not true for the first column of table 3.1, which is based on 1993 international dollars.

14. This study's qualitative conclusions about the composition of the middle class hold even if the authors adopt a relative definition of the middle class and confine their attention to the fifth decile of the world's income distribution—that is, the "median" individuals.

15. The authors' global middle class concept is in this sense similar to a poverty line, which is the amount of real income required to buy a fixed amount of calories. Poverty lines do not move through the periods of growth and decline, since the latter do not affect caloric intake requirements. Similarly, the study's definition of the middle class is based on the ability to afford a certain basket of goods and services, and anyone who can purchase this basket (whether in 2000 or in 2030) is a member of the middle class.

16. Note that the simulation design for China differs from the majority of countries in this study's sample. Because the authors do not have information on individual earnings, they cannot pass the changes in skill premia from the CGE model to the microsimulation. All other steps, including demographic change and growth in per capita incomes, remain fully consistent with the standard simulation approach. See box 3.1 and Bussolo and others (forthcoming) for more details.

17. The distribution is plotted as a kernel density function of the household per capita incomes.

18. In other words, the study results show that 13 percent of the middle-class population in 2030 will have completed less than a full cycle of primary education. The relevant population share for those earning more than middle class incomes is 12 percent.

19. As cited in Mayda and Rodrik (2002).

20. Note that the Africans of 2030 will be better off in absolute terms than in 2000, since the study forecasts non-negative real growth rates even at the bottom of the distribution.

21. There are 12 developing energy exporters in the study's 114-country database. These include three countries in the Middle East and North Africa, two in Sub-Saharan Africa, three in Latin America and the Caribbean, and four in Europe and Central Asia.

22. There are 15 developing-country agriculture exporters in the study sample. A country is defined as an agriculture exporter if its exports of any one agricultural commodity exceed 20 percent of total exports.

23. This is another case showing that this chapter's results should not be considered "forecasts" but *ceteris paribus* scenarios; a forecast should include at least some countries with negative performances.

24. Osberg (2003) measures polarization by the shares of population earning less than 50 percent and more than 150 percent of the median income. In both the United States and the United Kingdom, the shares of low and high earners increased substantially over the sample period.

25. These effects are somewhat ameliorated because with population aging, older and more experienced workers tend to become less scarce, reducing their wage premium (Higgins and Williamson 1999). Also, in 45 percent of the developing countries in the study sample, younger household heads tend to earn more than older ones, owing in part to higher education.

26. The maximum poverty elasticity (assuming that all migrants are poor and all poor migrants increase their incomes sufficiently to escape poverty) for developing countries is about 2—see table below, column (a). However, on average, of every 100 migrants only 20 are below the poverty line (column b). These results are based on the case where movers are selected according to their characteristics (that is, with a logit selection model). Furthermore, of the average 20 poor migrants among the movers, 7 remain in poverty in their new occupation (column c). This results in an observed poverty elasticity of 0.2 (column d).

27. By facilitating access to higher-paying jobs, education contributes to reducing poverty even for those workers who do not move across sectors.

28. This finding is informed by country-specific regression analysis focusing on the determinants of employment in farm and nonfarm sectors (probit models). Although this pattern is true for most countries, in some cases migrants tend to have different characteristics. For example, in a recent study for Brazil, Bussolo, Lay, and van der Mensbrugghe (2006) used a more complex behavioral model to show that, with only a few exceptions, poorer individuals are more likely to migrate to nonfarm occupations.

29. The authors of this study assume that, once the migrants are selected, in one way or another, they find a job in the rest of the economy and earn the modern sector's higher wage adjusted to take into account their personal characteristics.

30. See, for example, World Bank (2005) and Lopez and others (2006).

31. The relationship between household income and age of the household head is positive in approximately 70 percent of the sample countries, while the age-income profile is positive in 60 percent of the countries.

32. The literature on the evolution of income inequality identifies three channels that determine the effects of demographic change: first, given an upward-sloping age-earnings (incomes) profile, aging will increase inequality between old and young groups (Deaton and Paxson 1997); second, different age groups are characterized by different within-group inequality, and inequality tends to be higher among older

Moving from agricultural to nonagricultural occupations reduces poverty in some regions more than others

Migration-poverty elasticity when 10 percent of the population employed in agriculture migrates

Region	Maximum poverty elasticity (a)	Poverty among migrants before moving (b)	Poverty among migrants after moving (c)	Observed poverty elasticity (d)
Sub-Saharan Africa	1.60	0.35	0.14	0.36
East Asia and the Pacific	3.78	0.11	0.09	0.48
Europe and Central Asia	4.45	0.03	0.01	0.03
Latin America and the Caribbean	1.74	0.19	0.08	0.09
Middle East and North Africa	1.18	0.26	0.01	—
South Asia	1.81	0.23	0.07	0.15
Average in the developing world	2.03	0.19	0.07	0.20

Source: Authors' estimates from household surveys.
Note: Column (a) shows how much poverty could be reduced in percent terms with respect to the initial poverty headcount if all migrants are initially poor and all escape poverty after the move. Column (b) represents the actual poverty headcount of movers (accounting for the fact that many nonpoor migrate). Column (c) shows the poverty headcount among movers calculated after they are assigned the income of the new occupation. Column (d) is the actual migration-poverty elasticity (for a 10 percent migration rate). — = not available.

age cohorts (see Deaton and Paxson 1997; Jenkins 1995; and Mookherjee and Shorroks 1982). With everything else remaining constant, when older cohorts become more populous, as is the case with lower population growth rates, aggregate inequality increases. These two channels affect aggregate inequality without any change in the age premium, that is, with a fixed age-earnings profile; however, the third channel considers changes in inequality due to changes of the life-cycle income profile. As the population ages, older high-wage and more experienced workers tend to become less scarce and the wage premium they initially receive will be reduced (Higgins and Williamson 1999). This third channel works through the labor market and contributes to attenuating the inequality increases brought about by the first two channels. This channel is explored in more detail as part of the discussion on price-wage adjustments.

33. Some of the changes in inequality shown in figure 3.6 may seem implausible when compared with some ex post evidence; however, the aim of this figure is not to present forecasts of income inequality, but rather to show what may happen, *ceteris paribus,* to inequality in a specific scenario for the evolution of the global economy.

34. The simulated reduction of the gap between skilled versus unskilled workers' wages for Latin America is plausible and in line with recent evidence. Manacorda, Sanchez-Paramo, and Schady (2005), using micro-data for five Latin American countries, show that the relative rewards of workers who completed tertiary school have increased but, apart from Mexico, relative wages of workers who completed secondary school have decreased. In this study's micro-simulation the authors define a worker as skilled when his or her level of education is, at least, completed secondary. In Latin America, about 25 percent of heads of household have secondary education (without tertiary) compared with 12 percent of heads with tertiary schooling. Therefore, even with an increase of the tertiary-educated workers' wages, the average wage for the group defined in the study as skilled would still be reduced.

35. Notice that this is not the same as encouraging mobility by means of "forced urbanization," which is known to generate negative consequences. The focus here is on removing distortions rather than adding them.

36. These income dynamics—that is, the changes of the premia received by agricultural workers versus nonagricultural ones, as well as those obtained by skilled versus unskilled—are consistent with the CGE results of chapter 2.

37. Bourguingon, Levin, and Rosenblatt (2006) also show that although aid is often viewed as a zero-sum game, that is not the case if aid flows are measured in PPP terms, which account for lower prices of nontradable goods in the recipient countries.

38. This is given by the equation:

Gi = {Set of variables not related to aid} − 0.54 ∗ (ODAi/GDPi) − 0.02 ∗ (ODAi/GDPi)^2 + 0.31 ∗ (CPIAi ∗ ODAi/GDPi)

39. Institutional quality is captured by the World Bank's Country Performance and Institutional Assessment (CPIA) ratings. For International Development Association (IDA) member countries, CPIA scores are available online starting with 2005.

40. The assumption of equal distribution of ODA implies that the removal of aid flows does not change the income distribution within countries. On the one hand, assuming equal distribution may be too optimistic—aid may not reach the desired recipients owing to a host of factors including corruption and lack of access to infrastructure. On the other hand, it may be too pessimistic, since the rich in the recipient countries are assumed to derive some benefits from the aid that the donors never intended for them to obtain.

41. In estimating this effect, this study's methodology and the approach of Bourguignon, Levin, and Rosenblatt (2006) differ in two important ways. First, this study uses growth rates generated by the model of chapter 2 rather than historical growth rates. Second, while Bourguignon, Levin, and Rosenblatt (2006) disregard the within-country distribution of income (by assigning every individual within a country that country's per capita gross national income—GNI), this study's approach explicitly takes into account both between- and within-country distributions.

42. In 2004 only 10 of 66 low-income aid recipient countries received a "good enough" rating of their budget system according to the CPIA indicators (World Bank 2006). In the presence of bad policies, conventional aid delivery methods are unlikely to benefit the intended recipients, even if the aid is targeted toward human development–intensive sectors such as education and health (World Bank 1998). This is because aid is often fungible and can be easily reallocated away from target activities once it enters the public budget. At the same time, even the most distorted policy environments are likely to have "pockets of reform," which can become the focal point of donors' efforts to improve the overall policy environment. For example, efforts to improve public procurement—the mechanisms through which governments purchase goods and services—lie at the heart of the ability of aid to deliver the desired outcomes (World Bank 2006).

43. Notice that this implies a larger absolute cut in protection for developing countries, whose initial tariff levels are significantly above the high-income average.

44. In other words, figure 3.10 represents the difference between the growth incidence curve of the

trade reform scenario and the growth incidence curve of the baseline scenario. The horizontal line is the increase in the global average per capita income.

45. Figure 3.10 shows the dynamic gains from trade reform, which allow for feedback from increases in trade openness (exports-to-output ratio) to total factor productivity. Since low-income countries tend to have higher trade barriers, the trade reform scenario results in larger absolute tariff cuts in these countries and therefore greater increases in trade flows. The CGE model used to simulate the trade reform scenario does not capture the possibility of imperfect pass-through of price shocks to different individuals (because they are in remote areas, involved in subsistence activities and the like), and accounting for these imperfections would dampen the pro-poor potential of trade liberalization.

46. Engle, Galetoviv, and Raddatz (1998), cited in Lopez and others (2006).

47. Morley and Coady (2003) even attempt to estimate the future earnings of poor children receiving transfers under programs in Mexico and Nicaragua. In their words: "under the reasonable assumption that the wage structure of the future labor force will be the same as it was in the year of the most recent survey, we estimate that the additional education would add about 8 per cent to the average earnings of the poor in Mexico and about 9 per cent in Nicaragua."

References

Anderson, Kym, Will Martin, and Dominique van der Mensbrugghe. 2006. "Doha Merchandise Trade Reform: What Is at Stake for Developing Countries?" *World Bank Economic Review* 20: 169–95.

Atkinson, Anthony B. 2003. "Income Inequality in OECD Countries: Data and Explanations." Munich: CESifo Working Paper Series 881.

Atkinson, Anthony B., and Andrea Brandolini. 2004. "Global World Inequality: Absolute, Relative or Intermediate." Paper prepared for the 28th Conference of the International Association for Research in Income and Wealth, Cork, Ireland, August 22–28.

Bhalla, Surjit. 2002. *Imagine There's No Country: Poverty, Inequality, and Growth in the Era of Globalization.* Washington, DC: Institute for International Economics.

Bonaglia, Federico, Jorge Braga de Macedo, and Maurizio Bussolo. 2001. "How Globalization Improves Governance." CEPR Discussion Paper 2992, Centre for Economic Policy Research, London.

Bourguignon, François, Victoria Levin, and David Rosenblatt. 2004. "Declining International Inequality and Economic Divergence: Reviewing the Evidence through Different Lenses." *Économie Internationale* 100: 13–25.

———. 2006. "Global Redistribution of Income." World Bank Policy Research Working Paper 3961, Washington, DC, July.

Bourguignon, François, and Christian Morrison. 2002. "Inequality among World Citizens: 1890–1992." *American Economic Review* 92 (4): 727–44.

Bourguignon, François, and Luiz Pereira da Silva, eds. 2003. *The Impact of Economic Policies on Poverty and Income Distribution: Evaluation Techniques and Tools.* Washington, DC: World Bank and Oxford University Press.

Bruno, Michael, Martin Ravallion, and Lyn Squire. 1998. "Equity and Growth in Developing Countries: Old and New Perspectives on the Policy Issues." In *Income Distribution and High-Quality Growth,* ed. Vito Tanzi and Ke-young Chu. Cambridge, MA: MIT Press.

Burnside, Craig, and David Dollar. 2000. "Aid, Policies, and Growth." *American Economic Review* 90 (4) (September): 847–68.

Bussolo, Maurizio, Rafael De Hoyos, Denis Medvedev, and Victor Sulla. Forthcoming. "Demographic Change, Economic Growth, and Income Distribution: An Empirical Analysis Using Ex-Ante Microsimulations." Background paper for *Global Economic Prospects 2007: Confronting Challenges of the Coming Globalization.*

Bussolo, Maurizio, Jann Lay, and Dominique van der Mensbrugghe. 2006. "Structural Change and Poverty Reduction in Brazil: The Impact of the Doha Round." In *Poverty and the WTO: Impacts of the Doha Development Agenda,* ed. Thomas Hertel and Alan Winters. Washington, DC: World Bank.

Bussolo, Maurizio, and Denis Medvedev. 2006. "What Is the Role of Labor Markets in Making Trade Reform Pro-Poor in Latin America?" World Bank Policy Research Working Paper, Washington, DC. Draft.

Bussolo, Maurizio, and Jeffery Round, eds. 2005. *Globalisation and Poverty: Channels and Policy Responses.* London: Routledge/Warwick Studies in Globalisation, Routledge.

Chen, Shaohua, and Martin Ravallion. 2003. "Household Welfare Impacts of China's Accession to the World Trade Organization." Policy Research Working Paper 3040, World Bank, Washington, DC.

Chenery, Hollis, Montek Ahluwalia, C. Bell, John Duloy, and Richard Jolly. 1974. *Redistribution with Growth.* New York: Oxford University Press.

Collier, Paul, and David Dollar. 2002. "Aid Allocation and Poverty Reduction." *European Economic Review* 46 (8): 1475–1500.

de Ferranti, David, Guillermo E. Perry, Francisco H. G. Ferreira, and Michael Walton. 2004. *Inequality in Latin America: Breaking with History?* Washington, DC: World Bank.

Deaton, Angus, and Christina Paxson. 1997. "The Effects of Economic and Population Growth on National Saving and Inequality." *Demography* 34 (1) (February): 97–114.

Dollar, David, and Aart Kraay. 2002. "Growth Is Good for the Poor." *Journal of Economic Growth* 7 (3): 195–225.

Easterly, William, Ross Levine, and David Roodman. 2004. "Aid, Policies, and Growth: Comment." *American Economic Review* 94 (3) (June 1): 774–80.

Engle, E., A. Galetovic, and C. Raddatz. 1998. "Taxation and Income Distribution in Chile: Some Unpleasant Redistributive Arithmetic." NBER Working Paper 6828, National Bureau of Economic Research, Cambridge, MA.

Ferreira, Francisco H. G., and Phillippe G. Leite. 2003. "Meeting the Millennium Development Goals in Brazil: Can Microsimulations Help?" *Economía* 3 (2): 235–79.

———. 2004. "Educational Expansion and Income Distribution: A Microsimulation for Ceará." In *Growth, Inequality and Poverty,* ed. Anthony Shorrocks and Rolph van der Hoeven. London: Oxford University Press.

Higgins, Matthew, and Jeffrey G. Williamson. 1999. "Explaining Inequality the World Round: Cohort Size, Kuznets Curves, and Openness." Staff Reports 79, Federal Reserve Bank of New York.

Jenkins, Stephen P. 1995. "Accounting for Inequality Trends: Decomposition Analyses for the UK, 1971–86." *Economica* [London School of Economics and Political Science] 62 (245) (February): 29–63.

Li, Hongyi, Lyn Squire, and Heng-fu Zou. 1998. "Explaining International and Intertemporal Variations in Income Inequality." *Economic Journal* 108 (446): 26–43.

Lopez, J. Humberto, William F. Maloney, Guillermo E. Perry, Omar S. Arias, and Luis Servén. 2006. *Poverty Reduction and Growth: Virtuous and Vicious Circles.* Washington, DC: World Bank.

Lutz, Wolfgang, and Anne Goujon. 2001. "The World's Changing Human Capital Stock: Multi-State Population Projections by Educational Attainment." *Population and Development Review* 27 (2): 323–39.

Lutz, Wolfgang, Anne Goujon, Gabriele Doblhammer-Reiter. 1998. "Demographic Dimensions in Forecasting: Adding Education to Age and Sex." *Population and Development Review* 24 (Supplement: Frontiers of Population Forecasting): 42–58.

Manacorda, M., Carolina Sanchez-Paramo, and Norbert Schady. 2005. "Changes in Returns to Education in Latin America: The Role of Demand and Supply of Skills." CEP Discussion Paper dp0712, Centre for Economic Performance, London School of Economics.

Mayda, Anna Maria, and Dani Rodrik. 2005. "Why Are Some People (and Countries) More Protectionist than Others?" *European Economic Review* 49 (6) (August): 1393–1430.

Mayer, W., 1984. "Endogenous Tariff Formation." *American Economic Review* 74: 970–85.

Milanovic, Branko. 2002. "True World Income Distribution, 1988 and 1993: First Calculation Based on Household Surveys Alone." *Economic Journal* (Royal Economic Society) 112 (476) (January): 51–92.

———. 2005. *Worlds Apart: Global and International Inequality 1950–2000.* Princeton, NJ: Princeton University Press.

Milanovic, Branko, and Shlomo Yitzhaki. 2002. "Decomposing World Income Distribution: Does the World Have a Middle Class?" *Review of Income and Wealth* 48 (2): 155–78.

Mookherjee, Dilip, and Anthony Shorrocks. 1982. "A Decomposition Analysis of the Trend in UK Income Inequality." *Economic Journal* 92: 886–902.

Morley, Samuel A., and David Coady. 2003. *From Social Assistance to Social Development: Targeted Education Subsidies in Developing Countries.* Washington, DC: Center for Global Development and the International Food Policy Research Institute.

O'Rourke, Kevin. 2003. "Hecksher-Ohlin Theory and Individual Attitudes towards Globalization." CEPR Discussion Paper 4018, Centre for Economic Policy Research, London.

Olivera, Mauricio, and Eduardo Lora. 2005. "The Electoral Consequences of the Washington Consensus." Inter-American Development Bank Working Paper 530, Washington, DC.

Osberg, Lars. 2003. "Long Run Trends in Income Inequality in the United States, UK, Sweden, Germany and Canada: A Birth Cohort View." *Eastern Economic Journal* 29 (1): 121–42.

Pritchett, Lant. 1997. "Divergence, Big Time." *Journal of Economic Perspectives* 11 (3): 3–17.

Quah, Danny T. 1996. "Twin Peaks: Growth and Convergence in Models of Distribution Dynamics." *Economic Journal* [Royal Economic Society] 106 (437) (July): 1045–55.

———. 1997. "Empirics for Growth and Distribution: Stratification, Polarization, and Convergence Clubs." *Journal of Economic Growth* 2 (1): 27–59.

Ravallion, Martin. 2004. "Competing Concepts of Inequality in the Globalization Debate." In *Brookings Trade Forum 2004,* ed. Susan Margaret

Collins and Carol Graham. Washington, DC: Brookings Institution.

Ravallion, Martin, and Shaohua Chen. 2003. "Measuring Pro-Poor Growth." *Economics Letters* 78 (1): 93–99.

———. 2004. "China's (Uneven) Progress against Poverty." World Bank Policy Research Working Paper Series 3408, Washington, DC.

Sala-i-Martin, Xavier. 2002a. "The Disturbing 'Rise' of Global Income Inequality." NBER Working Paper 8904, National Bureau of Economic Research, Cambridge, MA. April.

———. 2002b. "The World Distribution of Income (Estimated from Individual Country Distributions)." NBER Working Paper 8933, National Bureau of Economic Research, Cambridge, MA. May.

Scheve, Kenneth, and Matthew Slaughter. 1998. "What Determines Individual Trade Policy Preferences?" NBER Working Paper 6531, National Bureau of Economic Research, Cambridge, MA.

Theil, Henri, and James Seale. 1994. "The Geographic Distribution of World Income, 1950–1990." *De Economist* 142 (4): 387–419.

Winters, L. A., N. McCulloch, and A. McKay. 2004. "Trade Liberalization and Poverty: The Evidence So Far." *Journal of Economic Literature* 42 (1): 72–115.

World Bank. 1998. *Assessing Aid: What Works, What Doesn't, and Why.* New York: Oxford University Press.

———. 2005. *World Development Report 2006: Equity and Development.* Washington, DC: World Bank and New York: Oxford University Press.

———. 2006. *Global Monitoring Report 2006: Millennium Development Goals—Strengthening Mutual Accountability, Aid, Trade, and Governance.* World Bank: Washington, DC.

World Tourism Organization. 2006. "Facts and Figures." Available at http://www.unwto.org/facts/menu.html.

4

New Pressures in Labor Markets: Integrating Large Emerging Economies and the Global Sourcing of Services

Rapid technological progress, trade in goods, and international sourcing of services come together to put new pressures in labor markets, pressures that will only become more acute in the next 25 years. Through these channels, globalization is creating a progressively more integrated global market for labor. The impact is tempered by differences in the skills, technology, and know-how available to workers.

Globalization offers opportunities for export growth and access to a wider range of cheaper imported products that can fuel productivity growth and rising average living standards. But globalization also imposes adjustment costs on certain groups within countries, primarily through labor markets by influencing wages and job security and by demanding retraining, and the upheaval of moving between jobs. The unskilled have seen their wages worsen relative to skilled workers and their jobs become less secure. This is true even in developing countries—contrary to expectations that the unskilled benefit relative to the skilled as labor-intensive manufacturing moves to low-wage countries. The projections in this report offer little reason to believe that this will change in the coming decade.

Two challenges are particularly demanding: one is the rise of China, India, and other emerging economies as manufacturing powerhouses, and the other is the emergence of global sourcing of services. While the qualitative implications of increasing exports of manufactured products from India and China are the same as

for the emergence of the Asian tigers, India and China's sheer size raises the specter of surging new export competition. Many developing countries fear that exports from these large new players may swamp their domestic markets, squeeze them out of the global market, foreclose avenues of diversification in manufactures as a road to higher growth, and gobble up all the investment flows. And high-income countries worry that if the large emerging economies can readily acquire and master the newest technologies, their exports may soon take over high-tech markets.

Global sourcing of services exerts pressures in the same direction. The transfer of relatively skilled service activities to firms in developing countries is putting new pressures on white-collar employment in both the high-income countries and advanced developing countries. This puts higher-paying and higher-skill jobs at risk in both high- and middle-income countries. Unlike displacement in low-skilled manufactures trade, services offshoring has the potential to destroy the previous investments of white-collar workers in firm-specific knowledge.

The analysis here suggests that three factors are likely to mitigate these effects in the medium and long term.

- First, the growth of the Chinese, Indian, and other emerging markets offers enormous offsetting opportunities for other developing and developed countries to increase exports. As China and India increase their exports, they will have to increase imports of intermediate inputs, energy, technology, and investment goods. Driven by China, Asia was the principal destination for accelerated exports from Africa and Latin America in the late 1990s and the early 2000s.

- Second, accompanying the rising value of exports and domestic living standards in emerging economies will be rising wages. This—together with the inevitable exchange rate adjustment to the rise in global demand for these countries' products and services—will create space for low-income countries to move into the lowest-skill activities vacated by producers in the large emerging countries.

- Third, developing the social institutions that support a dynamic market economy in China and India will take time, providing an opportunity for smaller, more flexible countries to progress faster in institutional development—and for rich countries to continue to lead in productivity-enhancing innovation. The flow of services activities from rich to poor countries, which entails some transfer of know-how, will be slowed to the extent that institutional frameworks discourage foreign direct investment (FDI) and in particular fail to protect the ownership of such assets.

The policies that countries adopt will determine whether they will be able to take advantage of these new opportunities. Effective policy responses will need to position countries to harness the opportunities from globalization while also addressing the adjustment tensions that inevitably arise from the unprecedented magnitude and speed of change in labor markets.

Policies to embrace, rather than resist, global integration will lay the foundations for future growth and job creation. Openness to trade and FDI will become ever more critical if the poorest countries are to absorb technologies

and know-how from abroad and seize the opportunities created by rising demand from—and production shifts in—India and China. But openness will not foster integration in the absence of an attractive investment climate, one with sound institutions and policies that allow labor, capital, and knowledge to flow from low-return to high-return sectors. Developing knowledge-intensive activities as future drivers of growth will require investing in the institutions and policy frameworks that foster innovation, and in education and lifelong learning for all workers. Developing countries with wages currently higher than those in China and India will have to place greater attention on their institutions and on education policies to create a climate for greater innovation and skill enhancement.

Social policies should focus on protecting workers rather than protecting jobs. Even in the most propitious policy and institutional environments, rapid growth, globalization, and labor-market flexibility are likely to quicken the pace of job creation and job destruction. This demands policies to cushion the adjustment costs associated with increased volatility and involuntary dislocation. The returns to skilled labor will continue to increase faster than those to unskilled labor, perpetuating a natural wage-widening tendency in many (if not most) countries and underscoring the need for measures to support workers at the low end of the scale. Rising wage inequality, together with volatile labor markets, are heightening insecurity among workers throughout the world.

The impact of globalization: the story so far

Globalization, coupled with technological change, has driven growth in the world economy, bringing new employment opportunities and enabling millions of people to escape absolute poverty. That said, impacts have varied across and within countries—and not all workers have benefited equally. While many countries have seized the opportunities offered by greater integration of markets in goods and services, others, especially in Sub-Saharan Africa, have remained marginalized. Meanwhile demand for skilled labor has increased in both developed and developing countries and greater global competition has become associated with a growing sense of insecurity for many workers worldwide.

Product markets are rapidly integrating . . . with a geographical redistribution of manufacturing

Developing countries' trade has accelerated over the last few decades. In the markets of developed countries, the share of developing countries in imports of manufactured products grew from barely 14 percent in 1973 to nearly 40 percent in 2003 (figure 4.1).[1]

Imports of developing countries have grown just as quickly as their exports to the rest of the world (Ghose 2003). Developing-country imports grew at about 2 percent per year during the 1980s, accelerating to 9.5 percent per year during the 1990s (Bhorat and Lundall 2004).

This increased two-way trade reflects the growth of outsourcing and global production chains (see *Global Economic Prospects 2003*). Enabled by falling barriers to trade and FDI, lower transport and communication costs, and new technologies, global chains break down goods into their constituent parts, each produced where it can be done most efficiently and at least cost, whether by an affiliate or by an independent supplier. Ghose (2003) sees a correlation between countries' share of world merchandise exports and their share of FDI inflows: between 1982 and 1999, foreign affiliates of transnational corporations increased their share of world exports from 31 percent to 45 percent.

At the same time, manufacturing employment has been redistributed between developed and developing countries. While the precise numbers are debated, the gain in the latter has been much larger than the loss in the former (Sapir 2005; Ghose 2003).[2] Overall, employment in manufacturing in developed countries declined from 28.7 percent in 1995 to 24.8 percent in 2005, while most developing regions saw gains (table 4.1).

Not all developing countries have experienced gains in manufacturing employment, however. Consider, for example, the striking differences between East Asia and Latin America. Over the 1990s, employment in manufacturing increased in China (by just under 15 percent cumulatively), India (by about 38 percent), Malaysia (40 percent), and Thailand (about 49 percent). In Latin America, however, aggregate manufacturing employment declined over the 1990s; increases in Chile (about 10 percent) were more than offset by declines in Brazil (about 50 percent) and Argentina (14 percent) (Bhorat and Lundall 2004).[3]

Services employment has increased in both developed countries and all developing regions, except the Middle East and North Africa, where it has remained the same (table 4.1). Over the 1990s, large increases in services employment were seen in Brazil (57 percent) and Mexico (62 percent), with smaller increases in China (about 13 percent) and India (25 percent) (Bhorat and Lundall

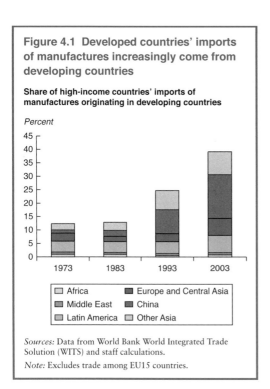

Figure 4.1 Developed countries' imports of manufactures increasingly come from developing countries

Share of high-income countries' imports of manufactures originating in developing countries

Percent

Sources: Data from World Bank World Integrated Trade Solution (WITS) and staff calculations.

Note: Excludes trade among EU15 countries.

Table 4.1 Employment in developing countries has shifted out of agriculture into manufactures and services

Trends in sectoral shares in employment, 1995–2005 (percent)

World region	Agriculture			Industry			Services		
	1995	2005[a]	Change (%)	1995	2005[a]	Change (%)	1995	2005[a]	Change (%)
World	44.4	40.1	−9.7	21.1	21	−0.5	34.5	38.9	12.8
East Asia	54.4	49.5	−9.0	25.9	26.1	0.8	19.7	24.4	23.9
South East Asia and the Pacific	55.3	43.3	−21.7	15.4	20.7	34.4	29.3	36	22.9
South Asia	64.1	61.2	−4.5	13.4	14.1	5.2	22.5	24.6	9.3
Latin America and the Caribbean	23.4	17.1	−26.9	20.2	20.3	0.5	56.4	62.5	10.8
Middle East and North Africa	30.8	26.3	−14.6	20.3	25	23.2	48.9	48.7	−0.4
Sub-Saharan Africa	70.1	63.6	−9.3	8.2	8.9	8.5	21.7	27.5	26.7
Developed economies and the European Union	5.1	3.7	−27.5	28.7	24.8	−13.6	66.1	71.4	8.0
Central and Eastern Europe and CIS	27.9	22.7	−18.6	27.5	27.4	−0.4	44.6	49.9	11.9

Source: ILO 2006; Bank staff calculations.
CIS: Commonwealth of Independent States.
a. Indicative.

2004). Also worthy of note are the relatively high levels of female employment in the sector.

To some extent, this increase may reflect changes in business organization, where functions once performed inside manufacturing companies are now outsourced to other firms on a contract basis, resulting in their reclassification as services. This change in business organization has also crossed borders, with multinational companies sourcing activities from subsidiaries or external firms around the globe. (The global sourcing of services will be revisited below.)

Globalization has generally been associated with rising average wages—but not all workers are benefiting equally . . .

While an economy's openness to trade and investment is in general associated with faster growth of average wages over the longer term, short-term impacts can vary. Although the initial impact of trade liberalization on wages may be negative in some countries, it becomes significantly positive over time. For FDI, the picture is reversed: an initial positive effect on wages is reduced to nothing after five years. This highlights the importance of the investment climate—if opening the economy does not attract FDI, potential short-term wage losses from opening the economy may not be offset (World Bank 2002).

While average wages rise more rapidly in open economies than in closed ones, increasing relative demand for skilled labor is widening the wage gap between skilled and unskilled workers in both developed and developing countries.[4] The latter is contrary to expectations based on traditional trade theory that globalization will increase the relative return to abundant unskilled labor in poor countries. While available evidence attributes wage widening primarily to technology, trade is also important. The relative impacts are hard to disentangle since technology can lead to trade, and technological innovation in turn can be a response to increased competition from trade (box 4.1).

A widening wage gap between skilled and unskilled workers is particularly evident in the United States, where lighter labor-market regulation permits faster adjustments in wages. In Europe, where labor markets are more tightly regulated, the outcome of rising relative demand for skilled labor has been

Box 4.1   What causes the gap between skilled and unskilled labor—technology or trade?

Traditional theory expects trade with low-wage countries to result in a shift in the composition of employment toward skilled labor *between* sectors (as industries expand or contract in response to foreign competition). In both developed and developing countries, however, labor composition *within* sectors has moved toward skilled labor (also reflected in a dramatic increase in their relative wages), suggesting that technological change has been the major force at work. Moreover, the sectors shifting toward skilled labor in developing countries in the 1980s had done so in the United States in the 1960s, suggesting a migration of technological change from developed to middle-income countries.

Technological change is generally viewed as the most important force in terms of the rising demand for skilled labor (Krugman 1995), as evidenced by the positive correlations between technology and growth of employment of skilled workers within industries, and by the fact that increases in the relative wages (cost) of skilled workers have been accompanied by an increase in their relative demand (Helpman 2004).

Trade, by contrast, is a less important force—although estimates vary. Feenstra and Hanson (2003) conclude that the offshoring of manufacturing accounts for 15–24 percent of the shift toward more skilled labor. Anderton and Brenton (1999), on the other hand, find that, when only offshoring to low-wage countries is included, trade may actually account for about 40 percent of the rise in the wage bill share of skilled workers and approximately one-third of the increase in their employment in the U.K. textiles sector. The OECD (2005d) finds that the average decline in employment in 15 Organisation for Economic Co-operation and Development (OECD) countries was 27 percent in industries characterized by high international competition compared with 16 percent in total manufacturing. Evidence from developing-country studies also suggests that technology and FDI, rather than trade, is the most important factor in wage inequality—for example in Chile (Reinecke and Torres 2001) and South Africa (Edwards 1999).

Trade plays an important role in disseminating new technologies, however. Robbins (1997), for example, finds that the amount of capital equipment imported into a subset of developing countries is a significant factor in raising the demand for tertiary-educated workers relative to demand for those completing only primary school. Moreover, technological upgrading can itself be a response to trade competition; there is substantial evidence that firms improve productivity following competition from imports (Hoekman and Winters 2005). Companies in high-wage countries facing import competition from lower-cost developing-country suppliers may engage in "defensive innovation," moving up the value chain and into more capital-intensive production. They may also respond by offshoring more production to reduce costs—generally the low-skilled activities, with the high-skilled activities remaining in the home market (Anderton, Brenton, and Whalley 2006).[a] This can occur in both high-skill-intensive and low-skill-intensive sectors so that trade with developing countries can thus potentially have an impact on a wide range of sectors—and even within low-skill-intensive sectors, the higher-skilled activities could still expand. In this sense, offshoring can have the same effect as technology in reducing the relative demand for unskilled labor *within* an industry (Feenstra and Hanson 2003), and reallocating away from high-wage economies to low-wage economies.

---

[a]Currency and exchange rate movements can also prompt a shake-out that leaves only higher technology firms in a sector. Disproportionate increases in offshoring can be seen during large exchange rate appreciations and the costs and difficulty of reversal may see offshoring remain after the currency has stabilized.

reflected in higher unemployment among the unskilled.[5] In the United States, increased demand for skilled workers since the mid-1980s has led to a relative increase in their employment and wages (Katz and Autor 1999).

Hence, while average U.S. real wages did not change significantly between the late 1970s and the mid-1990s, real wages of high-wage workers increased and those of low-wage workers declined (Helpman 2004)—despite

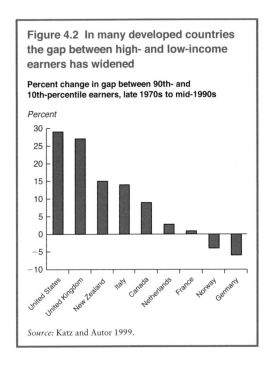

Figure 4.2 In many developed countries the gap between high- and low-income earners has widened

Percent change in gap between 90th- and 10th-percentile earners, late 1970s to mid-1990s

Source: Katz and Autor 1999.

the fact that the relative supply of skilled workers grew over the same period.[6]

The same decline in the relative wages of low-skilled workers is found in other developed countries, although to a lesser extent. While the gap increased by 29 percent in the United States and 27 percent in the United Kingdom (figure 4.2), it was only 15 percent in New Zealand, 14 percent in Italy, and 9 percent in Canada (Katz and Autor 1999).

The relative wages of skilled workers increased in developing countries in the late 1990s, along with a rise in their relative employment levels (Majid 2004; Bhorat and Lundall 2004). There are several possible reasons for this.

First, in some developing countries, notably in Africa, increased demand for low-skilled labor did not lead to wage increases because there was a large surplus of labor to be absorbed (Ghose 2003; Wood 1997; Fox and others 2004). Studies in Latin America and the Caribbean also suggest that the increased participation of women in the labor market may have contributed to a widening wage distribution. In that region,

women's skills tended to be lower than average and hence their entry in the 1990s depressed earnings to lower-skilled workers (although overall it raised the income of poor households) (de Ferranti and others 2002).

Second, demand for skilled labor increased (World Bank 2002). The share of skilled workers in total employment and the relative demand for these workers increased between the early and late 1990s in a range of countries—including Brazil, Chile, Malaysia, the Philippines, Singapore, and Thailand, with Mexico experiencing a slight decline. In all cases, including Mexico, the growth rate of relative wages of skilled workers exceeded that of unskilled workers.

The demand for skilled labor depends on the skill intensity of the export sector. In many countries in Latin America, increased exports based on abundant natural resources raised demand for complementary skilled labor and capital (Perry and Olarreaga 2006). Furthermore, activities considered relatively low skill in developed countries may nonetheless be relatively skilled in developing countries, especially in manufacturing. Transfer of activities considered relatively low skill in developed countries to developing countries raises the relative demand for and relative earnings of high-skilled workers in the latter (Feenstra and Hanson 2003).

Additionally, enhanced competition from trade can affect the relative demand for skilled labor by reallocating resources within sectors away from less productive, unskilled-labor-intensive firms toward more productive firms using more skilled labor. Trade also facilitates the transmission of skill-biased technological change. Protection in many developing countries favored unskilled-labor-intensive sectors, hence liberalization led to expansion of skilled-labor-intensive industries (Perry and Olarreaga 2006). Foreign direct investment can also increase the demand for skilled labor. In Eastern Europe, for example, privatization and FDI helped bias employment composition and relative wages significantly toward skilled labor as production facilities were upgraded with new technologies.[7]

Even outside the traded sector, globalization may have an impact on low-skilled workers in other ways. In all countries, wages in the non-traded sector may be affected by wages and employment in the traded sector if there is mobility between the two. In addition, international mobility in the form of migration may also have an impact on low-skilled workers, although there is considerable debate on this issue. Most studies focus on developed countries and tend to find small overall impacts—or indeed positive impacts—from migration on wages (see box 4.2).

Box 4.2   Workers in the nontraded sector—the role of migration

Even where workers do not experience increased competition from international trade, they may be affected by an increase in the supply of workers resulting from migration, although this impact may be positive. As immigration increases labor supply, and wages are reduced, more capital may be attracted and more jobs created. Moreover, consumption by migrants also increases the overall demand for native labor and capital. That said, many studies identify redistributional effects, with the impact of immigration concentrated on the lowest-skilled workers. The impact depends critically on the extent to which migrants and natives are substitutes for one another; that is, whether they are competing for the same jobs or operating in segmented markets (for a fuller discussion, see *Global Economic Prospects 2006*).

Borjas (2003) finds negative impacts on workers up to some college level, with immigration harming the employment prospects and lowering the wage of competing native workers (a 10 percent increase in supply reduces wages by 3–4 percent). The lowest-skilled were hardest hit: wages fell by 8.9 percent for high school dropouts, 4.9 percent for college graduates, and 2.6 percent for high school graduates while barely changing for workers with "some college." However, this analysis ignores, among other things, the long-run capital adjustments induced by immigration. If the capital stock does adjust, overall wages are unaffected and the loss of wages to high school dropouts is cut to below 5 percent (*The Economist*, "Economics Focus: Myths and Migration," April 8, 2006).

Borjas, Freeman, and Katz (1997) argue that the effect of immigrant-induced increases in relative labor supply are strongly concentrated on U.S. workers with less than 12 years of schooling, many of whom work in the nontraded sectors. Migration increased the supply of workers with less than high school education by 15 to 20 percent over 1980–95, leading to a 27–55 percent

decline in the relative wages of high school dropouts over 1980–95 (depending on wage elasticity). The effect of immigration is diffused throughout the economy, as natives move in response to immigration. Large immigrant flows to one region may discourage flows to that region of native workers, but may encourage flows of capital. Ottaviano and Peri (2005) find that migration increases total employment by 10 percent, and increases U.S.-born workers' wages by 3–4 percentage points, largely because U.S.- and foreign-born workers are not perfectly substitutable, even when they have similar observable skills. College graduates, high school graduates, and college dropouts all gain (about 2.4 percent real wage increase), but the low-skilled lose (by the same amount).

Cortes (2005) also sees sizeable wage effects on the low-skilled, but these are concentrated on other immigrants, as low-skilled immigrants and low-skilled natives are far from perfect substitutes. A 10 percent increase in the number of low-skilled immigrants in a city reduced the wages of low-skilled natives by 0.6 percent and of low-skilled immigrants by 8 percent. But migration also reduces the prices of non-traded goods and services. A 10 percent increase in the average city's share of low-skilled immigrants in the labor force decreases the price of immigrant-intensive services such as housekeeping and gardening by 1.3 percent, with about 50–80 percent of this net effect caused by reduction in wages.

Card (2005) argues that the wages of natives with less than a high school education relative to native high school graduates have remained nearly constant since 1980. This is despite immigrant inflows that have increased the supply of workers with less than high school education and despite the growing wage gap between other education groups. Most of the absorption of unskilled workers occurs in the form of city-specific, within-industry increases in low-skilled intensity.

. . . and workers are feeling less secure

Individuals are concerned not only about the level but also the security of their earnings. Greater global competition, along with more rapid technological change and diffusion, can increase wage and employment volatility,[8] although separating the effect of trade from technological change in volatility is difficult.

Labor turnover is high in many countries, fueling individuals' perceptions of economic insecurity. Available data show gross sectoral rates of job creation and destruction of between 5 and 20 percent, adding up to an annual job turnover of up to 40 percent in some countries. A significant part of that turnover (often 30–50 percent) can be traced to the entry and exit of firms, important for output and productivity growth. About 20 percent of firms are created and destroyed each year in many countries, involving 10–20 percent of the workforce (World Bank 2005). While evidence is not uniform, some studies of OECD countries find that increased trade exposure is associated with more labor churning (Hoekman and Winters 2005). Overall it is estimated that 3 to 5 percent of the OECD workforce experiences involuntary layoff in any given year (Kuhn 2002).

In the United States, more than 7 million jobs have been destroyed on average every quarter over the last decade as a result of the normal functioning of the economy (OECD 2005b), matched for the most part by equal or greater job creation. Among the unemployed, about 45 percent were laid off, 10–15 percent are persons voluntarily between jobs, and the remainder are persons entering or reentering the labor market as new job-seekers (Kletzer 2001). Voluntary attrition may account for up to two-thirds of employment reduction in the United States (OECD 2005d).

Falling transport and communication costs are creating new opportunities for developing countries to participate in global production chains by providing specific activities and tasks (see box 4.7). However, discrete activities are likely to be more footloose than whole sectors, so that while globalization can bring better

job prospects to developing countries, it can also bring greater volatility and insecurity. Bergin, Feenstra, and Hanson (2006) find that while offshoring of production from the United States to Mexico has been an important source of growth in Mexico, there is a high degree of volatility in these activities. Domestic demand shocks in the United States are amplified when they are transmitted to the offshored activities in Mexico. In this way, offshoring has led the United States to export to Mexico some of the employment fluctuations that it experiences over the business cycle.

In Latin America, overall labor turnover is higher than in OECD countries. However, turnover depends on education, per capita income, and other demographic and growth variables. For example, young workers change jobs more frequently than older workers and lower levels of education can imply lower levels of firm-specific capital and hence a higher incidence of voluntary separation. Adjusting for these factors, the region does not show conditionally higher turnover. There is only mixed evidence that either greater trade liberalization or exposure to technological change leads to greater overall turnover in the region; however, to the degree that trade liberalization has expanded the share of tradables in total output, it may have led to more churning in the job market (de Ferranti and others 2000).

To the extent that it reflects labor-market flexibility and the reallocation of resources to more productive sectors, increased turnover can be a sign of healthy adjustment, linked to further growth and job creation. However, churning can also be negative—for example, where job creation lags well behind job destruction, where high turnover lowers workers' and employers' incentives to invest in education and training (thus ultimately reducing productivity in a sector), or where churning results in labor moving into less productive sectors. In the absence of social safety nets, workers in developing countries may be unable to finance job searches and may be forced into the informal sector (where productivity is generally lower) or into low-productivity, relatively low-growth sectors such as agriculture.

The extent and nature of churning depend on the policy environment. Onerous labor-market regulations and restrictions on entry and exit of firms can discourage firms from hiring new regular workers, and workers from searching for jobs in the formal sector. They can also limit the movement of resources out of low-productivity sectors. Overly restrictive employment protection (such as restrictions on hiring and firing) tends to have the effect of protecting only *some* workers (insiders, usually prime-age males) at the expense of others (outsiders, usually youth, women, and low-skilled workers). Strict employment protection is associated with higher income disparities and a greater incidence of informal work (World Bank 2005). It also raises the costs of workforce reorganizations, thereby reducing incentives for innovation and implementation of new technologies (Arias and others 2005).[9]

The precise impact of strict employment protection on job creation depends on who bears the cost: where wages absorb less of the cost than firms, the disincentives to create employment are greater. In Latin America, firms can bear up to 50 percent of the cost of nonwage benefits, resulting in reduced wages, greater informality, or both (World Bank 2005). In the OECD countries, partial reforms have tended to reinforce labor-market inequality, with temporary contracts for new entrants (youth or women) but only limited access to more permanent jobs. Strict employment protection is also associated with a greater feeling of insecurity, perhaps because workers realize that their chance of long-term unemployment is higher (OECD 2005d, 2004).[10] A benefit of globalization is the pressure it exerts on institutions that cramp productivity growth and on governments to develop efficient safety nets that cushion workers from the worst aspects of economic insecurity, while preserving job creation and flexibility.

Today's global labor market is characterized by volatility, shifts in employment between developed and developing countries, and increasing wage gaps between low- and high-skilled workers worldwide. What will be the impact of the key challenges now facing global labor markets—namely absorption of large emerging economies and the global sourcing of services?

New challenge I—absorbing large emerging economies into the global market

By 2030 China and India together will account for about 40 percent of the world's workforce, which will remain predominantly unskilled

By 2030 the world's labor force will number some 4.1 billion workers, 90 percent of whom will live in the developing world. The global labor force is predicted to grow by about 1 percent per year over 2001–30, with higher growth in developing countries offset by some contraction in developed countries (table 4.2). East Asia, the Pacific, and South Asia together will account for just over half the world's workforce, with China and India alone representing 40 percent—although China's labor force will grow far more slowly than that of India. Sub-Saharan Africa will experience the highest rate of growth (about 2.4 percent per year) and will be the third-largest developing region.

Worldwide, the supply of skilled workers is likely to grow faster than that of unskilled workers, but the vast majority of the world's workforce will remain unskilled in 2030.[11] In the developing world, rates of growth in the number of skilled workers will be highest in Sub-Saharan Africa, South Asia, and the Middle East and North Africa. Given the large pool of unskilled labor, however, these increases will raise the share of skilled workers in developing countries' workforces only slightly (from 9.6 percent to 11.3 percent).

There will be significant regional variations in the developing world. The Middle East and North Africa, Latin America and the

Table 4.2 In 2030 most workers will be in developing countries and unskilled

Growth in the global labor force 2001–30

World region	All workers (millions)			Unskilled workers (millions)			Skilled workers (millions)		
	2001	2030	Growth (% per year)	2001	2030	Growth (% per year)	2001	2030	Growth (% per year)
World total	3,077	4,144	1.03	2,674	3,545	0.98	403	598	1.37
High-income countries	481	459	−0.16	327	276	−0.58	154	183	0.60
Developing countries	2,596	3,684	1.21	2,347	3,269	1.15	249	415	1.78
East Asia & the Pacific	1,060	1,279	0.65	988	1,163	0.56	71	117	1.70
China	773	870	0.41	740	816	0.34	33	54	1.72
South Asia	632	1,005	1.62	589	925	1.56	42	81	2.27
India	473	712	1.42	441	653	1.36	32	59	2.10
Europe & Central Asia	236	233	−0.04	195	192	−0.06	41	41	0.02
Middle East & North Africa	119	205	1.88	87	144	1.74	32	61	2.25
Sub-Saharan Africa	313	617	2.36	293	573	2.33	20	44	2.74
Latin America & the Caribbean	236	345	1.32	194	273	1.19	42	72	1.85

Source: World Bank staff calculations.

Caribbean, and Europe and Central Asia continue to have relatively high rates of skilled workers (30, 21, and 18 percent, respectively), compared to East Asia and the Pacific (9 percent), South Asia (8 percent), and Sub-Saharan Africa (7 percent). But in absolute numbers, India and China each have more skilled workers than Europe and Central Asia or Sub-Saharan Africa, and almost as many as the Middle East and North Africa. Overall, developing countries have more than twice as many skilled workers as developed countries, even though the proportion of skilled workers in the workforce is four times higher in the developed world.

Agricultural workers will constitute a shrinking share of the world's labor force, declining from about 43 percent in 2001 to about 30 percent in 2030. While the share of agricultural workers will fall by about half in developed countries, the stark decline is from an already low base (from 4 to 2.6 percent). The more significant change will occur in developing countries, where agricultural workers will shift from about 50 percent of the workforce in 2001 to 34 percent in 2030. The most notable shifts will occur in Sub-Saharan Africa (61 to 47 percent), East Asia and the Pacific (62 to 39 percent), and South Asia (55 to 35 percent)—with the latter

two driven by large changes in China (67 to 42 percent) and India (54 to 34 percent).

Moreover, while average incomes will continue to increase with new opportunities for growth, the skill premium—the ratio of skilled wages to unskilled wages—will also increase. Projections from the model developed in chapter 2 suggest that the skill premium in developing countries will rise from 3.5 on average in 2001 to 4.2 in 2030. In India the premium rises from 4.3 to 4.9 in 2030 while in China the increase is even larger, from 5.4 to 7.7. Developments in Sub-Saharan Africa are similar, with a rise from 5.1 to 6.8. The Middle East and North Africa sees only a modest increase in the skill premium from 1.3 to 1.5, while the premium remains constant at 2.2 in Latin America.

Pressures on unskilled workers will intensify in both developed and developing countries . . .

Between 1995 and 2005 the global labor force (employed and unemployed) grew by some 438 million workers, or 16.8 percent (ILO 2006). However, the effective increase in the global labor market is considerably larger, because many workers in the emerging economies were previously only weakly connected to the global economy. Freeman (2005) calculates that the integration of China, India, and the former Soviet Union has led to a "great doubling" of the global labor force.

The increasingly competitive global market for labor may be the most important issue facing workers worldwide. Freeman (2005) argues that because the workers in these countries brought little capital with them into the global labor force there has been a massive drop in the overall global ratio of capital to labor. In response to the huge amounts of new low-wage labor, therefore, capital should hemorrhage from rich countries and flow to China, India, and the ex-Soviet bloc. At the margin, new investment should take place in China and India, where returns should be highest.

The prognosis from this view is that developing countries with wages higher than those in China and India risk losing ground following the entry of these countries into global commerce. The sheer size of China and India may also preclude the diversification of the poorest countries into manufactures and so close off a route to growth and development (Cline 2006). In rich countries, low-skilled labor is expected to lose as well, and future growth opportunities will depend on whether the rich countries' comparative advantage in high-technology sectors can be maintained. According to this view, it is the *quantity* of new entrants from China and India that risks swamping the global market, undermining the prospects of unskilled workers in all other countries, both rich and poor. This may not be the case, however; competition is not always what it appears (box 4.3).

Box 4.3   Is the world flat . . . or just smaller?

In *The World Is Flat*, Thomas Friedman (2005) examines the rise of China and India in global supply chains for both goods and services, describing the increasing pace and intensity of competition across skilled activities as the "flattening" of the globe. But, as Leamer (2006) asks, is flatness the right metaphor? What if the world is not flat, but just smaller?

In the past, geography—physical, cultural, and informational—had limited competition by creating cost-advantaged relationships between proximate sellers and buyers. Three revolutionary forces are now driving a smaller world: (a) the presence of more unskilled workers in the global labor market resulting from liberalizations in China, India, the Russian Federation, and Latin America; (b) new equipment for knowledge workers (the Internet, computers) that has raised productivity, emphasized talent, and reduced the need for helpers; and (c) communications innovations that extend the geographic reach of suppliers and the competition for routine work and standardized products. In a smaller world, exchanges are more contested and relationships between buyers and sellers weaker. In a small world, wages in Los Angeles are set in Shanghai. Does everyone now live in a world in which distance—physical, linguistic and cultural—no longer isolates jobs from competition? Is the world flat or are jobs protected from competition by relationships and geography?

Competition is not always what it appears . . .
Smallness may confer a larger market without generating many new competitors in sectors where there are highly localized economies of scale, agglomeration (or cluster) effects, and first-mover advantages (consider the success of Hollywood in the global market for cultural products). Where you are still matters. Economic activity is dispersing around the globe, but with very strong clustering to benefit from agglomeration effects. Commerce still declines dramatically with distance (although cultural or linguistic forms of closeness can compensate for physical distance), and trade remains a neighborhood phenomenon, close to home both geographically and organizationally. Consumer preferences and trust contribute to this pattern—U.S. Web surfers still favor foreign sites close to the United States, particularly when financial transactions are involved.

(continued)

Box 4.3 *(continued)*

Moreover, competition in knowledge products is not necessarily a win-lose proposition: knowledge products have their value enhanced by the existence of other products (software is an example). And not all work is commoditized and sold in global markets. Most exchanges still rely on long-term relationships between buyer and seller—relationships that create the language needed to communicate, that establish the trust needed to carry out the exchange, that allow ongoing servicing of implicit or explicit guarantees, and that monitor and enforce the truthfulness of both parties. This is the difference between negotiated rather than contestable exchanges. Reliability—and liability—form limits to the contestability of high-skilled jobs. To date, global sourcing of intellectual work has been a small drop in a very large bucket, and the developed countries remain extremely well-positioned to compete in the Internet-based segment of the economy.

. . . but competition—or the threat of it—matters for routine tasks
Global competition is tight for standard tasks for which global markets exist, both in manufacturing and services. Movement of jobs is not the only indicator of global competition—contestability may be reflected in a deterioration of wages and working conditions, rather than the movement of jobs. That is, the possibility of factor mobility creates competitive pressure even in the absence of actual movement. Once this is factored in, the real effect of contestability—of global competition—is hard to assess.

Innovation is key, but innovation moves around the world, and its pace is quickening
Ideas stowaway with goods. As manufacturing work moves to China, so naturally do process innovations—as those closest to production are best placed to work out how to do it better. But will product innovation also move? The Internet has increased the speed and reduced the cost of distributing ideas (subject to the constraints of infrastructure and literacy). Add the integration of former outsiders that has increased the size of the global brain by

two-thirds, and the pace of innovation in the 21st century will be unlike anything previously seen.

Education, infrastructure, and safety nets are essential, but technology guarantees that inequality will persist
Global sourcing of services presents issues similar to those posed by manufacturing. The lessons are clear—make the education and infrastructure investments needed to keep high-paying, noncontestable, creative jobs at home, and argue for strong protection of intellectual property rights (IPRs) to preserve the value of knowledge goods sold abroad. But it is important to recognize that technology can accentuate inequality by magnifying the importance of talent and enabling it to reach a much larger customer base. Education may help to remedy the income-inequality problems caused by technology, but there are limits. First, if training is more effective for the talented, they are likely to receive more of it—and the amount of training needed to equalize incomes may be enormous and a great social waste. (How much training does it take to turn a World Bank economist into a Pavarotti? And is this a good use of resources?) Second, many jobs involve job-specific tacit knowledge gained only through on-the-job experience. But will workers invest in acquiring these skills if the job is likely to disappear? Will the incentives for skill acquisition also disappear? Policies are needed to facilitate the formation of long-term relationships between workers and employers and so instill the confidence to make relationship-specific investments from which great returns can flow.

Metaphors matter
The landscape of global competition is not flat, at least not much of it. The flat plains of open competition for mundane tasks certainly exist, but much of the landscape is hills and mountains—where endowments, human capital, and policy matter. That landscape is also constantly changing—today's hill might be tomorrow's plain, creating new opportunities and obstacles and demanding continual adaptation.

Source: Leamer 2006.

Productivity differences matter. Firms in rich countries combine unskilled workers in production with more and better capital and technical know-how than do firms in poor countries. What matters is whether the wage gap is greater than the difference in productivity—and whether productivity differentials can be maintained. Similarly, the least developed countries in Africa that have lower wages than China and India will be able to compete in the global market—but only if their levels of productivity are close to those in India and China. The sources of productivity differences across countries will be discussed in more detail below.

There is another problem with the view that the global market will be swamped by products from China and India. The law of comparative advantage implies that there will always be opportunities for other countries to export, even though China and India will come to dominate certain sectors. In general, as the global demand for Chinese manufactured products increases, dollar-denominated wages in China will tend to increase, in response to higher wage demands from Chinese workers (especially if the rural and urban labor markets remain partially segmented) and from the inevitable additional upward pressure on the yuan.

There is evidence that this process is already underway (figure 4.3). In 2004, real wages in China were 2.11 times the level of 1989, and the rate of wage increase accelerated in 2004–05, especially in the coastal regions (Yusuf, Nabeshima, and Perkins 2006). In 2005 alone, according to the People's Bank of China, average wages for Chinese workers rose by 14.8 percent (*China Daily*, "Worker Shortage Drives Salary Rise," May 27, 2006). Thus China's development should not keep the poorest countries from being able to export low-skill-intensive products, as long as these countries can manage to create and sustain a business climate that supports investment and trade. In Africa, competitiveness based on low-cost labor is undermined by high indirect costs, with the main barriers being corruption, crime, and inadequate

Figure 4.3 Average wages in China have increased more than in other countries

Internationally comparable average wage rates, indexed, 1998 = 100

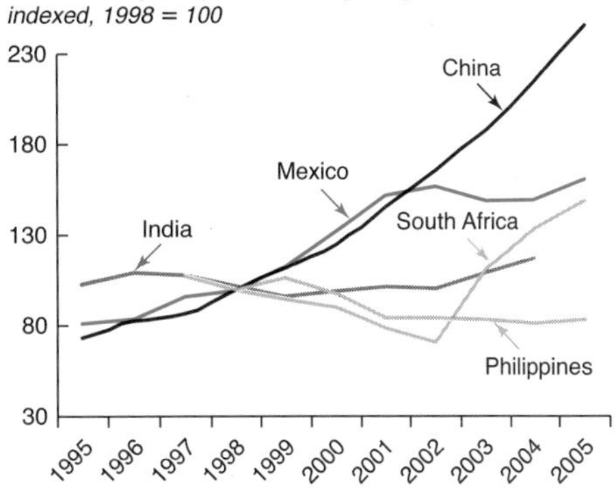

Sources: China Statistical Yearbook 2005, People's Bank of China, International Labour Organization (Philippines, South Africa), IBGE (Brazil), Banco de Mexico, Ministry of Statistics and Programme Implementation (India); exchange rates from IMF International Financial Statistics. Wages are average wages for China, the Philippines, and South Africa, average private sector wages in Brazil, and manufacturing wages for India and Mexico.

Note: 1998–2000 wages for the Philippines have been estimated using observed wages from 2001 and projecting them backward using GDP per capita growth rates.

infrastructure (Eifert, Gelb, and Ramachandran 2005). The poor business environment leads to lower returns to labor in production, depressing labor demand and real wages.

Even within sectors where China is expected to dominate world trade, there are examples of growing exports of other developing countries. The removal of quotas in the United States and the European Union on imports of textiles and clothing products from China and India was expected by some to decimate exports of these products from other developing countries. For example, it was suggested that one million jobs would be lost in Bangladesh and that half the factories in the industry in Sri Lanka would close down (Oxfam 2004). However, exports of clothing from both of these countries to the United States have increased since the quotas were dismantled. Sri Lankan exports in 2005 were 6 percent higher than in 2004 (with a further growth of 3 percent over the first six months of 2006 relative to the same period in 2005).

Exports of clothing from Bangladesh to the United States increased by 21 percent in 2005 and by a further 28 percent over the first six months of 2006.

Nevertheless, the growth of Chinese exports of textiles and clothing has had negative impacts on other countries. Many jobs have been lost in Mexico's *maquiladoras* because activities in sectors such as clothing have been unable to compete with China in the U.S. market. Clothing exports from African countries have declined substantially since 2004, amid reports of substantial loss of jobs in the sector. It is clear, therefore, that the emergence of China and India as major exporters will entail significant adjustment in some sectors in some countries. The adjustment costs are likely to be higher in countries that offer a less favorable climate for business and investment and that suffer from more rigidities in product and labor markets.

It should not be forgotten that trade and FDI have contributed to unparalleled reductions in poverty in China and can continue to do so. The poverty rate (people living on less than $1 a day) in China fell from almost 60 percent in 1980 to 17 percent in 2003. While lifting more than 400 million people out of poverty is a remarkable achievement, close to 200 million people still live on less than $1 a day, many of whom stand to benefit from China's continued trading strength.

For other countries the impact of the integration of the large emerging economies should not be qualitatively different from the pressures that globalization has exerted on labor markets over the past 30 years, as summarized above. Unskilled workers in both rich and developing countries are likely to face greater volatility of employment and continuing downward pressure on relative wages. The following section will discuss how policy makers can help to ameliorate these costs.

. . . *but opportunities for export and growth will remain for all countries*

The entry of large economic entities into the global market offers opportunities as enormous as the challenges it poses for developed and developing countries. The large markets of China and India have changed the dynamic of South-South trade and offer developing countries a route to decreased dependence on rich countries, whose demand for products produced in the poorest countries has been relatively stagnant for years. Demand in Asia, and primarily in China and India, has been the main source of the acceleration in African exports since 1990. Asia also has been a key source of recent export growth for Latin America. Overall, China's share of the world's non-oil imports grew from 1.8 percent in 1990 to 6.5 percent in 2004, implying substantial opportunities for its trading partners to expand exports and create jobs (figure 4.4).

As a result of Asia's increasing demand for resources there is an increasing correlation between growth in China and India and growth in developing countries that have a comparative advantage in natural-resource-intensive products (Lederman, Olarreaga, and Soloaga 2006). Even resource-abundant countries that have not increased exports to Asia—such as Bolivia, Colombia, and

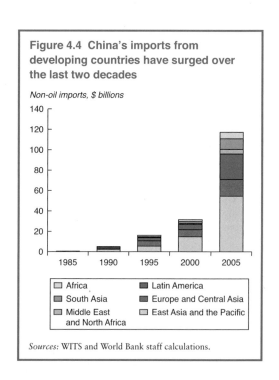

Figure 4.4 China's imports from developing countries have surged over the last two decades

Non-oil imports, $ billions

Africa
South Asia
Middle East and North Africa
Latin America
Europe and Central Asia
East Asia and the Pacific

Sources: WITS and World Bank staff calculations.

Ecuador—have seen benefits from higher world prices for their exports. Lederman, Olarreaga, and Soloaga (2006) also find fairly strong complementarity rather than substitutability between the exports of China and Latin America to third markets. They attribute this complementarity to the growing importance of production networks and the ability of Latin American firms to join them, the impact of cheaper imports of intermediate inputs on export competitiveness, and learning by exporting larger amounts to China. Nevertheless, they suggest that if Latin American and Caribbean countries were to refrain from protectionist policies that prevent them from using cheap inputs from China and India and were to invest more in skills, research and development (R&D), and institutions, they would be able to further exploit opportunities in the new global economy.

The surging demand in Asia for minerals has been the primary driver of growing South-South trade. But China and India offer huge potential for a range of other products as well, including agricultural products. However, trade restrictions keep many developing countries from gaining market access for many such products.[12] For most developing countries multilateral trade negotiations are potentially a major route to better access to growing markets in Asia and to better prices for traditional exports. The key feature of access to markets in Asia for developing countries in Africa and Latin America is that access should occur on a most-favored-nation basis—that is, each country should be entitled to the best trade terms an importer offers to any nation. Therefore market access is best addressed through multilateral trade negotiations, so that tariff concessions made by China and India are immediately available to all developing countries, regardless of their size and global importance.

Lower duties in Asia can buoy the export prospects of other developing countries in three ways. The first is through lower tariffs on products currently exported by these developing countries or that are the focus of export-diversification efforts. Markets in Asia are very large, but key products for developing countries face high tariff barriers. For example, cocoa beans face applied tariffs of 30 percent in India and 8 percent in China (in contrast to zero protection in developed countries). Second, for traditional commodities, even if the reduction in tariffs in Asia does not lead to new exports for a specific developing country, there will be a positive effect through the impact on world prices. Third, it is important to consider the tariffs on the final products that use resource-intensive inputs exported from developing countries. Reducing such protection will expand the demand for those inputs. It would also reduce tariff escalation and ease one of the constraints that limit higher value–added activities from being undertaken in developing countries.

Moreover, both China and India have become significant sources of FDI for both developing and developed countries. India's outward FDI stock grew from $0.6 billion in 1996 to $5.1 billion in 2003. China and India now occupy positions 54 and 72 (out of 132 economies) in terms of outward FDI performance (UNCTAD 2005).[13] About two-thirds of *cumulative* Indian FDI has gone to other developing countries, but developed countries (in particular the United States) are important markets at the moment. The leading developing country is Mauritius, which attracts about 10 percent of Indian investment flows. In the information technology sector, Indian firms' success in global sourcing exposed them to new knowledge and business methods from developed-country companies and induced outward FDI through demonstration and spillover effects. Liberalization of the Indian government's policies on outward FDI since 2000 also proved critical. Restrictions on maximum overseas investments as a percentage of net worth have been removed, as have the requirement to obtain prior approval for investments from the Reserve Bank of India and prohibitions against overseas investments in the same activity as the company's core activity in India (UNCTAD 2004).

Fears that China and India will quickly dominate high-technology sectors are misplaced

Some worry about the impact of the rising numbers of skilled workers in China and India.[14] Freeman (2006) suggests that the increase in these numbers together with increased capacity for technological advancement will undermine the advantage that rich countries have in high-tech, high-productivity activities. Trefler (2005) has put this issue concerning long-run comparative advantage in the following way: will China and India dominate high-tech goods and services to the west, leaving, for example, "Americans to mend the socks of Chinese business executives"? The prognosis that China and India will swamp the global market not only with low-skilled-intensive products but also skill-intensive high-tech products is based on the assumption that success in high-tech sectors depends on the absolute number of scientists and engineers rather than the relative number of such workers in the overall workforce. This view also fails to take account of a well-established literature that identifies the critical importance of domestic institutions in driving and sustaining innovation-based growth.[15]

Much evidence supports the view that growth and income levels do not depend solely on the physical amounts of capital and labor that are available in a country; instead, they depend on how those factors are combined in production. Cross-country variations in per capita income cannot be accounted for by differences in endowments of capital and labor, but by variations in productivity. For example, in 1988 output per Chinese worker was about 6 percent of that of the typical U.S. worker. Most of that difference was due to lower productivity in China rather than lower capital per worker or lower levels of human capital. If productivity levels had been the same, output per worker in China would have been more than 50 percent of that in the United States (Hall and Jones 1999).

Innovations matter. To understand differences in levels of income across countries and differences in rates of growth of per capita income, it is necessary to explain the sources of variations in productivity. Innovation is at the heart of such explanations. In recent models of endogenous growth, innovations lead to new products and processes that are to some extent protected by patents and other institutional mechanisms that return profit to the innovator and bolster the incentive to invest. Where protection of the innovation is less than full, a certain amount of "disembodied" knowledge becomes accessible to other innovators and so adds to the stock of knowledge available to all, reducing the costs of future research and development (see Helpman 2004 for a survey).

Some of a country's R&D effort may thus be accessed by other countries, even as it augments the national stock of knowledge. The main conduits for such technology transfer are FDI and trade. In this way the innovative efforts of rich countries push out the global technology frontier and support the growth of their total factor productivity. Developing countries, which invest little in R&D, can achieve long-run productivity growth through a process of continually catching up to the technology frontier. Policies that attract FDI from rich countries, openness to technology-intensive imports, and learning by exporting into the most demanding markets are crucial for this catching up. This learning can also be enhanced by temporary movement of people.[16]

Multinational firms exhibit the highest levels of total factor productivity and create more knowledge inputs than other types of firms. Criscuolo, Haskel, and Slaughter (2004) find that globally engaged firms generate more ideas than their purely domestic counterparts, not only because they employ more researchers, but also because they have access to a wider pool of knowledge. That pool is deepened by contacts with suppliers and customers and, for multinationals, by the intrafirm stock of ideas. Others (Bernard, Knetter, and

Slaughter 2004, cited in Criscuolo, Haskel, and Slaughter 2004) find that the parents of U.S.-based multinationals perform about two-thirds of all private R&D in the United States but are a small fraction of 1 percent of the total number of U.S. firms. Thus, it appears that openness to trade is important not only for poor countries to absorb new technologies created by firms in developed countries, but also for wealthier countries to stimulate investment and productivity growth.

So do institutions. Even after taking into account innovation efforts, a substantial amount of the variation in per capita income levels and growth rates across countries remains unexplained. What accounts for the rest of the variance? Institutions and institutional quality are now accepted as the reason why some countries have higher productivity than others and why growth rates have differed across countries, even when factor endowments and rates of innovation are similar (Helpman 2004). For example, Hall and Jones (1999) conclude that "a country's long-run economic performance is determined primarily by the institutions and government policies that make up the economic environment within which individuals and firms make investment, create and transfer ideas, and produce goods and services."

To compete with the United States, the European Union, and Japan in innovation and high-tech products, China and India will require institutions similar to those of the OECD countries. The two countries are a long way from having such institutions at present. Moreover, building them takes a long time and is unlikely to occur within 25 years (Trefler 2005). Thus the United States leads in innovation-based growth not because it has more scientists and engineers, but because it has an institutional framework that allows companies such as Microsoft, Apple, and Yahoo to exploit new ideas.

Recent research has highlighted how institutional quality can determine comparative advantage and so influence the commodity structure of trade. Nunn (2005) shows that countries with a good institutional environment for contract enforcement will tend to have a comparative advantage in producing and exporting goods that require relationship-specific investments.[17] Countries with poor contract enforcement will suffer from underinvestment and thus higher costs of production for goods that require relationship-specific investment. Such investments are more likely to be necessary in industries in which firms have some form of firm-specific asset, which in turn are more likely to be high-technology and innovation-intensive industries. The same is equally true for services.

The structure of all countries' exports is thus influenced by the nature of domestic institutions. The growth of exports from China and India in some products and services that require relationship-specific investment has been facilitated by having good institutions in particular enclaves of the economy such as special economic zones. The ability of these countries to substantially increase exports of these goods and services further will depend on the ability to engender economywide institutional change, something that will be much harder to achieve and will occur more slowly.

Continual technological innovation and changes in demand make comparative advantage a dynamic concept. It is very difficult to predict in which sectors and tasks countries will be efficient producers. Thirty years ago, who could have predicted the emergence of the iPod or known how the value added in production and the return to knowledge would be distributed across countries (box 4.4)?

The opportunities of global production chains will encourage the upgrading of domestic institutions, as countries compete on quality and efficiency as well as price—just as they have for another set of domestic institutions related to labor standards. Rather than a race to the bottom, with declining

Box 4.4   Global production and the iPod

Take just one component of the iPod nano, the central microchip provided by the U.S. company PortalPlayer. The core technology of the chip is licensed from British firm ARM and is modified by PortalPlayer's programmers in California, Washington State, and Hyderabad. PortalPlayer then works with microchip design companies in California that send the finished design to a "foundry" in Taiwan (China) that produces "wafers" (thin metal disks) imprinted with hundreds of thousands of chips. The capital costs of these foundries can be more than $2.5 million. These wafers are then cut up into individual disks and sent elsewhere in Taiwan (China) where each one is tested. The chips are then encased in plastic and readied for assembly by Silicon-Ware in Taiwan (China) and Amkor in the Republic of Korea. The finished microchip is then warehoused in Hong Kong (China) before being transported to mainland China where the iPod is assembled.

Working conditions and wages in China are low relative to Western standards and levels. Many workers live in dormitories and work long hours.

It is suggested that overtime is compulsory. Nevertheless, wages are higher than the average of the region in which the assembly plants are located and allow for substantial transfers to rural areas and hence contribute to declining rural poverty. PortalPlayer was only established in 1999 but had revenues in excess of $225 million in 2005. PortalPlayer's chief executive officer has argued that the outsourcing to countries such as India and Taiwan (China) of "non-critical aspects of your business" has been crucial to the development of the firm and its innovation: "it allows you to become nimbler and spend R&D dollars on core strengths."

Since 2003, soon after the iPod was launched, the share price of Apple, the company that produces and sells the iPod, has risen from just over $6 to over $60. Those who own shares in Apple have benefited from the globalization of the iPod.

Sources: C. Joseph, "The iPod's Incredible Journey," *Mail on Sunday,* July 15, 2006; "Meet the iPods's 'Intel,'" *Business Trends* 32(4)(April), 2006.

wages and standards as countries compete on trade and investment, globalization is encouraging gradually *higher* labor standards, both directly in terms of attracting FDI and indirectly, through higher growth (box 4.5).[18]

Implications for middle-income countries. While China and India are unlikely to threaten Western dominance of "big idea" innovation, Puga and Trefler (2005) suggest that the great capacity of these countries for lower-level incremental innovations may have important implications for middle-income developing countries. The presence of many well-trained scientists and engineers in China and India means that Western firms looking to invest will tend to be attracted to these countries—for their greater capacity to assist the firm in incremental innovation—rather than to other countries, such as Thailand and Mexico. Puga and Trefler refer to the rapidly increasing number

of U.S.-owned patents with at least one inventor who is a resident of China or India. Thailand and Mexico have not witnessed such growth.

But Cravino, Lederman, and Olarreaga (2006) find no evidence that FDI by Western firms in China and India is displacing FDI in Latin America. In a detailed econometric exercise, Bravo-Ortega and Lederman (2006) find no statistical evidence that current patenting activity by China and India has had an impact on the number of patents of Latin American countries. They do find some evidence, however, that the stock of patents to which China and India have contributed is feeding the innovation process in Latin America. In other words, innovators in Latin America can learn from innovations undertaken in China and India.

Thus both economic theory and the available evidence suggest that while the sheer size of new entrants into the global economy poses

Box 4.5   Does globalization lead to a race to the bottom on labor standards?

Looking at the relationship between core labor standards (freedom of association and collective bargaining; and elimination of forced labor, child labor, and discrimination in employment) and trade, the OECD (1996) finds no empirical support for the view that low-standards countries will enjoy gains in export-market shares to the detriment of high-standards countries. There is also no evidence that low core labor standards are associated with low unit labor costs: real wages actually grew faster than productivity growth in a number of low-standards countries from the mid-1980s to the mid-1990s. While core labor standards will not necessarily affect comparative advantage negatively and indeed may have a positive affect, noncore or economic standards such as working time and minimum wages may affect trade performance negatively (OECD 2000a).[a] However, the picture is not clear; Dehejia and Samy (2002) find no clear link between labor standards and a country's competitiveness. Rodrik (1996) finds that labor standards are a significant determinant of labor costs when one controls for productivity, but not of comparative advantage, which is mostly determined by factor endowments.

Evidence on FDI also suggests that firms are attracted to countries with higher, not lower, labor standards (OECD 2000b; Aggarwal 1995; Rodrik 1996; Brown, Deardorff, and Stern 2002).[b] Multinationals invest principally in the largest, richest, and most dynamic markets; with the significant exception of China, countries where core labor standards are not respected receive a very small share of global flows. Even in China, the average foreign affiliate pays wages 30 percent higher than the average in state-owned enterprises and has higher occupational safety and health standards than Chinese-owned firms (Lardy 2004). Overall, multinational firms provide incentives to improve, rather than worsen working conditions; pay higher wages than alternative employment; and tend to promote, rather than repress worker rights (Brown, Deardorff, and Stern 2002).

In some countries, labor regulations do not apply and a range of labor standards issues still arise in export processing zones (EPZs), which now employ around 50 million persons worldwide. That said, the majority of EPZs are covered by national labor laws, and physical conditions and wages tend to be better than in the rest of the economy (ILO 1998). EPZs with poor working conditions do not attract long term investment—"smart" EPZs have introduced measures to continuously upgrade labor (OECD 2000b).

Why not a race to the top?

Globalization may be forcing a race to the top, as it places a new emphasis on speed, efficiency, and quality as well as cost, shifting the focus from cheap labor to productive labor (ILO 1998; Aggarwal 1995). Countries can gain an advantage by improving labor standards. Strengthened core labor standards can increase economic growth and efficiency by raising skill levels, thereby creating an environment that encourages innovation and higher productivity (Stiglitz 2000; OECD 2000a). At the same time, in the sectors with a reputation for poor labor standards (clothing, footwear, and sporting goods) consumers are increasingly demanding products produced under acceptable working conditions, with monitoring and certification, often by trusted nongovernmental organizations.

Indeed, efforts to promote labor standards at a global level have been increasing: examples include the 1998 International Labour Organization (ILO) Declaration on Fundamental Principles and Rights at Work (under which monitoring and reporting on core labor standards is extended to all members) and development cooperation programs to reduce child labor. More controversially, trade agreements have been used to promote compliance with labor standards. The United States suspends access under the Generalized System of Preferences (GSP) in the event of noncompliance, while the European Union grants additional access for compliance. Labor provisions or side agreements figure in U.S. free trade agreements. Links to the World Trade Organization (WTO) have faced strong resistance from developing countries.[c] Other market-based mechanisms, such as labeling schemes or codes of conduct for firms (at the OECD, ILO, and firm level) have expanded, with

(continued)

Box 4.5   (*continued*)

most U.S. Fortune 500 companies now embracing such codes (see OECD 2000a; Stern 2003).[d]

Labor standards rise with income (Stern 2003; OECD 2000a), and the path to higher growth for developing countries lies in seizing the opportunities of global production networks in goods and services. But this in turn requires efforts to raise productivity and create a stable and attractive environment for FDI. And the evidence suggests that improving core labor standards and creating frameworks for sound and stable labor relations can contribute to both of these goals, with the potential to create a virtuous circle of rising wages and standards for workers in developing countries.

[a]Bates (2000) distinguishes between core labor standards, which are viewed as fundamental human rights and can create the framework conditions for the economy to operate efficiently, and developmental or economic labor standards

(for example, minimum wages), which will vary depending on the level of income in a given society.

[b]Data on freedom of association rights in 75 countries that represent virtually all of world trade and all inward and outward FDI show no significant deterioration in these rights in any of the 75 countries between 1980 and 1999 (the period during which competition for FDI heated up). Data show significant improvement in those rights in 17 countries (OECD 2000b).

[c]Moran (2004) provides a persuasive analysis of the practical problems of using dispute settlement under trade agreements to enforce labor standards, given the lack of international agreement on exactly what core labor standards mean and what is required for adequate implementation and the reliance on incomplete, nonrepresentative, noncomparable, and potentially biased sources of information.

[d]More recently, attention has shifted beyond core labor standards to the concept of decent work (work that is freely chosen, provides an income sufficient to satisfy basic economic and family needs, respect for rights and representation, basic security through some form of social protection, and adequate conditions) (ILO 2004).

---

a number of challenges to other countries, both developed and developing, there are enormous opportunities. To grasp these opportunities requires that countries have in place a policy environment that allows competitive advantages to be exploited and the key sources of growth to flourish, while ensuring that those workers adversely affected are assisted in adjusting by moving to new sectors and/or by augmenting their particular skill set. In other words, while aggregate gains are available to all countries, some industries, firms, and workers will incur some pain. Appropriate policy responses are discussed further below.

New challenge II—global sourcing of services

Workers in previously sheltered services face international competition

The global competition in goods that has been under way for decades is now visible in services, as falling telecommunications costs and greater openness to FDI enable different parts

of the services value chain to be performed in different locations around the globe—a phenomenon that has come to be known as "outsourcing" or "offshoring," but could perhaps be most accurately termed "global sourcing of services."[19] Global sourcing has increased competition in services markets for a wide variety of activities, from low-skilled functions such as data entry, word processing, and call centers to higher-skilled activities such as software development, consultancy, medical services, and R&D. A range of services previously thought to be nontradable are now being provided electronically over large distances.

Global sourcing allows firms to benefit from around-the-clock production (for just-in-time delivery of both goods and services) and lower wage costs. Estimates of the total cost savings from global sourcing vary across a wide range—for example, from 15–30 percent (Atkinson 2004) to 30–60 percent (industry estimates cited in Kirkegaard 2005).

While absolute numbers to date are not large, growth rates have been high, and global sourcing of services is expected to grow by

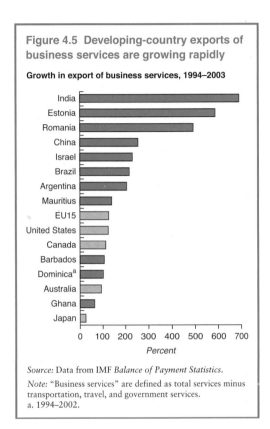

Figure 4.5 Developing-country exports of business services are growing rapidly

Growth in export of business services, 1994–2003

India
Estonia
Romania
China
Israel
Brazil
Argentina
Mauritius
EU15
United States
Canada
Barbados
Dominica[a]
Australia
Ghana
Japan

0   100 200 300 400 500 600 700
Percent

Source: Data from IMF *Balance of Payment Statistics.*

Note: "Business services" are defined as total services minus transportation, travel, and government services.

a. 1994–2002.

30 percent per year over 2003–08.[20] While developed countries still dominate the trade, some developing countries experienced fast growth in exports of business services between 1994 and 2003: nearly 700 percent for India; more than 200 percent for China, Brazil, and Argentina; and more than 100 percent for Mauritius, Barbados, and Dominica (figure 4.5).

Sourcing locations expand and change over time, and technology advances are likely to allow more services to be provided offshore. As costs in Ireland rose, activities moved to India and the Philippines. Now, as costs in India rise, other locations, including some in Eastern Europe, are becoming popular (Atkinson 2004). Language patterns influence location decisions, but these are not immutable.[21] Against this backdrop, countries across all regions and levels of development—from Senegal to Sri Lanka, Argentina to Zambia—are now seeking to become sites for services sourcing.

The number of service jobs that migrate from rich to poor countries could be large

Estimates to date of the scale of potential job movements from global sourcing of services vary widely according to the definitions and methodology used. A great deal of attention was initially given to a report by Forrester Research (2002) that estimated that 3.3 million service jobs would move offshore from the United States by 2015. However, when put into perspective—the U.S. economy creates about 30 million jobs per year—that number is quite small. Even for the job categories deemed to be vulnerable to outsourcing, including management and computer operations, the predicted impact amounts to just over 0.5 percent of existing employment (see Bhagwati, Panagariya, and Srinivasan 2004).

Blinder (2006) asserts that a much broader range of services will be liable to global sourcing (almost all of those activities that do not require direct personal delivery) as communications costs decline further and technology continues to advance. His rough estimate is that between 28 and 42 million jobs in the United States could move overseas as a result of global sourcing. OECD (2005c) concludes that close to 20 percent of total employment could potentially be affected by information and communications technology–enabled offshoring of services.

The potential size of the future market for global sourcing of services remains a matter of debate, reflecting uncertainties over how the dividing line between tradable and nontradable services will shift over time (see box 4.6).

Even if these higher predictions come to fruition they do not imply a corresponding lower level of employment. The impact of global sourcing of services on the overall level of unemployment in rich countries may be small, especially in countries that are effective in generating new jobs.

Global sourcing will benefit both developed and developing countries

The shift in jobs resulting from global sourcing of services is unlikely to be a zero-sum

Box 4.6   The number of services jobs liable to be moved abroad: large or small?

To identify the tradability of industries and occupations, Jensen and Kletzer (2005) use indicators of regional concentration of production in the United States to group industries into three categories of tradability, leaving a similar number of industries in each category (the more the geographical concentration, the higher the degree of tradability). They then use this degree of tradability of the sector to estimate the number of jobs that are prone to global sourcing.

Results are very sensitive to assumptions about what is considered tradable. The first figure below presents possible effects for the U.S. economy (excluding public administration), distinguishing between the agriculture and manufacturing sector, nonpersonal services, and personal services. For each category, the first bar shows the number of workers currently employed, while the second bar shows the number of jobs that may potentially be globally sourced under three possible scenarios. The lowest part considers only the highly concentrated industries as tradable; here fewer than 4.5 million jobs in the nonpersonal services sector could be lost overseas. In contrast, the middle part of each

second bar adds those jobs that could potentially be lost if all jobs in all tradable sectors (including those where production is only relatively geographically concentrated) could be sourced globally. This changes the picture dramatically; more than half the jobs in nonpersonal services could be affected by globalization (about 30 million jobs).

In Jensen and Kletzer's analysis there is a distinct difference in the vulnerability to global sourcing between wholesale and retail activities, which are less concentrated and therefore deemed less prone to global sourcing (about 36 percent of jobs in these sectors are at risk), and professional services (where 71 percent of jobs are at risk). However, technological change may make global sourcing more relevant to the wholesale and retail activities. The top part of the second columns shows that an additional 9.7 million jobs could be lost if the sensitivity to global sourcing for professional sectors were equal to that of the other nonpersonal services (the light gray part in the second column for nonpersonal services). The second figure below shows the same analysis for the European Union (EU15). The figure suggests that the

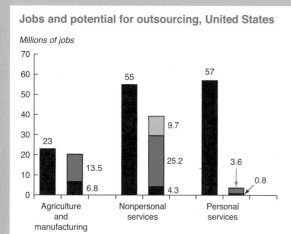

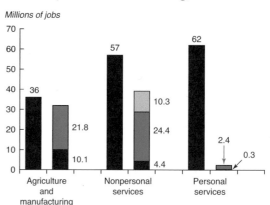

Sources: Jensen and Kletzer 2005; World Bank staff calculations.

Note: The first, black bar for each sector represents the number of workers currently employed in that sector. The second bar indicates the number of jobs potentially globally sourced. The black section represents only workers in highly geographically concentrated industries subject to global sourcing; the other two sections represent workers in less geographically concentrated industries (see text).

Box 4.6   *(continued)*

potential future adjustment for the EU15 is somewhat skewed toward the agricultural and manufacturing sectors, where currently a higher share of total employment can be found than in the United States.

A further important caveat to these estimates is that only certain elements of production in tradable sectors can be sourced overseas. Equally, there could be activities in the production process of largely nontradable services sectors that could be globally sourced. For these reasons it is preferable to identify tasks, rather than sectors, as tradable or nontradable (see box 4.7). Jensen and Kletzer make a crude attempt at this by repeating their exercise for broad occupational groups. They find that 11 percent of total employment is represented by tradable occupations in industries that are classified as nontradable. Similarly, about 22 percent of the total workforce is found in nontradable occupations in tradable industries.

game, owing to the presence of significant offsetting factors. While workers whose jobs are liable to offshoring will face lower labor demand and downward pressure on their relative wages, workers who are *complementary* to the offshored activities will see a rise in their productivity and an increase in relative wages. In addition, global sourcing will augment the productivity of firms that utilize the opportunities presented by lower labor costs overseas. These firms are more likely to expand than other firms, increasing their demand for labor, some of which will be for local tasks that can be fulfilled by the type of worker affected by offshoring, thus offsetting, to some extent, the impact of offshoring on wages (Grossman and Rossi-Hansberg 2006).

Moreover, demand is not inelastic—lower wages for software workers in developing countries raise global demand for software, benefiting all countries. Some OECD countries are experiencing a net inflow of service jobs from outsourcing (Amiti and Wei 2004); investment by foreign companies in the United States, for example, exceeded investment by U.S. companies in foreign countries every year over 1996–2001 (Atkinson 2004),[22] and several OECD countries have experienced double-digit growth in exports of business services. For example, exports grew at 11 percent in both the United States and Australia (OECD 2005a).[23]

There is also little evidence to date that tradable service activities have lower employment growth than other service activities, or that net outward investment or imports of business services are associated with significant declines in the share of employment potentially affected by outsourcing (Jensen and Kletzer 2005; OECD 2005a; Amiti and Wei 2004). However, growth is lower at the lower end of the skill distribution—although this may also indicate that these jobs are most readily substituted by technology. Worker displacement rates are higher in tradable services, but affected workers have higher skills and higher predisplacement earnings than displaced manufacturing workers (Jensen and Kletzer 2005).

The key labor-market issues raised in rich countries by the global sourcing of services are the nature of the new jobs that will replace those transferred overseas, and the difficulties that firms and workers may face in adjusting to this new facet of globalization. Workers previously sheltered from global competition are facing greater job insecurity, downward pressure on their wages, and potential costs of adjustment in moving from one job to another or in upgrading their skills to obtain new employment following displacement. These issues are explored in more detail below, following a brief discussion of an appropriate framework in which to assess the nature and impacts of global sourcing.

Global sourcing of services offers opportunities as well as challenges

Global sourcing of services is creating considerable opportunities for development in poor, low-wage countries, through export possibilities and through access to cheaper service inputs that raise productivity when used in other sectors. Global sourcing is providing important new employment—in India, employment in the information technology (IT) sector is now three million, although this is concentrated in five or six urban centers (Yusuf, Nabeshima, and Perkins 2006). Employment creation is at a wide range of skill levels, reflecting the range of activities open to global sourcing. In the relatively low-value segments such as call centers, wage costs are important determinants of location (along with language skills), and competition is fierce among developing countries. At the high end, global sourcing of services may be reducing incentives for skilled migration by creating new opportunities at home. A large number of those employed as a result of global sourcing are women, offering a different route to development than those based on the growth of agriculture and manufacturing.

While India and China are likely to come to dominate the market for global sourcing of services, comparative advantage will ensure that there are opportunities for many developing countries. Small island economies in the Caribbean, for example, have been able to attract certain back office activities from the United States, such as data entry. The services revolution and global sourcing are offering opportunities for new exports and for attracting services-related foreign investment for a range of poor countries. IT and global sourcing offer new and alternative drivers of development that circumvent some of the key constraints to growth driven by the expansion of exports of agricultural and manufactured goods.

This is most apparent for landlocked countries and small (often island) economies that face very high transport costs. For example, development in Rwanda has to confront an extremely adverse location, one of the highest population densities in the world, and a high population growth rate. While increasing the quality and quantity of exports of traditional agricultural exports (coffee) and minerals is crucial to increases in incomes for the poor in the short to medium term, the government of Rwanda has identified the provision of IT-intensive services, both locally and abroad, as a base for growth in the long run, to provide for employment and turn the country's large, but very young, population into a driver of development rather than a constraint.

The important new opportunities for developing countries are accompanied by considerable challenges related to the provision of necessary infrastructure, the design and implementation of appropriate regulation, better education to increase the supply of human capital, and the creation of strong marketing profiles and reputations for reliability.[24] Access to relatively cheap and reliable electricity, a critical problem for many poor countries, will be necessary. High-quality telecommunications infrastructure must be accompanied by a competitive framework for the provision of telecommunications services. Liberalization of the trade and investment regime, complemented by an appropriate and effective regulatory environment, can help ensure the efficient and competitive provision of the telecommunications backbone services.

Many developing countries could assist their nascent IT sectors by joining the Information Technology Agreement (ITA) of the WTO. The agreement covers the main categories of IT products, computers, telecommunications equipment, semiconductors, semiconductor manufacturing equipment, software, and scientific instruments, and commits members to bind tariffs at zero on these items. Joining the ITA can provide a strong signal to investors, both domestic and foreign, of a country's commitment to an open IT environment by ensuring access to necessary equipment at world prices. The ITA has 43 members (with the European Union treated as one), among them industrial countries and some large and small developing countries, such as China, the Arab Republic of Egypt, El Salvador, India, Mauritius, Moldova, and Morocco. As yet, however, none of the least developed countries is a member.

But does the global sourcing of services have different implications for labor in developed and developing markets?

Trade in services that use skilled labor intensively is not new. In the standard analysis of multinational firms, parent companies in developed countries are seen as exporting a range of services such as design, management and engineering consultancy, marketing, and finance to their overseas subsidiaries in poorer countries. What is new is trade in the opposite direction, as services both within multinationals and through arm's-length trade flow from low-wage countries to richer markets.

An immediate implication of this new development is that the standard factor-endowments model of trade (countries export goods and services that make intensive use of factors abundant in their country) cannot explain why skilled-labor-intensive services are being exported from countries with very scarce skilled labor. A common explanation involves the absence in developing countries of the knowledge-based assets that are complementary to skilled labor. The lack of these assets limits the use of skilled labor at home and keeps such workers cheap even though they are relatively more scarce than in rich countries. Globalization in the form of the transfer of know-how to complement cheap skilled labor in poor countries leads to trade in skilled-labor-intensive services.

There is much discussion of whether the global sourcing of service activities to low-wage countries presents features and issues different from those associated with global trade in goods. Bhagwati, Panagariya, and Srinivasan (2004), for example, argue that global sourcing of services has effects that are not qualitatively different from those emanating from the sourcing of goods. In both cases, there are gains from trade and national incomes rise, but displaced workers face some costs of adjustment.

For Trefler (2005), by contrast, the fact that skilled workers lose their jobs when services are sourced from low-wage countries has important economic implications that do not arise when low-skilled jobs disappear. The loss of relatively high-wage jobs and the pressure on the wages of high-skilled workers may reduce economic incentives to invest in and to acquire skills. In addition, in knowledge-intensive service activities skilled workers are more likely to have obtained some industry- and firm-specific knowledge that is lost when the job is lost. This may have a direct negative impact on productivity, especially if the knowledge is complementary to other skills or factors. In developing countries the opposite will tend to occur. The transfer of know-how, the increasing demand for skilled workers, and the upward pressure on skilled wages will tend to increase the incentives to acquire skills. This will increase demands on the education system in developing countries, which in many cases is likely to become a constraint on this process.

The rapid pace of change and flexibility demanded by competitive global markets, along with new trends such as global sourcing of services, will lead to potentially rising adjustment costs falling on a wider range of—more highly skilled—workers. These trends all argue for countries to review their domestic policy and institutional frameworks to ensure that their advantages can be exploited and that affected workers are supported when they incur adjustment costs.

Policies to confront the labor market challenges of globalization

Focusing on factors that determine the growth of productivity will be key to confronting the challenges of globalization without neutralizing its opportunities. This will require a change of mindset by policy makers, who must grasp and internalize the fundamental changes in the nature of international production and trade (see box 4.7).

Box 4.7   Trading goods and services or trading tasks?

In the classic conception, international trade is the exchange of complete goods and services across national boundaries. Countries gain from specialization in particular sectors of the economy, such as textiles and steel. Within firms, gains are had from higher productivity, that is, by allowing workers to specialize in particular tasks. In the past, effective coordination of these efforts, and the combination of tasks to produce a product, required proximity. Communication required physical presence and the transportation of intermediate inputs was slow and costly. Specialization led to geographic concentration of production. International trade occurred if consumers lived in another country.

However, the nature of production has changed. Revolutions in transport and communications technologies have led to enormous reductions in cost, allowing tasks to be separated in time and space, and weakening the link between specialization and geographic concentration. Instructions and information can be effectively conveyed over long distances and intermediate inputs can be transported quickly and much more cheaply than before. Thus, increasingly it is *tasks* in addition to final goods and services that are exchanged across national boundaries, resulting in global production networks of activity in a wide range of sectors. In this new global economy there are additional gains from specialization, as firms take advantage of differences in the cost of labor and skills across countries to allocate tasks internationally.

Some tasks can be offshored more easily than others. What matters is the extent to which a particular task is contested globally (Leamer 2006). This is more likely for standard, mundane tasks that can be coordinated through codifiable information and less

likely for complex tasks that require tacit information. The latter often require relationships and are often best performed in clusters of individuals. Your neighbors matter. Even for some mundane tasks, such as mowing the grass, physical presence is required.

In this new global environment, interventions that target particular sectors will be ineffective relative to initiatives to provide an environment that supports activities and tasks. This entails greater emphasis on a business environment that facilitates the entry and exit of firms across all sectors and policies and infrastructure and regulations that support the free flow and low cost of imported inputs (whether physical or information) to which domestic workers can contribute their tasks. What matters is the quality of roads, ports, telecommunications, and electricity together with relatively low tariffs on imported inputs and effective regulation of key backbone services.

Finally, the increasing importance of trade in tasks creates a challenge for the measurement of international trade flows. Currently imports of goods are recorded according to their invoice value as they cross the border and the whole value of the import is attributed to the country in which the last substantial transformation occurred. There is no system by which the countries that contributed value added to the product are identified. Thus, for example, the value of the iPod discussed in box 4.4, when imported into the United States, is attributed to China, where it is assembled. Yet most of the value of the iPod is added by tasks undertaken in other countries.

Sources: Grossman and Rossi-Hansberg 2006; Leamer 2006.

In the new environment, productivity growth requires openness to new ideas and the ability to exploit new technologies and opportunities. Economies need to be sufficiently flexible to enable resources to move from low-productivity to high-productivity tasks and activities, which policy makers cannot identify beforehand. This places a premium on institutions and policies that encourage innovation,

investments in human capital, and reductions of barriers to the flow of knowledge, capital, and labor. This process is not without adjustment costs, and complementary policies are needed to ensure that particular groups in society do not bear a disproportionate share of the pain.

The appropriate policy mix that provides a framework for productivity growth will vary over time and according to country characteristics, such as level of development and size. Nevertheless, key ingredients will be openness to trade and FDI and an attractive climate for investment and for innovation, investing in education, and repositioning labor-market policies to focus on protecting workers, not jobs. Rich countries have a particular responsibility to maintain and, indeed, increase the openness of their markets to goods and services produced in poor countries. A related issue is the impact that globalization and openness may have on a country's capacity to raise tax revenues to fund infrastructure for trade or training for affected workers.

Supporting open access to markets, innovation, and a strong business climate

Openness to trade in goods, services, and ideas provides a critical stimulus to innovation and productivity growth, both for countries at the global technology frontier and those catching up. But because trade and technology can lead to lower relative wages and greater employment volatility for some workers, policy makers are often tempted to meet the challenges of globalization by increasing trade protection. Doing so compromises a key source of growth. As a former finance minister of a developing country that undertook successful reforms stated, "Trade shocks are better dealt with through more, rather than less, trade."[25]

Trade policies interact critically with other elements of the business and investment climate. Reaping the benefits of globalization requires not only openness to trade and investment but also physical infrastructure and a policy framework that enables actual and potential exporters to effectively exploit their advantages. High costs of clearing customs, poor port infrastructure, weak telecommunications services, and poor regulation, for example, raise costs and hamper competitiveness. These major challenges for developing countries, particularly the least developed, must be addressed if trade liberalization is to be effective in stimulating trade,

investment, and growth. Domestic policy reforms, underpinned where necessary by increased "aid for trade" from the international community, will be essential in helping the poorest countries benefit from the opportunities of new global markets.

In addition, policies that affect innovation and access to technology are crucial. For the least developed countries, moving up the technology ladder by acquiring technological know-how from overseas through trade and FDI will be a key driver of growth over the next 20 to 30 years. Innovation and learning will continue to play essential roles in raising productivity and sustaining growth in rich countries and increasingly in the middle-income countries, placing emphasis on the institutions that frame incentives to invest in R&D and in the acquisition and application of knowledge.[26] In the middle-income countries there will be opportunities to be had from incremental innovations to processes that improve the tasks undertaken for foreign firms and to products that can be tailored for growing domestic markets. In the richer countries it is innovation and learning creating new goods, services, and new processes for producing them, that will be of greater importance. The key elements of a policy framework to support innovation and learning will differ between countries according to level of development as well as size but to varying degrees will include the following:

- *Investing in human capital* to overcome shortages of skilled labor, including due to migration. Learning-by-doing in firms increases with its workers' human capital.
- *Supporting public research through universities and research centers, and facilitating interaction with private businesses* to ensure dissemination of "basic" knowledge that stimulates research for commercially exploitable innovations.
- *Defining—and enforcing—adequate intellectual property rights* to encourage domestic investment in innovation and acquisition of technology through FDI.[27]

- *Promoting access to finance,* especially for new entrants and small and medium enterprises (SMEs), which are more likely to be innovative (Geroski 1990).
- *Careful review of fiscal incentives to stimulate R&D and innovation,* taking into account that evidence of effectiveness is scarce (de Ferranti and others 2002) and that there could be crowding out or in of private investment (Jaumotte and Pain 2005).

Providing more people with lifelong learning

In all countries investment in education will become an ever more critical determinant of labor-market performance in the context of greater global competition and increasing rewards to skills. Higher-skilled workers are better at dealing with changes, including adoption of new technologies, new workforce organizations, and ongoing pressures for adjustment and shocks, and also support the creation of well-functioning institutions (World Bank 2006; Hoekman and Javorcik 2006).[28] Countries need to focus not only on enrollment in education but also on quality and relevance, a fact underlined by the prevalence of youth unemployment in both developed and developing countries.

Education systems everywhere face new challenges, however. In the face of rapid changes in technology and business organization, these systems struggle to keep pace with demand for new skills—a trend likely to be exacerbated by global sourcing of services. For individual workers, this means rapid changes in the value of their skills, demanding constant retraining and skill upgrading. But workers facing more rapid obsolescence or devaluation of skills may have lower incentives for skill acquisition. Moreover, firms already faced with competitive cost pressures and concerns that they will not benefit from their investment in training as their workers leave for other firms, will increasingly have access to a global pool of workers with the desired skills to substitute for the existing workforce. This could place greater pressure on the education system to provide the industry-specific skills previously provided by firm-level training; while continuing volatility could also place a premium on providing workers with the general skills that enable continuous adaptation.

In sum, education systems will be expected to provide more people with more opportunities to learn across a broader menu of educational and skill-development options at more stages of their lives than ever before. This will require a new model of education and training, as well as ongoing reform of traditional methods, providers, and financing of education (box 4.8).

Protecting workers, not jobs

While globalization offers new opportunities for workers, it can also entail greater movement—for example, between jobs, sectors, or regions—and this brings with it additional risk. This calls for policies that shift the emphasis from measures designed to protect those in employment—which, as discussed earlier, can discourage job creation—to mechanisms aimed at ameliorating the potentially negative effects of greater labor movement through targeted labor-market policies and social safety nets. While the precise combination of labor-market programs and income support measures will need to be determined at the national level—taking account of local circumstances and involving all relevant stakeholders—and there can be important differences in the types of programs that are most effective in developing and developed countries, some general lessons can be drawn.

In all countries, income support programs will remain the core of worker assistance. In OECD countries, the redistributive impact of the tax-transfer system increased in the late 1980s and 1990s (Brenton 2006). In developing countries, the design of such programs raises specific challenges.

- *Unemployment benefits* can ease adjustment and maintain public support for structural change, but if set too high

Box 4.8 Key challenges for education systems in the new global economy

While some of the key challenges relate to problems that education systems have traditionally faced, such as increasing access to and quality of education, others relate to revisiting the nature, type, and purpose of educational offerings to equip a globally competitive workforce. In key respects, traditional educational methods are ill-suited to providing the lifelong learning that is necessary in the new global economy (World Bank 2003).

Increase access. In Sub-Saharan Africa and South Asia, more than 40 percent of those aged 25 and over in 2000 had not completed any formal education. In developing countries, public funding—directed through public educational institutions or to individuals (loans or vouchers)—can help expand access (World Bank 2005). Recent policies in Brazil that addressed supply-side constraints in the education system by establishing a minimum spending level per student have proven successful in increasing enrollment rates substantially (de Mello and Hoppe 2005). While the central government transfers funds to the local governments in case these are unable to finance the prescribed spending levels, demand for education is increased by using school attendance as a requirement for certain types of income transfers to low-income households.

Provide access at all ages. Preschool and early childhood programs establish a solid basis for subsequent learning[a] while primary and secondary education give workers the basic skills that enable them to learn new skills required by technology-induced changes (OECD 1996).[b] Lifelong learning helps workers to adjust, but government support (for instance, via a training levy) may be needed (World Bank 2005). In many emerging economies, improving the access to secondary and postsecondary education will be critical in view of the rising skill premium.

Improve quality.[c] Efficient increased spending should be combined with strengthened incentives to teach and learn, and with improved accountability (World Bank 2006). Quality assurance mechanisms (including regionally) and national qualifications frameworks raise standards and facilitate international recognition.

Focus on learning to learn, equipping workers to learn throughout their working lives, and continuously upgrade how they produce in whatever sector they might be employed (de Ferranti and others 2002). This means moving away from a model in which the teacher is the source of knowledge to a system where educators function as guides to multiple sources of knowledge.

Include a range of providers. Including private sector as well as public sector providers can promote greater access to education and greater variety in educational offerings. Additionally, foreign institutions can help upgrade standards, although sound regulation is needed to ensure quality and access, and to provide clear and nondiscriminatory conditions for investors. Here again, government measures to ensure broad access may be necessary.

Strengthen the links between education and work. The mismatch between graduates' skills and labor-market needs in many developing countries argues for greater links between the private and public sectors. In the Middle East and North Africa, skills geared toward public sector jobs are ill-suited to the needs of industry, while the traditional focus on law, philosophy, and theology in education in much of Latin America and the Caribbean is argued to have slowed the development of natural resource sectors (de Ferranti and others 2002). Postsecondary education should be balanced between academic and technical-vocational training (OECD 1996), with the latter assessed, certified, and formally recognized.

---

[a]In developing countries, early childhood and preschool programs show returns of $2–5 for every $1 invested (World Bank 2006).

[b]For a full discussion of ensuring access and quality in education, see World Bank (2006). For a discussion of issues in the delivery of basic education services, see *World Development Report 2004: Making Services Work for Poor People.*

[c]Children in Argentina, Chile, and Mexico perform about two standard deviations below children in Greece, one of the poorest-performing countries in the OECD. In reading competence (based on the OECD's Programme for International Student Assessment [PISA] 2001), the average Indonesian student performed at the level of a French student at the seventh percentile (World Bank 2006). More than 20 percent of firms in many developing countries rate inadequate skills and education of workers as a major or severe obstacle to their operations (World Bank 2005).

and given for too long, can slow down adjustment. In developing countries, informality makes targeting of benefits difficult as the unemployed may also have jobs in the informal sector, and the registered unemployed may be middle- rather than low-income workers (Hoekman and Winters 2005).[29] However, unemployment insurance may also be an alternative source of credit for self-employment. Individual savings accounts or similar types of unemployment insurance may be a better solution for developing countries, although there is a risk that workers have insufficient resources.

- *Mandatory severance pay* is the most common income support program in developing countries, as compliance is complaint-driven and an expensive bureaucracy is not required. However, if overly large, severance pay may discourage hiring or reforms as costs become unmanageable.

- One-off *compensation programs* have also been used in both developing (public sector downsizing) and developed (restructuring of declining industries) countries. While supporting relatively well-off workers (the previous beneficiaries of rents), they are often seen as politically necessary for reform—although experience suggests that they have often not succeeded in attaining their stated goals.[30]

- *Wage insurance* gives workers a proportion of their former wage for a set period of time, conditional upon their finding new employment. This eases adjustment, provides an incentive to take a new, albeit lower-paying, job and (in effect) subsidizes on-the-job retraining—the most effective kind (Kletzer 2001).

Global competition and movement of workers argues for separating health care from employment status. The possibility that in future more types of workers could experience periods of unemployment or more frequent job change argues for new mechanisms to ensure that they are not left without access to essential health services. Moreover, health care benefits provided by firms are a burden on globally contestable jobs and make employers wary of forming long-term relationships with prospective employees (Leamer 2006). In developing countries, extending universal basic medical care not linked to other aspects of formality could help to reach the poorest, but risks increasing incentives for informality (Arias and others 2005). One option is general health provision, funded by tax revenue rather than attached to employment; a more modest alternative is the creation of a health insurance subsidy for displaced workers, as proposed by Kletzer (2001).[31]

Active labor-market programs can be effective in keeping workers in the labor market and upgrading their skills, but experience has been mixed and programs need to be designed to suit the conditions in developing countries.[32] While there is considerable experience in the OECD countries,[33] less is known about policies in developing countries.[34] For the latter, the key issues are the size of the informal sector, limited administrative capacity, and the absence of broader social safety nets. Leakage risks are higher, as the unemployed may also have informal jobs and may not be low-income. Policies need to improve conditions in the informal sector, but avoid creating additional incentives for informality.

In both developed and developing countries successful interventions are comprehensive, oriented to labor demand, linked to real workplaces, and carefully targeted (box 4.9). Interventions are also more effective when the economy is growing. But longer-term assessments are needed (most cover one to two years) and a range of effects—deadweight (impact would have been achieved in the absence of the program), substitution (participants substitute for nonparticipants in the labor market and the employment effect is zero), and displacement (firms with subsidized

Box 4.9 Overview of the impact of active labor-market programs

Employment services. Generally have a positive impact on employment and earnings and are cost-effective. But they are of limited use where structural unemployment is high and labor demand low. May be less effective in developing countries where informality is high and implementation capacity limited.

Public works. Effective, including for informal workers, as a short-term safety net in developing countries but do not improve future labor-market prospects, especially where a stigma is attached to participation. Wages need to be sufficiently low to target those with low incomes and few job prospects, and projects should also target poor areas. Can be most redistributive, but require government expenditure.

Training. Can result in higher employment rates, if not earnings. Programs work best with active employer involvement (on-the-job training), and limited evidence from developing and transition economies suggests better results for women than men. But firms are reluctant to train lower-skilled workers; in the OECD countries the least qualified are only a quarter to a third as likely as the highly qualified to participate in job-related training. A growing number of countries fund enterprise-based training via compulsory levies (usually 1 percent of payroll), with reimbursement based on training provided in some cases (examples include Singapore and Mauritius).

Retraining after mass layoffs. No positive impact, except with a comprehensive package of employment services, and expensive. Workers are often geographically concentrated with industry-specific skills. Best results have been achieved with longer programs that include some worker contribution to costs.

Training for youth. Less successful than earlier investments in the education system. Some success in Latin America with programs that integrate training with remedial education, job search assistance, and social services. For example, the "Jovenes" programs of Argentina, Chile, Peru and Uruguay are targeted at disadvantaged youth. They combine training and work experience with other services, include the private sector, and are financed by tripartite levy-grant schemes or the government. They have substantial and positive impacts on employment and earnings, but can be small scale, may not be cost-effective, and participants can displace other workers.

Employment subsidies. Mostly for disadvantaged groups, although some countries (Belgium, France, the Netherlands) provide for all low-paid work. A significant share of overall active labor-market program (ALMP) spending in several OECD countries. Most do not have a positive impact and have substantial deadweight (workers would have been employed without the subsidy) and substitution (worker displaces a nonsubsidized worker) costs.

Microenterprise development and self-employment assistance. Some evidence of positive impacts for older and better-educated workers, but take-up is low and business failure rate is high.

Sources: Betcherman, Olivas, and Dar 2004; World Bank 2005; Rama 2003; Arias and others 2005; OECD 2005a, 2005d; Heckman and Pagés 2000.

Note: Betcherman, Olivas, and Dar (2004) build on an earlier World Bank study of 72 scientific (that is, using a control group) evaluations of ALMPs by Dar and Tzannatos (1999) by adding 87 new studies, 39 of which cover programs in developing and transition economies. Similar conclusions on a number of points have been made in OECD reviews (see Martin 2000).

workers displace those without)—need to be taken into account. Given their mixed record, and the challenges of appropriate design, governments need to be realistic about what active labor-market policies can achieve.

Globalization may undermine funding for programs to support labor

While integrating into the world economy requires that import taxes be kept low and relatively uniform, for the least developed

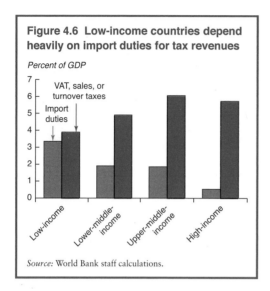

Figure 4.6 Low-income countries depend heavily on import duties for tax revenues

Percent of GDP

Source: World Bank staff calculations.

countries they are a key source of revenue relative to value-added tax (VAT) and sales taxes (figure 4.6). High-income countries are able to recover revenues lost from trade liberalization from other sources: on average, middle-income countries recover 45–60 percent of lost tariff revenues while least developed countries recover less than 30 percent (Baunsgaard and Keen 2005).

But many countries collect far less in tariff revenue than the applied tax rates would suggest, owing to the widespread (discretionary) granting of exemptions. Exemptions make the tax regime opaque and difficult to administer and can lead to a distorted incentive structure that discriminates against small firms with less influence. Further, there is little evidence that exemptions have a significant impact on investment, their primary justification. Many countries could substantially reduce applied tariffs while maintaining or even increasing revenue if exemptions were removed and collection improved. However, it is still necessary to address the development challenge highlighted in figure 4.6 of moving from easy-to-collect trade taxes to harder-to-collect consumption and income taxes.[35] Simply implementing a VAT is not sufficient; a high degree of collection efficiency (the ratio of actual to potential revenues) is needed.[36]

While feelings of greater economic insecurity among workers may lead to greater demands for social insurance, it has been argued that globalization is limiting the capacity of governments to fund such protection—and to support the productivity-enhancing measures discussed above. The fear is that globalization and greater mobility of capital and wealthy workers will undermine the tax base, as these factors move to the lowest tax locations, compromising social welfare programs for those bearing the burden of adjustment. There is little evidence of this process in developed countries (OECD 2000b), however, and the preferences of wealthy individuals for education, health, law and order, and social welfare suggest that fears of large numbers of skilled workers emigrating to low tax havens are unlikely to be justified. Moreover, much of the knowledge of these workers is gained and creates value from interactions and synergies with clusters of other similar workers. As Leamer (2006) says, it matters who your neighbors are.

The international community—working together—can help realize the potential of globalization

The rise of China, India, and other emerging economies amounts to a huge increase in the supply of unskilled labor on a global scale. This could heighten the existing—and growing—inequality between skilled and unskilled workers in both developed and developing countries that has resulted from a mix of technology and trade effects. There are fears that there will be no space for other countries, particularly developing countries, to compete in low-wage exports or in attracting global capital flows. In addition, because China and India are rapidly upgrading the skills of their workforce, and services activities along the value chain are being globally sourced, skilled workers everywhere are increasingly facing competitive pressure. There are mitigating forces, however; China and India offer huge markets for the exports of other countries, their own wages are bound to grow rapidly, and developing the full range of institutions needed to underpin a modern, dynamic market economy will take time.

This new global climate poses challenges—but also offers considerable opportunities—for all countries. The countries best placed to address the challenges will be those best able to seize the opportunities and generate the new sources of growth and wealth needed to finance additional investments in social safety nets and education. In many developing countries, domestic reforms to reduce rigidities in the labor market and improve the climate for business and innovation will be critical. All countries will need better mechanisms to cushion adjustment costs and distribute the benefits of growth to offset the tendencies toward inequality and volatility. But collective action by the international community will also be needed in two important respects. First, as the pressures of globalization increase the calls for beggar-thy-neighbor protectionism, the international community will need to band together to preserve and extend the open markets that have underpinned recent advances in growth and poverty reduction. In the absence of open global markets, many of the new opportunities from the coming globalization will disappear. Second, the international community needs to provide the financial and technical support—the "aid for trade"—to enable the poorest countries to overcome the infrastructure and capacity constraints that limit their ability to take advantage of new trade opportunities.

Notes

1. Trade among developing countries is also growing significantly; South-South trade now constitutes one-quarter of developing-country exports, and this trade is growing 50 percent faster than world trade.

2. A recent U.S. study (Brofenbrenner and Luce 2004) concludes that the Bureau of Labor Statistics (BLS) grossly underestimates the total number of jobs lost to global production shifts. While the BLS reported 4,633 private sector workers in establishments with 50 or more employees who lost their jobs because of global outsourcing from January to March 2004, the authors, drawing on media reports, find evidence of a minimum of 25,000 jobs lost over that period. Moves were often to several destinations

simultaneously and most were in manufacturing, although there was a significant increase in shifts of white-collar-services jobs to India.

3. Ghose (2003) identifies a group of manufacturing-exporting developing countries that have shown impressive growth in employment in the sector, from about 50.9 million in 1980 to 82.8 million in 1997 (or from 79 to 88.7 percent of total employment over the same period). In this group are China, the Arab Republic of Egypt, India, Indonesia, Israel, the Republic of Korea, Malaysia, Mauritius, Morocco, the Philippines, Singapore, Sri Lanka, Taiwan (China), Thailand, and Turkey. However, other manufacturing-exporting countries have witnessed declines of 13.5 to 10.6 million (21 to 11.3 percent) over the same period—this group consists of Argentina, Brazil, Hong Kong (China), Malta, Mexico, Pakistan, and South Africa. Note that Mexico's figures do not include the *maquiladora*; if they did, the country would have appeared in the first group.

4. A further question is the distribution of gains between labor and capital. However, this issue has proven difficult to analyze and beyond the immediate scope of this chapter, which focuses on the distribution within labor markets between skilled and unskilled workers.

5. Whether the impacts of greater openness operate more or less through wages as opposed to employment depends on labor-market institutions, the efficiency of capital markets, and social policies. Hence in the United States, the more flexible labor market and more efficient financial sector mean that wages bear a greater share of shocks than in the European Union. In developing countries, it also appears that wage responses are greater than employment impacts, suggestive both of labor-market rigidities and industry rents engendered by trade policy (Hoekman and Winters 2005).

6. For full-time workers in the United States between 1979 and 1995, real wages of those with 12 years of education fell by 13.4 percent, and real wages of those with less than 12 years of education fell by 20.2 percent. During the same period, real wages of workers with 16 or more years of education rose by 3.4 percent so that the wage gap between these groups grew significantly (Feenstra and Hanson 2003).

7. Some of the overall increases in the skill premium could also be related to the artificially low prices for skilled labor prior to opening. Modest increases are also found in China and Vietnam (World Bank 2002).

8. Economic literature has mainly focused on the impact of globalization on labor demand elasticities. Authors such as Rodrik (1997) argue that globalization has led to an increase in the labor demand elasticity, with the result that changes in product prices now have magnified impacts on wages and employment. The

empirical support for this link is mixed, although estimating elasticities is prone to difficulties. Rodrik (1997) finds that the interaction between trade openness and variation in a country's terms of trade is positively linked with volatility of growth and government expenditures. The latter, Rodrik argues, reflects the increasing demand for social protection as globalization increases insecurity. On the other hand, Iversen and Cusack (2000) argue that what is required is to show that volatility from international markets is greater than that in domestic markets; they find that in developed countries there is no correlation between trade openness and output, earnings, or employment volatility. Others have tried to link trade liberalization to changes in labor demand elasticities. Slaughter (2001) finds that labour demand elasticities for low-skilled workers in the United States have increased over time but with no clear link to trade variables. Fajnzylber and Maloney (2005), for a set of Latin American countries, and Krishna, Mitra, and Chinoy (2001) for Turkey do not find strong support for this link. On the other hand, Hasan, Mitra, and Ramaswamy (2003) find a strong link between trade reform and wage and employment volatility in India. Nevertheless, even though a positive link between globalization and observed measures of volatility has not been found, globalization may still have contributed to greater risks and to heightened economic insecurity (Scheve and Slaughter 2002).

9. Data for 19 developed and developing economies suggest that flexible hiring and firing rules are positively associated with higher rates of entry of new firms, which are often better at harnessing new technologies (World Bank 2005).

10. Alternatively, of course, it could be argued that strict employment protection is a response to the higher level of anxiety of workers in these countries. If that is the case, however, one would also have to conclude that protection has not been very effective in reducing that anxiety.

11. Skilled workers are considered to be those with some secondary education, plus those with secondary education or above. This selection does not take into account the quality of the education received or comparability among countries.

12. This is notwithstanding the fact that trade liberalization in India and especially China has advanced greatly over the last 15 years, in China driven in part by World Trade Organization (WTO) accession and in India by unilateral reforms.

13. It should be noted that Hong Kong (China) is the world's third-largest outward investor, with flows of about $40 billion in 2004 (UNCTAD 2005).

14. There is controversy around the exact number of graduates from Chinese and Indian institutions. For example, a recent study by Duke University indicated that engineering graduates from Chinese universities numbered only 351,000 per year as opposed to previous estimates of over 600,000. Note that the new number is still two and a half times as many graduates as in the United States; however, China's population is four times as large.

15. It is interesting to note that the Soviet Union overtook the United States in the number of research workers (Nolting and Feshbach 1980) but did not succeed in achieving strong and sustained innovation-driven growth.

16. Migration of skilled workers can be positive for the country of origin when those workers come back. In Morocco, high-skilled labor has started to return, bringing substantial know-how and technological knowledge into the country, increasing productivity and boosting innovation in terms of improved business practices.

17. The value of a relationship-specific investment is significantly higher within a buyer-seller relationship than outside it. An example is where suppliers or subcontractors to a car producer make investments in design modifications that improve the fit or ease of assembly with other parts but which are not relevant to the production process of other car makers. Such investments tend to be associated with longer-term contractual commitments between producers and their suppliers and less repeated bargaining (Joskow (1987)). Spencer and Qui (2001) find that such relationships in the Japanese car industry tend to limit the range of imports to less important parts and that it is possible that no parts are imported despite lower production costs overseas.

18. Looking at U.S. imports from 10 major developing countries (which together accounted for 26.5 percent of U.S. imports at the time of the cited study), Aggarwal (1995) noted that sectors with egregious labor conditions were not a primary share of these countries' exports; that standards were often lower in less export-oriented or nontraded sectors; and that, within the export-oriented sector, labor conditions in firms more involved in exporting were either similar to or better than those in other firms. Raynauld and Vidal (1998) showed that, since 1980, countries with low standards had not increased their share of global exports and two-thirds of 39 countries with low labor standards had seen their international competitiveness (as measured by unit labor costs) stagnate or decline (decline reflects either a decline in labor productivity relative to the nominal cost of labor or a rise in the nominal cost of labor relative to its productivity) while 14 of the 18 high-standards countries had increased their international competitiveness.

19. "Outsourcing" or "offshoring" have both been used to refer to the global sourcing of

services—technically "outsourcing" refers to the sourcing of an activity outside a company (such as the contracting out of billing services), which can also take place within the domestic market, while "offshoring" is the movement of production of a service outside a country. For firms, offshoring need not be outsourcing when the activity stays within a foreign affiliate; from the perspective of national labor markets, it is the movement of production to another territory that is the focus of interest. Strictly speaking, not all FDI is offshoring, as in cases where a foreign affiliate is built to service the local market in the host country (Kirkegaard 2005).

20. Note that balance of payments (BOP) statistics imperfectly measure the full extent of global sourcing of services because of classification and data limitations; figures should be taken as an underestimate.

21. Atkinson (2004) notes that a concerted effort by the Chinese government to expand acquisition of English could see China moving beyond non-language-based services to other business services.

22. Care needs to be taken with comparisons between outsourcing and inward FDI, as the foreign establishment may be created primarily to serve the domestic market (see note 19). That said, the comparison may be more relevant in terms of the contribution of foreign companies to job creation within the United States, to offset the movement of jobs overseas.

23. For every $1 of call-center work offshored by U.S. firms, an estimated $1.43 is reinvested in the U.S. economy; the amounts are $1.33 and $1.42 for information technology services and high-end knowledge services (such as equity research, tax preparation, and risk management), respectively. The net benefit to the U.S. economy of shifting $1 previously spent in the United States to India could be as high as 12–14 cents per dollar (*McKinsey Quarterly*, October 2003).

24. The absence of international standards for many service sector activities reinforces the importance of reputation in attracting new clients.

25. Nicolás Eyzaguirre, former Minister of Finance from Chile, comparing the experiences of Chile and Argentina, in a presentation to the Mauritius High Level seminar in September 2006.

26. Rates of return can also be influenced by the lack of competition. If incumbents are able to extract large rents that are not endangered, the incentive to innovate is severely restrained because the returns will replace some of the rents they are actually collecting, reducing the net value of innovation. Evidence indicates that monopolies are not particularly innovative and that small firms stimulate innovation (Geroski 1990). Opening markets by reducing external barriers and creating better regulatory frameworks for natural monopolies is hence likely to raise rates of innovation.

27. However, IPR protection must be balanced against the need to avoid stifling competition.

28. Education can also promote access to technology and development of new sectors: in 21 countries in Latin America and the Caribbean, an increase of five years in the average level of education in those above 15 was associated with an increase in FDI of 3 percent of GDP (de Ferranti and others 2002).

29. While the informal sector can also be a way of managing risk, there are limits to its role as a safety net, as it often generates most of the flows into unemployment (about 60 percent in Argentina, Brazil, and Mexico) and is ineffective in cases of multiple/covariate shocks (Arias and others 2005).

30. In the United States, the structure of the political system (including, for example, passage of Trade Promotion Authority in Congress) and nature of pressures have led to the development of trade-specific adjustment measures (Brenton 2006). Under the U.S. Trade Adjustment Assistance (TAA) program, qualified workers can receive an additional 52 weeks of unemployment insurance provided they are enrolled in an approved training program; a similar program was created for the North American Free Trade Agreement (NAFTA) in 1993. TAA and NAFTA payments are about $300 million annually (Kletzer 2001). The European Union is also now considering a Globalization Fund of half a billion euros to help retrain and relocate 35,000–50,000 workers a year whose jobs are lost to global sourcing and trade. Money would be available in the case of layoffs of at least 1,000 people in regions with a population of at least 800,000 where the unemployment rate was already higher than the European or national average; or where several companies in a sector laid off at least 1,000 workers over six months in regions with a population of up to three million and where the job losses added up to 1 percent of total employees in that sector. While the fund will cover a relatively small number of workers, it is seen as important in resisting growing calls for protection (Kanter 2006). It is not clear, however, that there is an equity argument for distinguishing between trade-affected and other workers, such as those affected by technological change. In some circumstances—such as mass layoffs—trade-specific assistance may be more cost-effective. However, it should be used sparingly, aimed at orderly adjustment, be time-limited, and include both services and manufacturing workers as well as workers who have lost their jobs from both import and export competition (OECD 2005d).

31. Under Kletzer's proposal for the United States, all full-time displaced workers would be eligible to receive a health insurance subsidy for up to six months, or until they found a new job, whichever is earlier.

32. ALMPs include employment services, training, public works (which offer short-term employment on

community projects in sectors such as construction, rural development, and community services), wage and employment subsidies, and self-employment assistance.

33. Over 1990–2002, average national expenditure on ALMPs in OECD countries remained relatively constant at about 0.75 percent of gross domestic product (GDP). This average masks wide differences, however, with some European countries spending over 1 percent of GDP while the United States, Japan, Korea, and the United Kingdom spent under 0.4 percent. Training accounted for the bulk of spending (36 percent), followed by public employment services (24.5 percent) and job subsidies (19.5 percent). Transition economies show similar (but lower) patterns of spending (Betcherman, Olivas, and Dar 2004).

34. There is some evidence that Latin American countries have been investing significantly in youth training and public works programs, but in Africa there is very little active programming on any significant scale (Betcherman, Olivas, and Dar 2004).

35. For many resource-rich developing countries facing rising demand from China and India and higher world prices, a crucial opportunity that has to be addressed is translating higher revenues into investments in social and educational programs that enhance competitiveness and support diversification. For these countries, the priority for domestic reform must be to address governance and corruption issues associated with distributing the revenues from resources. This must be supported by the global community through increased efforts to discipline the activities of firms and governments in countries demanding these resources.

36. Countries with smaller agricultural and larger urban sectors, with strong political institutions, with higher per capita incomes, and that are more open to trade tend to have higher collection efficiencies for VAT (Aizenman and Jinjarak 2006).

References

Aggarwal, M. 1995. "International Trade, Labor Standards and Labor Market Conditions: An Evaluation of the Linkages." U.S. International Trade Commission, Office of Economics Working Paper No. 95-06-C, Washington, DC.

Aizenman, Joshua, and Yothin Jinjarak. 2006. "Globalization and Developing Countries—A Shrinking Tax Base?" NBER Working Paper No. 11933, National Bureau of Economic Research, Cambridge, MA.

Amiti, Mary, and Shang-Jin Wei. 2004. "Fear of Outsourcing: Is It Justified?" NBER Working Paper No. 10808, National Bureau of Economic Research, Cambridge, MA.

Anderton, Robert, and Paul Brenton. 1999. "Outsourcing and Low-Skilled Workers in the UK." Bulletin of Economic Research 51: 267–86.

Anderton, Robert, Paul Brenton, and John Whalley. 2006. Globalisation and the Labour Market: Trade, Technology and Less-Skilled Workers in Europe and the United States. London and New York: Routledge.

Arias, Omar, Andreas Blom, Mariano Bosch, Wendy Cunningham, Ariel Fiszbein, Gladys Lopez Acevedo, William Maloney, Jaime Saavedra, Carolina Sanchez-Paramo, Mauricio Santamaria, and Lucas Siga. 2005. "Pending Issues in Protection, Productivity Growth, and Poverty Reduction." World Bank Policy Research Working Paper No. 3799, Washington, DC. December.

Atkinson, Robert. 2004. "Understanding the Offshoring Challenge." Progressive Policy Institute Policy Report, May, available at www.ppionline.org.

Bates, Jenny. 2000. "International Trade and Labor Standards." Progressive Policy Institute (PPI) Policy Report, available at www.ppionline.org.

Baunsgaard, Thomas, and Michael Keen. 2005. "Tax Revenue and (or?) Trade Liberalization." International Monetary Fund (IMF) Working Paper No. 05/112, Washington, DC.

Bergin, Paul, Robert Feenstra, and Gordon Hanson. 2006. "Outsourcing and Volatility." University of California.

Betcherman, Gordon, Karina Olivas, and Amit Dar. 2004. "Impacts of Active Labor Market Programs: New Evidence from Evaluations with Particular Attention to Developing and Transition Economies." Social Protection Discussion Paper Series, World Bank, Washington, DC. January.

Bhagwati, Jagdish, Arvind Panagariya, and T. N. Srinivasan. 2004. "The Muddles over Outsourcing." Journal of Economic Perspectives 18: 93–114.

Bhorat, Haroon, and Paul Lundall. 2004. Employment and Labour Market Effects of Globalization: Selected Issues for Policy Management. Employment Strategy Papers No. 2004/3, ILO, Geneva.

Blinder, Alan. 2006. "Offshoring: The Next Industrial Revolution?" Foreign Affairs 85(2): 113–28.

Borjas, George. 2003. "The Labor Demand Curve Is Downward Sloping: Reexamining the Impact of Immigration on the Labor Market." Quarterly Journal of Economics 118(4): 1335–74.

Borjas, George, Richard Freeman, and Lawrence Katz. 1997. "How Much Do Immigration and Trade Affect Labor Market Outcomes?" Brookings Papers on Economic Activity 1: 1–90, Washington, DC.

Bravo-Ortega, Claudio, and Daniel Lederman. 2006. "The Effect of Chinese and Indian Patenting

Activity on Latin America's Patent Counts: Estimating the Effects of Cumulative Learning and Contemporaneous Patent Tournaments." Background paper for the Office of the Chief Economist for Latin America and the Caribbean Regional Study: "Latin America and the Caribbean Respond to the Growth of China and India." World Bank, Washington, DC.

Brenton, Paul. 2006. "Adjusting to Globalisation: Policy Responses in Europe and the US." In *Globalisation and the Labour Market: Trade, Technology and Less-Skilled Workers in Europe and the United States*, ed. Robert Anderton, Paul Brenton, and John Whalley. London and New York: Routledge.

Brofenbrenner, Kate, and Stephanie Luce. 2004. "The Changing Nature of Corporate Global Restructuring: The Impact of Production Shifts on Jobs in the US, China and Around the Globe." Washington, DC: US-China Economic and Security Review Commission.

Brown, D., A. Deardorff, and R. Stern. 2002. "The Effects of Multinational Production on Wages and Working Conditions in Developing Countries." In *Challenges to Globalization*, ed. Robert Baldwin and L. Alan Winters. Chicago: University of Chicago Press.

Card, David. 2005. "Is the New Immigration Really So Bad?" NBER Working Paper No. 11547, National Bureau of Economic Research, Cambridge, MA.

Cline, William. 2006. "Exports of Manufactures and Economic Growth: The Fallacy of Composition Revisited." Institute for International Economics, Washington, DC.

Cortes, Patricia. 2005. "The Effect of Low-skilled Immigration on US Prices: Evidence from CPI Data." Massachusetts Institute of Technology, Cambridge, MA.

Cravino, Javier, Daniel Lederman, and Larcelo Olarreaga. 2006. "Substitution between Foreign Capital in China, India and the Rest of the World: Much Ado about Nothing?" Background paper for the Office of the Chief Economist for Latin America and the Caribbean Regional Study, "Latin America and the Caribbean Respond to the Growth of China and India," World Bank, Washington, DC.

Criscuolo, Chiara, Jonathan Haskel, and Matthew Slaughter. 2004. "Why Are Some Firms More Innovative? Knowledge Inputs, Knowledge Stocks and the Role of Global Engagement." University College London.

Dar, Amit, and P. Zafiris Tzannatos. 1999. "Active Labor Market Programs: A Review of the Evidence from Evaluations." Social Protection Discussion Paper No. 9901, World Bank, Washington, DC. January.

de Ferranti, David, Guillermo Perry, Indermit Gill, and Luis Servén. 2000. *Securing Our Future in a Global Economy*. Washington, DC: Latin American and Caribbean Studies, World Bank.

de Ferranti, David, Guillermo Perry, Daniel Lederman, and William Maloney. 2002. *From Natural Resources to the Knowledge Economy: Trade and Job Quality*. Washington, DC: Latin American and Caribbean Studies, World Bank.

de Mello, Luiz, and Mombert Hoppe. 2005. "Education Attainment in Brazil: The Experience of FUNDEF." OECD Economics Department Working Papers No. 424, OECD, Paris.

Dehejia, Vivuk, and Yiagadeesen Samy. 2002. "Trade and Labour Standards—Theory, New Empirical Evidence and Policy Implications." CESifo Working Paper No. 830, December.

Edwards, L. 1999. "Trade Liberalization, Structural Change and Occupational Employment in South Africa." Paper presented at the Trade and Industrial Policy Secretariat (TIPS) Annual Forum, Muldersdrift, September 19–22.

Eifert, Ben, Alan Gelb, and Vijaya Ramachandran. 2005. "The Business Environment and Comparative Advantage in Africa: Evidence from Investment Climate Data." Paper presented at the 17th Annual World Bank Conference on Development Economics (ABCDE), January 27, Dakar, Senegal.

Fajnzylber, Pablo, and William F. Maloney. 2005. "Labor Demand and Trade Reform in Latin America." *Journal of International Economics* 66: 423–46.

Feenstra, Robert, and Gordon Hanson. 2003. "Global Production Sharing and Rising Inequality: A Survey of Trade and Wages." In *Handbook of International Trade*, ed. E. K. Choi and J. Harrigan. Blackwell Publishing.

Forrester Research. 2002. "3.3 Million US Services Jobs to Go Offshore." Cambridge, MA.

Fox, L., G. Betcherman, V. Chandra, B. Eifert, and A. Van Adams. 2004. "Realizing the Potential of the Labor Force in Africa: Barriers and Opportunities." World Bank, Washington, DC.

Freeman, Richard. 2005. "The Great Doubling: Labor in the New Global Economy." Harvard University, Cambridge, MA.

_____. 2006. "Labor Market Imbalance: Shortages, or Surpluses, or Fish Stories?" Paper presented at Boston Federal Reserve Economic Conference, "Global Imbalances—As Giants Evolve," Chatham, MA.

Friedman, Thomas L. 2005. *The World Is Flat: A Brief History of the Twenty-First Century*. New York: Farrar, Straus and Giroux.

Geroski, P. A. 1990. "Innovation, Technological Opportunity, and Market Structure." *Oxford Economic Papers* 42(3): 586–602.

Ghose, Ajit K. 2003. *Jobs and Incomes in a Globalizing World*. Geneva: International Labour Office.

Grossman, G., and E. Rossi-Hansberg. 2006. "The Rise of Offshoring: It's Not Wine for Cloth Anymore." Princeton University, Princeton, New Jersey.

Hall, Robert, and Charles Jones. 1999. "Why Do Some Countries Produce So Much More Output per Worker Than Others?" *Quarterly Journal of Economics* 114: 83–116.

Hasan, Rana, Devashish Mitra, and K. V. Ramaswamy. 2003. "Trade Reforms, Labor Regulations, and Labor-Demand Elasticities: Empirical Evidence from India." East-West Center Working Papers No. 59. Honolulu, Hawaii.

Heckman, James, and Carmen Pagés. 2000. "The Cost of Job Security Regulation: Evidence from Latin American Labor Markets." NBER Working Paper No. 7773, National Bureau of Economic Research, Cambridge, MA.

Helpman, Elhanan. 2004. *The Mystery of Economic Growth*. Cambridge, MA: Harvard University Press.

Hoekman, Bernard, and Beata S. Javorcik. 2006. "Lessons from Empirical Research on International Technology Diffusion through Trade and Foreign Direct Investment." In *Global Integration and Technology Transfer*, ed. Hoekman and Javorcik. Washington, DC: World Bank.

Hoekman, Bernard, and L. Alan Winters. 2005. "Trade and Employment: Stylized Facts and Research Findings." Mimeo.

ILO (International Labour Office). 1998. *Labor and Social Issues Relating to Export Processing Zones*. Geneva: ILO.

———. 2004. *A Fair Globalization: Creating Opportunities for All: Report of the World Commission on the Social Dimension of Globalization*. Geneva: ILO.

———. 2006. *Competing for Global Talent*. Geneva: ILO.

Iversen, Torben, and Thomas Cusack. 2000. "The Causes of Welfare State Expansion." *World Politics* 52: 313–49.

Jaumotte, Florence, and Nigel Pain. 2005. "An Overview of Public Policies to Support Innovation." OECD Economics Department Working Papers No. 456, OECD, Paris.

Jensen, J. Bradford, and Lori Kletzer. 2005. "Tradable Services: Understanding the Scope and Impact of Services Outsourcing." IIE Working Paper Series No. WP05-9, Institute for International Economics, Washington, DC.

Joskow, P. L. 1987. "Contract Duration and Relationship-Specific Investments: Empirical Evidence from Coal Markets." *American Economic Review* 77: 168–85.

Kanter, James. 2006. "EU Fund to Ease Globalization Pain." Reprinted from *The International Herald Tribune*, March 2, 2006, available at Yale Global Online (http://yaleglobal.edu).

Katz, Larry F., and David H. Autor. 1999. "Changes in the Wage Structure and Earnings Inequality." In *Handbook of Labor Economics*, Vol. 3A, ed. Orley C Ashenfelter and David Card. Amsterdam: Elsevier.

Kirkegaard, Jacob Funk. 2005. "Outsourcing and Offshoring: Pushing the European Model Over the Hill, Rather than Off the Cliff!" IIE Working Paper Series No. WP05-1, Institute for International Economics, Washington, DC.

Kletzer, Lori. 2001. "A Prescription to Relieve Worker Anxiety." Institute for International Economics Policy Brief No. 01-2, Institute for International Economics, Washington, DC.

Krishna, Pravin, Devashish Mitra, and Sajjid Chinoy. 2001. 'Trade Liberalization and Labor Demand Elasticities: Evidence from Turkey." *Journal of International Economics* 55: 391–409.

Krugman, Paul. 1995. "Technology, Trade and Factor Prices." NBER Working Paper No. 5355, National Bureau of Economic Research, Cambridge, MA.

Kuhn, P. J., ed. 2002. "Losing Work, Moving On." W. E. Upjohn Institute for Employment Research, Kalamazoo, MI.

Lardy, Nicholas. 2004. "Do China's Abusive Labor Practices Encourage Outsourcing and Drive Down American Wages?" Senate Democratic Policy Committee Hearing, March 29. Available at www.iie.org.

Leamer, E. 2006. "A Flat World, A Level Playing Field, a Small World After All, or None of the Above?" Forthcoming in *Journal of Economic Literature*.

Lederman, Daniel, Marcelo Olarreaga, and Isidro Soloaga. 2006. "The Growth of China and India in World Markets: Opportunity or Threat for Latin American Exporters?" Background paper for the Office of the Chief Economist for Latin America and the Caribbean Regional Study, "Latin America and the Caribbean Respond to the Growth of China and India." World Bank, Washington, DC.

Majid, Normaan. 2004. "What Is the Effect of Trade Openness on Wages?" Employment Strategy Papers No. 2004/18, Employment Analysis Unit, ILO, Geneva.

Martin, J. 2000. "What Works among Active Labour Market Policies: Evidence from OECD Countries'

Experiences." *OECD Economic Studies*, No. 30. OECD, Paris.

Moran, Theodore. 2004. "Trade Agreements and Labor Standards." The Brookings Institution Policy Brief No. 133, available at www.brookings.edu.

Nolting, Louvan, and Murray Feshbach. 1980. "R and D Employment in the USSR." *Science* 207 (Feb. 1): 493–503.

Nunn, Nathan. 2005. "Relationship Specificity, Incomplete Contracts and the Pattern of Trade." University of British Columbia. Forthcoming in *Quarterly Journal of Economics*.

OECD. 1996. *Trade, Employment and Labour Standards: A Study of Core Workers' Rights and International Trade*. Paris: OECD.

_____. 2000a. *International Trade and Core Labour Standards*. Paris: OECD.

_____. 2000b. *Policy Competition and Foreign Direct Investment: A Study of Competition among Governments to Attract FDI*. Paris: OECD Development Centre Studies.

_____. 2004. *OECD Employment Outlook*. Paris: OECD.

_____. 2005a. "The Impact of Structural Policies on Trade-Related Adjustment and the Shift to Services." Economics Department Working Papers No. 427, OECD, Paris.

_____. 2005b. *Trade and Structural Adjustment: Embracing Globalization*. Paris: OECD.

_____. 2005c. "The Share of Employment Potentially Affected by Offshoring—An Empirical Investigation." Working Party on the Information Economy, DSTI/ICCP/IE(2005)8/FINAL.

_____. 2005d. *OECD Employment Outlook*. Paris: OECD.

Ottaviano, Gianmarco, and Giovanni Peri. 2005. "Rethinking the Gains from Immigration: Theory and Evidence from the US." NBER Working Paper No. 11672, National Bureau of Economic Research, Cambridge, MA.

Oxfam. 2004. "Stitched Up: How Rich-Country Protectionism in Textiles and Clothing Trade Prevents Poverty Alleviation." Briefing Paper No. 60, Oxfam, U.K. Available at http://www.oxfam.org.uk/what_we_do/issues/trade/downloads/bp60_textiles.pdf.

Perry, Guillermo, and Marcelo Olarreaga. 2006. "Trade Liberalization, Inequality and Poverty Reduction in Latin America." Paper presented at the Annual World Bank Conference on Development Economics (ABCDE) 2006.

Puga, Diego, and Daniel Trefler. 2005. "Wake Up and Smell the Ginseng: The Rise of Incremental Innovation in Low-Wage Countries." Department of

Economics Working Papers tepica-193, University of Toronto, Ontario.

Rama, Martin. 2003. *Globalization and Workers in Developing Countries*. World Bank Policy Research Working Paper No. 2958, Washington, DC. January.

Raynauld, André, and Jean-Pierre Vidal. 1998. *Labor Standards and International Competitiveness: A Comparative Analysis of Developing and Industrialized Countries*. Cheltenham, U.K. and Northampton, MA: Edward Elgar.

Reinecke, G., and R. Torres. 2001. *Studies in the Social Dimension of Globalization: Chile*. Geneva: International Labour Office.

Robbins, Donald. 1997. "Trade and Wages in Colombia." *Estudios de Economia* 24(1): 47–83.

Rodrik, Dani. 1996. "Labor Standards in International Trade: Do They Matter and What Do We Do about Them?" In *Emerging Agenda for Global Trade: High Stakes for Developing Countries*, Overseas Development Council Essay No. 20, ed. R. Z. Lawrence, D. Rodrik, and J. Whalley. Washington, DC: John Hopkins University Press.

_____. 1997. *Has Globalization Gone Too Far?* Washington, DC: Institute for International Economics.

Sapir, André. 2005. "Globalization and the Reform of European Social Models." Background document for the presentation at ECOFIN Informal Meeting in Manchester, U.K., September 9.

Scheve, Kenneth, and Matthew Slaughter. 2002. "Economic Insecurity and the Globalization of Production." NBER Working Paper No. 9339, National Bureau of Economic Research, Cambridge, MA.

Slaughter, Matthew J. 2001. "International Trade and Labor-Demand Elasticities." *Journal of International Economics* 54: 27–56.

Spencer, Barbara, and Larry Qui. 2001. "Keiretsu and Relationship-Specific Investment: A Barrier to Trade?" *International Economic Review* 42: 871–901.

Stern, Robert M. 2003. "Labour Standards and Trade Agreements." RSIE Discussion Paper No. 496, available at www.spp.umich.edu.

Stiglitz, J. 2000. "Democratic Development as the Fruits of Labor." Keynote Address, Industrial Relations Research Associations, Boston, January.

Trefler, Daniel. 2005. "Offshoring: Threats and Opportunities." Paper presented at the Brookings Trade Forum, May, Washington, DC.

UNCTAD (United Nations Conference of Trade and Development). 2004. *India's Outward FDI: A Giant Awakening?* UNCTAD/DITE/IIAB/2004/1. New York and Geneva: United Nations.

_____. 2005. *World Investment Report: Transnational Corporations and the Internationalization of R&D*. New York and Geneva: United Nations.

Wood, Adrian. 1997. "Openness and Wage Inequality in Developing Countries: The Latin American Challenge to East Asian Conventional Wisdom." *World Bank Economic Review* 11(1): 33–58.

World Bank. 2002. *Globalization, Growth, and Poverty: Building an Inclusive World Economy*. Washington, DC: World Bank.

_____. 2003. *Lifelong Learning in the Global Economy: Challenges for Developing Countries*. Washington, DC: World Bank.

_____. 2005. "Workers and Labor Markets." In *World Development Report 2005*. Washington, DC: World Bank.

_____. 2006. *World Development Report: Equity and Development*. Washington, DC: World Bank.

Yusuf, Shahid, Kaoru Nabeshima, and Dwight Perkins. 2006. "China and India Reshape Global Industrial Geography." In *Dancing with Giants: China, India, and the Global Economy*, ed. L. Alan Winters and Shahid Yusuf. Washington, DC and Singapore: World Bank and the Institute of Policy Studies.

5

Managing the Environmental Risks to Growth

The gains from growth and globalization could be undermined by their environmental side effects. Because increases in production magnify cross-border pollution, while improvements in technology make it possible to expand or intensify the exploitation of scarce global resources, decisions at the national level are having a growing impact on other countries. International institutions will thus be required to play a larger role in a wide spectrum of issues—all involving global public goods—where exclusive reliance on the decisions of individual governments or the private market can lead to adverse outcomes. Such goods include maintaining global security, keeping the trading system open and nondiscriminatory, and ensuring global financial stability. As developing countries enlarge their role on the global stage, their integration as full partners in multilateral solutions to global problems will be essential.

Mitigating climate change, containing infectious diseases, and preserving marine fisheries are three additional global public goods that demonstrate the need for—and benefits of—international policy cooperation. Rising industrial output means increasing concentrations of greenhouse gases in the atmosphere, which will have detrimental effects on future productivity and—more generally—on human welfare around the globe. Even in the next decade or two, scientists underscore the (unlikely) possibility that global warming could cause natural disruptions severe enough

to depress growth rates below the low-growth scenario presented here. It is more likely that decades will pass before the most severe effects of climate change begin to be felt. Even so, the collective response of today's global leaders is almost certain to have far-reaching implications for the welfare of future generations.

Technological progress and rising demand have increased efforts to harvest fish from the open seas, degrading ocean environments and driving some valuable species to near-extinction. Longstanding efforts to limit marine catches to sustainable levels have met with only a few successes. Why? Because institutional weaknesses, technical difficulties, and fishing subsidies impede sustainable management.

The growing interaction of national economies through trade and movements of people, while broadly beneficial, has increased the risk of spreading contagious diseases. HIV/AIDS (human immunodeficiency virus/acquired immune deficiency syndrome) is one example. The severe acute respiratory syndrome (SARS) is another. The most prominent current threat is the avian influenza virus.

These examples of the side effects of globalization—one long-term, one medium-term, and one immediate—pose risks to the progressive expansion of the global economy, and to developing countries in particular. Some of the more catastrophic climate-change scenarios, if they materialize, could undermine the development prospects of whole countries and even regions through their effects on agriculture, water, and ecosystems. Similarly, failure to contain an epidemic could bring global commerce to a sudden halt, isolate some populations, and impose huge losses on affected developing countries. Unrestrained marine fishing, while less potentially calamitous than climate change or a flu pandemic, could permanently exhaust a critical global food source and destroy irreplaceable deep-sea habitats and biodiversity.

Effective multilateral collaboration is needed to ensure that economic growth and poverty reduction will proceed without causing irreparable harm to future generations. Developing countries are central to the management of these risks. Although these countries are relatively small contributors to global warming today, the projections in chapter 2 imply that they will soon enough become large contributors to global warming. And if no action is taken, the standard of living that they could otherwise expect may well be put at risk. Given the limited supply of medical facilities and nursing care in the developing world, a flu pandemic could have horrific consequences. In many developing countries, people depend on fish for an important share of their diet, and the poor would suffer if the price of fish, as well as substitutes, were to skyrocket as supplies dwindled.

The degree of international coordination required varies greatly from issue to issue, depending on the nature of the issue and the geographical spread of its causes and effects (table 5.1). The need for international coordination falls with the degree to which an individual country can benefit from its own efforts to provide the good (or mitigate the evil), and rises with the number of countries involved (Barrett 2004). For example, the U.S.-Canadian agreement on reducing acid rain was facilitated in part because only two countries had to agree and because each country gained an important benefit from its own efforts to reduce pollution. By contrast—as shown below—negotiations over climate change are intractable in part because even

though every country will be affected, there is little systematic relationship between the size of most countries' efforts to reduce carbon emissions and the damage these countries experience from climate change.

Ensuring that developing countries reap the benefits from global public goods is particularly difficult. Developing countries typically account for a small share of international transactions, so they often lack the clout to ensure that decisions made in international fora adequately reflect their interests. Many developing countries lack the financial and technical resources to participate effectively in international negotiations on many issues. For example, the simultaneous negotiations on a variety of critical environmental issues forces governments with inadequate resources to limit their participation (Esty and Ivanova 2002). Developing countries also lack the resources required to effectively address many common problems. For example, malaria kills millions in developing countries, but research on pertinent vaccines is limited, although some efforts are now under way.

While the three cases spotlighted here differ in the agreement on the extent of risks, there is a sufficient scientific consensus to move forward on all of them. The needs and the methods to protect against the spread of (selected) contagious diseases are well known, although the efficacy of particular strategies (quarantine, stockpiling of available vaccinations) in limiting the spread of avian flu is in dispute. The overexploitation of marine fish stocks is well understood, although disagreement remains on the amount of resources to commit, the limits on fishing to impose, and how to allocate access to fisheries. There is an international consensus that human activity is contributing to climate change, but the precise implications of different levels of greenhouse gas concentrations for climate change remain uncertain. While disagreements over the facts of each case have affected efforts at international cooperation, they have not been the major impediment to progress. In reviewing the state of knowledge in each area, this chapter

Table 5.1 Progress in providing many global public goods is limited

Examples of global public goods

Good	Role of developing countries	Progress of international efforts
Global commons		
Climate change	Limited current contributors, but major future source, of carbon emissions; potentially disastrous impact on many countries	Current mitigation efforts insufficient to stabilize global temperature
Biodiversity and ecosystems	Main reservoir of many species	Rate of species extinction rising; tropical forest cover declining
Water resources	Over 600 million people face acute freshwater shortage	Little international effort beyond increasing awareness; 2–3 billion people may face severe freshwater shortage by 2020
Fisheries	Many countries dependent on ocean fisheries for exports and domestic consumption	75 percent of commercial fish stocks exploited at or above sustainable levels
Human issues		
Infectious diseases	Developing countries could suffer severe losses in a global flu pandemic; already suffer millions of deaths from tropical diseases	Flu pandemic avoided (for now); limited progress in containing malaria, measles, AIDS in developing countries
Peacekeeping	Millions killed in civil wars and intercountry conflicts	Some interventions successful (Kosovo in the Republic of Serbia); others less so (Sierra Leone)
Poverty	1 billion people living on less than $1 a day	Asia expected to see continuing decline in people living in extreme poverty; Africa likely to see rise
Regulatory framework		
Trade	Developing countries account for 27 percent of global merchandise exports; goods and services exports represent 33 percent of developing countries' gross domestic product	Trade rules effective, but limited progress on removing trade barriers critical to developing countries
Financial architecture	Total fiscal costs of systemic crises in developing countries since 1975 exceeds $1 trillion	Crisis interventions have mixed success; little change in global rules that would dampen volatility

Sources: Rischard 2002; World Bank, World Development Indicators; Honohan and Laeven 2005.

discusses some of the key economic issues that constrain or support effective action to protect the environment and sustain growth.

The immediate risk of epidemics

Globalization has increased the volume and speed of cross-border transactions, thus increasing the potential for the transmission of contagious diseases. The international transmission of disease is nothing new.[1] But air travel and international contacts have greatly accelerated its potential speed. Over the next quarter-century the global economy will continue to be at risk of sharp downturns from disruptions caused by contagious diseases. For example, a human flu pandemic similar to the 1918 Spanish flu could reduce global GDP by 3 percent over a one-year period, with the more severe effects (in percentage terms) felt in developing countries (World Bank 2006).

The potential for a devastating global outbreak of contagious disease underscores the importance of international cooperation. Individuals benefit directly from access to vaccination, and individual countries benefit from controlling disease within their borders—both benefits reduce the role that international institutions must play. Nevertheless, other countries do have a critical interest in containing disease, as containment reduces the probability of further transmission. Measures by individual countries to contain infectious disease may be insufficient from a global perspective, in part because individual countries may lack the resources to take all measures that the international community might consider prudent. And the supply of informational goods—for example, research on vaccines and knowledge of treatment and quarantine procedures—is likely to be impaired in the absence of effective international cooperation. This section discusses these issues in the context of the recent SARS epidemic and the potential for an avian flu pandemic.

SARS was a case study in virus proliferation and containment

Five months after initial reports from East Asia (in February 2003) of an atypical respiratory disease, more than 8,000 cases had been reported in close to 30 countries.[2] The disease, labeled SARS, was highly contagious and life threatening: almost 10 percent of reported cases ended with the patient dying.

The global response to the rapidly spreading disease was swift and determined. Many countries—whether they had reported SARS cases or not—designated special treatment centers ("SARS hospitals") and put in place quarantine procedures. In some of the places most severely hit, the measures were very strict. Hong Kong (China) imposed restrictions on peoples' movement between city districts, and Singapore used TV surveillance and radio bracelets to monitor and control the movements of persons who had come in contact with SARS patients and of patients discharged from SARS hospitals. The World Health Organization (WHO) collected and disseminated up-to-date information on the development of the disease and how to respond, and coordinated scientific efforts to control and identify the virus causing the sickness. Given the crucial role of air traffic in the spread of SARS between countries and continents, WHO issued the first emergency travel advisory in its history. Travel bans were imposed for major affected areas in April 2003 (Bell and Lewis 2004).

The combined efforts by local, national, and international authorities to contain the threatening pandemic were successful: newly reported cases, which increased rapidly in March and April of 2003, peaked in early May and thereafter declined rapidly (figure 5.1). Although no cure has yet been found

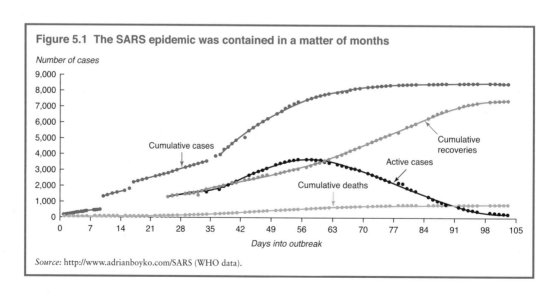

Figure 5.1 The SARS epidemic was contained in a matter of months

Number of cases

Days into outbreak

Source: http://www.adrianboyko.com/SARS (WHO data).

for the disease, it was successfully contained by late 2004, and no new cases have been reported since 2005. The containment of SARS was facilitated by the fact that the disease is less transmissible than some influenzas experienced in the past. The SARS experience highlights the role of the technological developments and rapid communications that promote globalization both in speeding the spread of contagious diseases and in providing the tools to combat them.

Has the risk of avian flu been contained?

The virus causing avian flu (H5N1) affects primarily birds, although cases of human infection, recorded since 1997, have increased significantly since 2003, while remaining low. An outbreak of avian flu through human-to-human transmission could have catastrophic implications for welfare, particularly in developing countries where public health systems are weak, and could result in a sharp, short-term interruption in global growth.

Possible pandemic. The avian flu is a subject of great concern principally because more than half of all infected persons have died from the disease, and flu viruses have the potential to mutate into a form that is easily transmitted between humans (the "Spanish flu" pandemic of 1918–19 killed up to 50 million people). The rapid expansion of the poultry population, and in particular the close proximity between humans and animals in East Asia, has increased the likelihood that such a mutation may occur.[3] And if it does, the greatly increased speed and scope of human travel would facilitate a rapid spread of the disease worldwide. WHO projections reckon that the mutation of the avian flu virus permitting human-to-human transmission would, under best-case scenarios, entail the spread of the disease among humans across all continents (WHO 2005). Other estimates that assume a more virulent virus involve much higher numbers of deaths.

Prevention and countermeasures. Alternative measures of preventing or responding to an outbreak have been discussed widely at both the national and international level (WHO 2006; CDC 2004; Osterholm 2005; Sturm-Ramirez 2006). A large number of actions to address a potential avian flu pandemic can be envisaged:

- Reducing the incidence of avian flu in birds would reduce the probability of human infection. Effective systems to monitor flocks is required, coupled with compensation for damage if birds have to be slaughtered, and punishment for failure to report, as otherwise breeders are likely to conceal incidences of the disease in their flock. There also is a need to regulate bird breeding and marketing methods that facilitate the occurrence or spread of the disease.

- Developing a vaccine that is certain to be effective is impossible, given present knowledge, because the form of the future mutation of the virus is unknown. There is hope among researchers that it may be possible to develop flu vaccines that will be effective against whole classes of flu viruses, including future mutations. Many experts argue that the likely success rate from the use of existing vaccines is sufficiently high to make stockpiling vaccines a key ingredient in a comprehensive response strategy.

- An effective surveillance system will be essential to detect and report cases—even suspected cases—before they have a chance to spread. The SARS episode showed how important early detection can be for an effective containment strategy.

- Steps to treat victims and contain the disease may range from administering appropriate medicines to implementing quarantine procedures for contagious patients. It is uncertain whether current antiviral drugs would be effective against a future mutation of the avian flu virus. Even so, many experts argue that existing antiviral drugs are sufficiently likely to be effective to justify stockpiling them as part of any response strategy.

- Should both prevention and containment in the early stage of the disease fail, trade and travel restrictions, quarantine procedures, the transformation of existing buildings into emergency hospitals, and general efforts to deal with the multitude of disruptions accompanying any such catastrophe would be required.

Avian flu threat receding. At this writing there are encouraging reports that the avian influenza is indeed in retreat. New cases are rarely reported, and the countries where the most human infections have occurred (Vietnam, Thailand, and China) report that cases observed in both poultry and humans have declined steeply.[4] Officials of WHO and the World Organisation for Animal Health (OIE) credit countries' aggressive countermeasures for the apparent success in getting the disease under control. Global communications and cooperation clarified the risks, publicized advanced methods to contain it, and induced valuable international cooperation at various levels. Virtual unanimity among national administrations on the need to act rapidly enabled WHO and OIE to implement appropriate supranational measures without delay. Nevertheless, these efforts have failed to prevent the disease from becoming fully endemic in several countries, and reducing the scope of the disease remains a high priority to limit the risk of another flu pandemic.

Global cooperation may prevent contagion

The success of international efforts to contain infectious disease is in part rooted in the nature of the problem. The threat of a global pandemic is immediate, well understood, and potentially catastrophic for the industrial countries that have the resources to act. In addition, while international cooperation has played a critical role in reacting to SARS and avian flu, individuals and individual governments have been willing to make major,

independent efforts because they benefited directly, thus reducing the burden on international cooperation. Contrast this (so far) success story with the failure to eradicate other endemic diseases.[5] The burden of infectious diseases is greatest for developing countries, which often lack the resources to effectively distribute vaccines and treatments. Would these diseases still be so prevalent if industrial countries continued to be vulnerable to them?

The medium-term risks to marine fisheries

Marine fishing, on the high seas and within many nations' 200-nautical-mile exclusive economic zone (EEZ), is reaching its limits. Increased demand and technological improvements have led to increasing pressures on marine fish, as well as on the fragile ecosystems in which they live.[6] Excluding data from China, the accuracy of which has been questioned, production has declined since about 1990 (FAO 2004 and figure 5.2). The acceleration of global growth envisioned in chapter 2 is likely to increase pressures on marine fisheries over the medium term. Without efforts at conservation, the global economy is likely to confront dwindling supplies of commercially exploited marine fish, coupled with rising demand for fish with growing incomes.

Marine fish are under increasing pressure

A significant number of the world's most valuable fish stocks have been depleted through overfishing, habitat degradation, pollution, or other causes (Bolton 2005). Fully 75 percent of the world's marine fish stocks are being exploited either at or above their maximum sustainable level (FAO 2004). While reductions in fish stocks from fishing are not new, they have accelerated over the past few decades owing to technological advances that have enabled large-scale commercial fishing fleets to increase their exploitation of traditional waters and expand to new areas

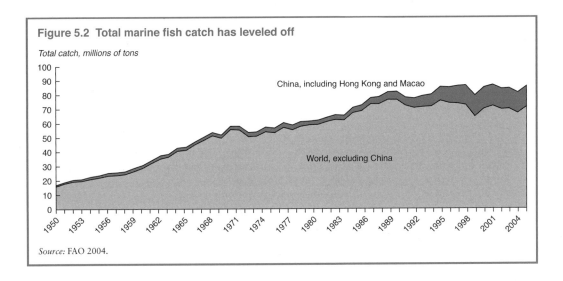

Figure 5.2 Total marine fish catch has leveled off

Total catch, millions of tons

Source: FAO 2004.

in the Indian Ocean and the seas around Antarctica.[7] And improvements in fishing gear and onboard storage technology have made new species commercially viable (Kura and others 2005). Natural phenomena, for example the impact of El Niño on Chilean and Peruvian fisheries and of warmer water in the North Atlantic on North Sea cod, have contributed to the reduction in fish stocks (Schmidt 2002). Climate change (discussed below) will increase the acidity of the ocean as increasing amounts of carbon dioxide dissolve in sea water, with potentially serious implications for ocean environments and the sustainability of some fish species (U.K. Government 2006). And some deep-sea fish are particularly vulnerable to overfishing owing to their long lives and few offspring (Shotton 2006). Subsidies, estimated globally at between $12 and $20 billion a year, have also contributed to overexploitation of fish resources (Milazzo 1998; APEC 2000; WWF 2001).[8]

Managing high-seas fisheries is not easy

The UN Convention on the Law of the Seas (effective in 1994) helped define property rights by enabling coastal states to establish EEZs of up to 200 miles.[9] The UN Agreement for the Conservation and Management of Straddling Fish Stocks and Highly Migratory Fish Stocks, called the UN Fish Stock Agreement (effective in 2001), established basic standards for fisheries management for highly migratory species, such as tuna, and for so-called straddling stocks—species that range between EEZs and the high seas (Lodge 2005). But high-seas bottom-dwelling species are in a jurisdictional vacuum. Few of the regional fisheries management organizations are mandated to manage bottom fishing on the high seas (Gianni 2004), and most of these fisheries should be considered unregulated (FAO 2004). Even when a mandate exists, the regional fisheries management organizations established for this purpose often suffer from inadequate resources or insufficient political support, and face several important obstacles:

- Data on catch volume and area, the number and size of fish, the number of juveniles that develop to maturity, interactions with other species, and the impact of environmental factors are often inadequate to define sustainable catches (Kura and others 2005). Overall, estimates of fish stocks may be off by as much as 30 percent (Berrill 1997), and single-species stock assessments have failed to predict rapid stock declines in a number of cases (Pauly and others 2002).

- It can be difficult to set limits on fish catch that impose the right incentives. The allocation of licenses, the most common system for controlling fish effort (Cunningham and Greboval 2001), can be thwarted by expanding the capacity of individual boats or improving technology. Limits on the total catch (at which point a fishery is closed) can result in the harvest being caught more rapidly and using more resources than would be the case if quotas were allocated to individual fishers (difficult for regional fisheries management organizations, though it is done in areas controlled by single countries), and may encourage more dangerous fishing, such as during inclement weather (Kura and others 2005).[10]

- Monitoring and enforcing limits on fishing can be problematic, because fishers understandably are reluctant to provide information that can affect their competitiveness (Shotton 2006). Some fishers report data to national authorities under confidentiality agreements that prohibit release to international authorities.

- Fishers can attempt to evade enforcement of conservation measures by registering under a flag of convenience (with countries that exercise little control over their ships); at least 2,800 large fishing vessels either have a flag of convenience or no registry at all (WWF 2001).

Developing countries are particularly vulnerable

Developing countries, important participants in large-scale commercial fishing, confront particular weaknesses in managing fishery resources. In 2001, 6 of the top 10 marine fishing nations were from the developing world, with China and Peru (numbers 1 and 2) alone accounting for more than a quarter of total marine capture in metric tons. Developing countries also account for the vast majority

of the increased trade in highly migratory species since the late 1970s (Webster 2006).[11] About 250 million people in developing countries depend directly on the fishing sector (including inland fishing) for food and income, and fish provide nearly 20 percent of animal protein consumed by people in developing countries (World Bank 2004).

Many developing countries lack the resources to police their own coastal waters and economic zone, much less establish effective regional institutions to manage nearby marine fisheries. The expansion of distant-water fishing fleets to new, mostly unregulated areas has spawned conflicts with traditional fishers in the poorer developing countries, while largely uncontrolled fishing has led to the depletion of valuable fishery resources in the southern seas—for example, the sharp decline in orange roughy and in Patagonian toothfish (Chilean sea bass), as worldwide demand for them increased. While some developing countries earn significant foreign exchange by selling fishing rights in their waters (several West African nations without significant industrial fleets have done so), this practice has intensified competition for small-scale fishers (Kura and others 2005).[12] Fish resources in the shallow waters off the west coast of Africa may have declined by half from 1985–90 because of distant-water fleets.

International cooperation aims to ensure sustainable fishing

There is a global consensus, expressed at the World Summit on Sustainable Development in Johannesburg in 2002, that depleted fish stocks should be restored to levels that can produce their maximum sustainable yield by 2015. Progress has been considerable in setting the institutional framework for conserving the ocean's fish, both through defining ownership rights (setting an EEZ of 200 miles) and in setting up multilateral institutions (regional fisheries management organizations). Effective management plans have been implemented for a few highly migratory fish stocks, for example the North Atlantic swordfish and Atlantic bigeye tuna (Webster 2006). Still, most commercially exploited marine fish species face increasing pressures. Regional management is clearly inadequate in many fisheries. And further uncontrolled exploitation could lead to the irretrievable loss of valuable sources of the world's food. A further strengthening of domestic and multilateral institutions, particularly the regional fisheries management organizations, is a high priority for international action.

The long-term risk of climate change

Climate change induced by carbon emissions already has had significant impacts on the global environment, and continuing emissions at current levels are likely to have severe implications for human welfare over the long term. The threat of climate change is inextricably linked with the scenario for global growth over the next 25 years, because there is a risk that climate change could accelerate, entailing greater-than-expected near-term

consequences for growth. Moreover, the approach adopted to reducing carbon emissions could entail costs to growth, particularly if political constraints prevent the adoption of efficient policies. Developing countries, at the center of this issue, are likely to suffer the worst consequences of climate change and have the least ability to adapt. They also are the largest future source of additions to carbon emissions, and thus will have an important role in negotiations to limit emissions.

Global temperatures are rising

The burning of fossil fuels produces gases that trap incoming solar radiation, leading to a rise in global average surface temperature.[13] Measurements show that the average world temperature has increased since the start of the Industrial Revolution (figure 5.3). Models of the determinants of temperature change that take into account the addition of greenhouse gases (GHGs) into the atmosphere from human activities (second panel of figure 5.4) provide much more accurate explanations of historical trends in temperature than models

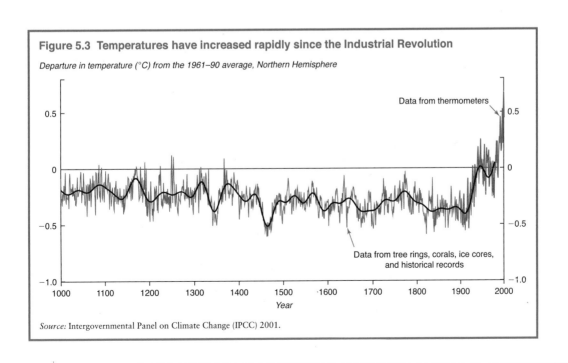

Figure 5.3 Temperatures have increased rapidly since the Industrial Revolution

Departure in temperature (°C) from the 1961–90 average, Northern Hemisphere

Source: Intergovernmental Panel on Climate Change (IPCC) 2001.

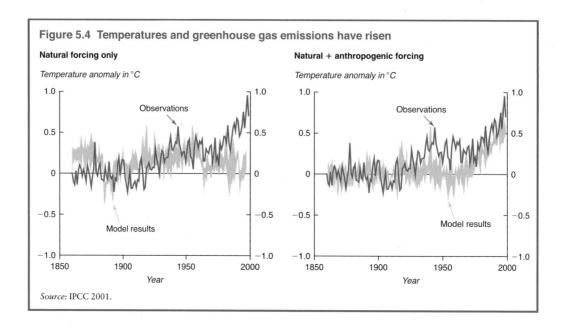

Figure 5.4 Temperatures and greenhouse gas emissions have risen

Source: IPCC 2001.

that ignore this addition (first panel of figure 5.4). There is general agreement that human activity has contributed to the rise in GHG concentrations and climate change since the start of the Industrial Revolution.

Climate change, while generally viewed as a long-term problem, has already had significant effects. Ice coverage has declined at the two poles (box 5.1), mountain glaciers are retreating worldwide, ocean temperatures are rising, the sea level is rising, the permafrost is thawing, growing seasons in mid- to high-latitude areas are lengthening, and the ranges of some animal and plant species are moving toward the poles and higher altitudes (IPCC 2001). Controversy remains about the precise quantitative impact of anthropogenic GHG emissions on the climate. Nevertheless there is widespread concern that a continuation of the rapid economic growth experienced since the beginning of the Industrial Revolution (and as a second industrial revolution unfolds in China and other major rapidly growing developing countries), supported by the continuing exploitation of fossil fuels, will induce significant changes in global and regional climates.[14]

Temperatures will continue to rise

The extent of climate change will depend on future GHG emissions (which will be determined largely by growth, technological developments, and policies that determine incentives for carbon efficiency) and on the ultimate effect of those emissions on climate. The Intergovernmental Panel on Climate Change (IPCC) has developed scenarios that relate forecasts of output, population, and technological developments to future CO_2 (the most important GHG) concentrations in the atmosphere, and thus to climate change. While the scope for limiting future GHG concentrations and the associated climate change remains great, past and current GHG emissions will continue to influence the global climate for some time. Even if emissions peak in the 21st century and then decline below current levels, global surface temperature will continue to rise for centuries, and sea levels will rise for several millennia (figure 5.5).

The IPCC scenarios cover a wide range of growth paths, with the four principal scenarios ranging from 1 percent to 3 percent growth in per capita income during 2000–30. Although these scenarios were developed in the

Box 5.1   The vanishing polar ice

One effect of the rise in global temperatures has been the drastic reduction in large bodies of ice in the Arctic and in Antarctica, which appears to have accelerated recently. Average temperatures in the Arctic region are rising twice as fast as elsewhere in the world. Arctic ice is thinning, melting, and rupturing. The largest single block of ice in the Arctic, the Ward Hunt Ice Shelf, had been around for 3,000 years before it started cracking in 2000. Within two years it had split all the way through and is now breaking further into smaller pieces.

The polar ice cap as a whole is shrinking. Images from National Aeronautics and Space Administration (NASA) satellites show that the area of permanent ice cover is contracting at a rate of 9 percent each decade. If this trend continues, summers in the Arctic could become near ice-free by the end of the century.

Consecutive satellite images also have revealed the collapse of the Larsen B ice shelf on the Antarctic Peninsula during the 2002 Antarctic summer, fulfilling predictions made by British Antarctic Survey (BAS) scientists. The collapse of the 3,250 km^2 ice shelf is part of the ongoing developments in a region of Antarctica that has experienced unprecedented warming over the last 50 years.

Continued melting of polar ice could induce significant rises in sea levels, with potentially catastrophic implications for many coastal areas, and raise the possibility of interrupting the Gulf Stream, which could drastically reduce European temperatures.

The summer arctic ice field is shrinking

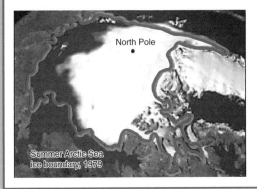

North Pole

Summer Arctic Sea ice boundary, 1979

The Larsen B ice shelf collapsed

March 5, 2002
February 17, 2002
January 31, 2002

late 1990s, a recent review finds that they are roughly consistent with projections undertaken since then (Van Vuuren and O'Neill 2006). The scenario outlined in chapter 2 envisions global per capita growth of 2.2 percent. Thus, the path of carbon emissions implicit in this scenario is roughly similar to that envisioned in many of the IPCC scenarios. As discussed in chapter 2, this scenario assumes a steady improvement in the technical efficiency of energy use but no major policy initiatives that would raise the price of fossil fuels. Thus, the forecasts in this book would imply considerable potential for reining in carbon emissions over the medium term, given strong international efforts to slow climate change. While achieving reductions in emissions (as envisioned in figure 5.5) by improving efficiency holds considerable promise, the near-term prospects for reducing carbon emissions through alternative energy sources are limited (box 5.2). The world is not yet on a path toward the emissions reductions that will be essential even to stabilize global temperatures (at significantly higher levels than at present).

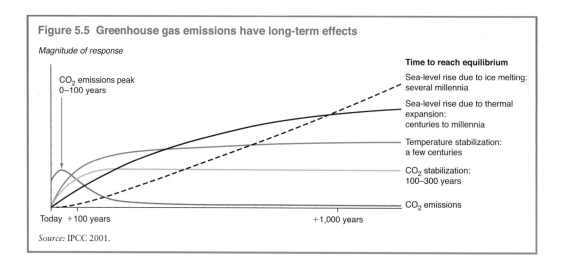

Figure 5.5 Greenhouse gas emissions have long-term effects

Source: IPCC 2001.

Box 5.2   Can efficiency and renewables be the answer?

Significant reductions in GHG emissions can be achieved through improvements in energy efficiency and increased use of renewable energy sources. Nevertheless, the share of renewables in energy use is not expected to increase much within the forecast period, and the demand for hydrocarbons is set to rise by more than 50 percent (IEA 2004, 2005). This underlines the need for policies to encourage energy savings and improve the profitability of alternative energy sources.

Developing countries have much greater potential than industrial countries for reducing emissions, in great part because they are moving toward the technological frontier in existing industry and infrastructure. For example, China could use some 20 percent less coal if its plants were as efficient as the average plant in Japan, and the potential for adopting proven energy savings in cement and pulp and paper is significant. Moreover, rapidly growing developing economies can invest directly in energy-efficient technologies, thereby leapfrogging earlier, inferior processes. For example, expansion of low-power, white-light-emitting diodes that run on batteries charged by solar panels could enable the rural poor in some countries to bypass the need for centralized electrical grids. Developing countries

have the opportunity now to adopt more efficient choices for infrastructure and technology that could drastically reduce GHG emissions for decades to come.

Energy efficiency is often the most cost-effective and low-risk approach to reducing the need for energy, and can also generate significant environmental benefits. Considerable potential exists for adopting more efficient technologies in transport, industry, buildings, and power generation.

- In *transport*, new materials, compact engines, and advanced fuel systems can lead to lighter and more fuel-efficient vehicles, while hybrid vehicles can provide substantial fuel savings. If all technical means were implemented, the International Energy Agency estimates that a 40 percent improvement in fuel economy of gasoline engines is achievable in the coming decades. The prospects for hydrogen and fuel cell vehicles are less promising over the forecast period because they require significant cost reductions, performance improvements, and development of fuel cell vehicle markets and hydrogen infrastructure.
- Many new *buildings* could be 70 percent more energy efficient than the existing stock through the use of new technologies in windows,

Box 5.2 *(continued)*

insulation, furnaces, air conditioners, appliances, lighting, and standby power.

- In *industry* there is a large potential to improve the efficiency of motors, boilers, pumps, and heating and cooling systems. In addition, large amounts of energy can be saved through new processes in individual sectors, such as direct casting in iron and steel, and biofeedstocks in the production of petrochemicals.

- In the *electric power* sector, switching from coal to natural gas would reduce emissions, both because natural gas emits only about half as much CO_2 as coal per kilowatt hour and because the latest combined-cycle gas plants attain efficiencies of 60 percent, compared to 46–49 percent for the best available coal-fired plants. Nuclear energy offers emission-free technology but faces high capital costs, problems of waste storage, risks of accident, public opposition, and possible proliferation of nuclear weapons.

Renewable energy sources. Renewable energy now accounts for 14 percent of world energy demand, and while the authors of this chapter anticipate that its use may rise by 50 percent by 2030, its share of total energy is not expected to change greatly unless vigorous policies encourage switching from nonrenewable energy sources.

- Renewable electricity generation is dominated by *hydropower,* which accounts for 16 percent of global electricity production. Hydropower is the cheapest source of power in many areas. There is considerable potential for expansion, particularly in the form of small hydro plants, although concerns over undesirable environmental and social impact have been important barriers.
- *Biomass* generation can be highly economic, particularly for co-firing other hydrocarbon-based plants. New technologies are expected to reduce costs further, but the largest barrier

to accelerated expansion is competition with other demands for biomass, particularly for use as food.

- *Wind* generation is expected to rise, buoyed by sharp declines in the cost from economies of scale with the use of larger turbines. Nevertheless, wind still has problems of intermittency, low reliability, problems connecting to the grid, and (more recently) difficulties in siting land-based turbines.
- Generation from *geothermal* sources is concentrated in a few countries. While geothermal is a very competitive and reliable source of power, and its potential is enormous, it is a site-specific resource that can only be accessed in certain parts of the world.
- *Solar* power is expected to account for less than 0.5 percent of total power supplies by 2030, as its investment and generating costs are the highest of all commercially deployed renewable energy sources, although the range of costs varies widely depending on the amount of sunshine available. There will also be some rise in solar thermal power, whose generation costs are typically double those of conventional energy sources.
- *Tide and wave* generation is still in its infancy. Projects need to be large-scale if they are to withstand offshore conditions, and these are very costly and carry high risks. Site-specific environmental effects also need careful assessment.

Biofuels may provide a significant alternative fuel option for transportation over the forecast period, with ethanol from sugarcane (from Brazil, for example) offering the best chance of commercial viability. Other feedstocks, such as corn, have much higher costs owing to lower yields and are unlikely to be financially viable without government support. If ethanol can be produced from cellulose using biomass as the fuel for the conversions process, net GHG emissions from well to wheel basis (that is, through the complete chain of fuel production and use) could be reduced to zero, according to the International Energy Agency.

Climate change could have a catastrophic impact on some countries

The effects of climate change on human welfare are uncertain, depending as they do on the magnitude and timing of increased

temperatures, the precise climate changes involved, and the links between climate change and human activity. Available calculations indicate that the *aggregate* global economic impact of a small rise in temperatures would be significant, but not enormous. Tol (2002) finds that the impact of a rise in the global mean surface air temperature of 1 degree Celsius (the temperature rise anticipated over the first half of the 21st century) could range anywhere from an annual increase of world GDP by 2.3 percent to a decrease of 2.7 percent, depending on assumptions made about the value of nonmarket goods and services. Examples include how to value human lives lost and gained, and the damage to ecosystems and biodiversity—a quarter of the world's known animals or plants, or more than a million species, are likely to die out because of the forecast warming over the next 50 years (Grubb 2006b).[15] A more recent analysis estimates that failing to address climate change could reduce welfare by an amount equal to a 5–20 percent fall in per capita consumption (box 5.3).

These estimates also do not capture low-probability risks that could imply severe consequences for the global economy over a relatively short timeframe. For example, if the Gulf Stream stalls as melting ice introduces more fresh water into the northern Atlantic, European temperatures could plummet. And there is potential for a rapid, almost self-perpetuating acceleration of climate change if the large methane deposits in arctic tundra are released as climate change proceeds.

Estimates of the aggregate economic impact of climate change mask extreme variations in costs and benefits for different countries. The brunt of the damage from climate change will be felt by low-latitude developing countries, with the extent of harm critically dependent on how much temperatures increase (so that damages are likely to rise as time goes on). Many developing countries are more vulnerable to climate change because they are already warmer than developed countries and suffer from high rainfall variability, they are heavily dependent on agriculture (the sector most vulnerable to climate change), poor public services increase the potential welfare loss, and low incomes impede adaptation (U.K. Government 2006). Countries near the poles could

benefit from a modest rise in temperatures, while mid-latitude countries, many of them high-income, are likely to face small *net* effects from climate change through this century (the rise in the sea level may inundate some coastal areas and increasing severity of hurricanes and cyclones could increase coastal damages, while agricultural yields in other areas could improve). Over the long term, and in the absence of successful mitigation efforts, climate change is likely to be disastrous for all countries. Examples of the possible damage include the following:

- A rise of 1 degree Celsius could lead to an 80 percent loss of coral reefs; further increases in extreme precipitation causing drought and landslides; a 20 to 35 million ton loss in cereal production and an approximately 10 percent decline in yields of various African crops (such as barley and rice).
- A rise of 2 degrees Celsius could lead to large-scale displacement of people in the Mahgreb as rainfall declines by at least 40 percent; the total loss of summer Arctic sea ice; the likely extinction of the polar bear and walrus; millions more people at risk to malaria, particularly in Africa and Asia; and a 50 percent loss of the Chinese boreal forest.
- A rise of 3 degrees Celsius could lead to massive changes in habitats, such as the collapse of the Amazon rainforest and the Great Lakes wetland systems; the inundation of the Ganges delta region, undermining the agricultural system that feeds a quarter of a billion people; the spread of desert-like conditions in Africa as the Kalahari dunes become mobile; additional millions of people at risk of hunger; two to three hundred million more exposed to malaria; hundreds of millions more exposed to dengue; several tens of millions displaced from coastal areas because of rising sea levels; and billions more subject to increased water stress (Warren 2006).

Box 5.3 Stern Review: The Economics of Climate Change

The government of the United Kingdom recently issued a report on the economics of climate change prepared by Sir Nicholas Stern at Treasury. The report underlines the very serious global risks posed by climate change, and the urgency of steps to reduce carbon emissions. The principal finding is that the benefits of strong, early action on climate change exceed the costs involved, reflecting two insights.

First, the continued growth of carbon emissions at current rates raises the risk of serious, irreversible damage to global welfare. Absent changes in policies, carbon emissions could rise by the middle of this century to a level that would eventually commit the world to a rise in average temperatures of more than 5 degrees Celsius above preindustrial revolution levels, equal to the amount of global warming that occurred between the last ice age and today. The total cost of the climate change resulting from "business as usual" emissions over the next two centuries is estimated to equal a minimum reduction in global per capita consumption of 5 percent. Taking into account the nonmarket impacts (on the environment and human health) of these emissions, the potential for feedbacks that would amplify climate change, and an increase in the weight accorded to the poorer regions, and "business as usual" climate change results in a reduction of about 20 percent in global per capita consumption.

Second, atmospheric greenhouse gas concentrations could be stabilized at levels that greatly reduce the risk of climate change damages, at relatively low cost. Carbon emissions can be cut by reducing the demand for emissions-intensive goods and services, increasing energy efficiency, switching to low-carbon technologies, and reducing non–fossil fuel emissions (from deforestation and in agriculture). A series of model-generated estimates of the annual cost of cutting emissions to a level consistent with stabilizing atmospheric greenhouse gas concentrations at 550 parts per million average 1 percent of global GDP by 2050.[a]

Reducing emissions efficiently requires pricing carbon to reflect fully the risks of climate change. This can be done through *setting a tax on emissions* or through *establishing tradable quotas*, although regulation may also be used where market-based mechanisms are ineffective. However, setting an appropriate price for carbon may not lower emissions sufficiently, due to uncertainty on future pricing policies, barriers to technology development in key sectors related to climate change, and external benefits to technology development (for example, inspiring ideas for new technologies) that are not captured by investors. Thus, the public sector also should *promote low-carbon and high-efficiency technologies* through increasing support for research and development, demonstration projects, and early-stage commercialization investments in some sectors. Governments also should focus on *removing barriers to behavioral change*—such as transaction costs, organizational inertia, and a lack of reliable information—through regulation (for example, minimum standards for buildings and appliances), labeling, and sharing best practices, and financing the upfront costs of efficiency improvements.

Adaptation also will be essential to limiting the negative impact of inevitable climate change. While individuals will undertake adaptation in reaction to market or environmental changes, governments can provide policy guidelines as well as economic and institutional support.

The Stern report emphasizes the importance of *international collective action* to respond to climate change. Cooperation should cover all aspects of emissions reductions policies. It is necessary to create a broadly similar carbon price signal around the world, and to promote carbon finance to accelerate action in developing countries. An equitable distribution of effort that takes into account income, historic responsibility, and per capita emissions would have industrial countries undertaking emissions reductions of 60 to 80 percent (from 1990 levels) by 2050.

---

[a]Anything higher than 550 parts per million would substantially increase the risk of harmful impacts on global welfare while reducing the expected costs of mitigation by comparatively little.

These measurements generally consider the welfare impacts of a particular level of global average temperatures, and thus may exclude some significant risks. Climate change may increase the uncertainty surrounding, and variability of, weather, which could increase costs. For example, a higher mean sea level could make storm surges more devastating; and higher average temperatures may have a smaller impact on agricultural productivity than increases in long, hot, dry spells (Weyant 2000). The speed of climate change is also important, as many species may have trouble adapting to rapid increases in temperatures.

What can be done to reduce GHG emissions?

In the absence of intervention, global CO_2 emissions could reach between two and four times current levels by 2100, resulting in much greater GHG concentrations than envisioned in most models of climate change (Grubb 2006b). Thankfully, there is a wide variety of possible methods to reduce GHG emissions, for example improving energy efficiency and relying more on renewable energy sources (see box 5.2), switching to fuels with lower GHG emissions (from coal to natural gas, for example), capturing and storing carbon emissions, sequestering carbon through reforestation, changing lifestyles to reduce demand for energy, reducing growth in output, and geoengineering (to change the reflectivity of the atmosphere, oceans, and land).[16] Some measures, such as reducing subsidies that support high levels of energy intensity, may have low or even negative costs, while others involve very expensive regulatory intervention.

The costs of measures to achieve a given level of emissions reductions, and thus the consistency of mitigation efforts with an acceleration of global growth, will depend critically on technological developments and the policies adopted. Technological developments are uncertain, although the dangers posed by climate change encourage attention to subsidizing research. Policies that would induce

polluters to seek the least costly method of reducing the risk of climate change are

- Setting a uniform price for the emission of GHG (a uniform global carbon tax, for example), and an equivalent subsidy for measures reducing atmospheric GHG concentrations and other conditions that can cause climate change.[17]
- Setting a global emissions target and establishing a market for emission permits. Industries and nations with high (or low) abatement costs would buy (sell) such permits, up to the point where abatement costs were equalized across industries and national economies, resulting in a uniform price of emissions permits.[18]

Location is important in determining costs because the marginal cost of combating climate change differs widely between countries and economic sectors. For example, the cost of a 100-million-ton reduction in carbon emissions by 2010 was estimated to be less than $5 per ton of carbon (in 1985 dollars) for the United States, about $40 for the European Union, and almost $400 for Japan (Ellerman, Jacoby, and Decaux 1998). Costs tend to be even lower for developing countries. The time span over which emissions are required to fall also affects the cost of abatement: longer time spans reduce costs because existing plants and equipment need not be retired before the end of their useful life, while shorter time spans improve the credibility of compliance targets. The future path of global growth may well be affected by efforts at mitigation, depending on their severity and the attention paid to ensuring that mitigation is achieved at least cost.

In addition to reducing carbon emissions, efforts to adapt to climate change will also be required. Even if the world succeeds in markedly reducing carbon emissions in the near future, the GHGs already in the atmosphere imply increases in global temperatures and rises in sea level for many years to come (see figure 5.5). The welfare impact of climate change on developing countries is likely to be all the more devastating because developing countries bear the brunt of the anticipated damages and have less ability than industrial countries to adapt, and because the welfare impacts of income declines are greatest for the poor.

Given the critical nature of this issue for developing countries, the World Bank Group is rapidly expanding its activities to achieve a low-carbon economy. The Bank currently manages nine funds devoted to developing the carbon market, with a total investment of $2 billion. The Global Environment Facility is the largest source of multilateral grant financing for low-carbon technologies, with a total investment of $1 billion. The Bank is on track to meet its 2004 commitment to a 20 percent average annual growth in new renewable energy and energy-efficiency commitments between fiscal year 2005 and fiscal year 2009 (Sierra 2006).

Agreeing on policy is difficult

Model-based analyses suggest that the global net benefits of a coordinated international policy regime to reduce GHG emissions far exceed the benefits of individual countries acting on their own (Nordhaus and Yang 1996). However, as there is no systematic relationship between the locations where GHG emissions originate and where major damages induced by climate change are likely to occur, most countries gain very little direct benefit from their own mitigation efforts. Individual countries thus face a strong incentive not to make efforts to reduce emissions, and to minimize their own commitments to international efforts. The problem is exacerbated because likely damages are distributed unevenly around the globe. While the very existence of some island states may be threatened by rising ocean levels, countries with large Arctic areas may actually benefit from (modest) climate change.[19]

Developing countries can be major players in global efforts to reduce global climate change—they certainly will be greatly affected by success or failure. As discussed, developing countries are likely to bear the worst costs of climate change. At the same time, they bear little responsibility for the current stock of GHGs in the atmosphere and are understandably loath to impede their own growth to resolve a problem that is largely the creation of industrial countries. Still, future increases in GHG emissions will occur mainly in developing countries (figure 5.6), so that any policy strategy that excludes these major future emitters is unlikely to be effective. Moreover,

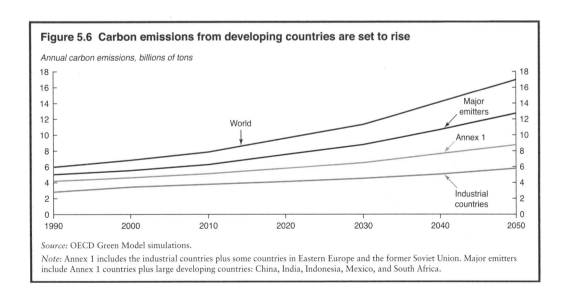

Figure 5.6 Carbon emissions from developing countries are set to rise

Annual carbon emissions, billions of tons

Source: OECD Green Model simulations.

Note: Annex 1 includes the industrial countries plus some countries in Eastern Europe and the former Soviet Union. Major emitters include Annex 1 countries plus large developing countries: China, India, Indonesia, Mexico, and South Africa.

agreements with limited geographic coverage may lead to the migration of key polluting industries to nonparticipating countries, thereby undermining success.[20]

Other aspects of climate change impede international agreement. With a few highly hypothetical exceptions, the most severe impacts of climate change are not expected for several decades, which raises uncertainty, leads to disagreement on how costs should be distributed over time and across generations, and discourages action by political leaders concerned with short time horizons (the next election). And as elaborated above, considerable uncertainty remains over the costs of mitigation and the precise impact of different levels of GHG concentrations on human welfare.

What has been done to reduce GHG emissions?

Despite the difficulties involved in reaching international agreements and the incentives for free riding, some progress has been made in reducing GHG emissions, both through international agreements and by individual countries and regions.

Kyoto Protocol. The Kyoto Protocol, which came into force in February 2005, committed most industrial countries and some of the transition economies (together referred to as the "Annex B countries") to targets that implied reductions by 2008–12 of some 5 percent of the GHG emissions recorded in these countries in 1990. Countries may either reduce actual GHG emissions or enhance the amount of carbon captured in "carbon sinks" (by sequestering GHG from the atmosphere), for example, through reforestation programs. The protocol also allows countries to achieve their emission-reduction obligations together, to buy emission rights from other Annex B countries whose emissions are below the limits, and to receive emission reduction credits for sponsoring GHG mitigation or sequestration projects in other Annex B countries (Joint Implementation Framework) or in developing countries (the Clean Development

Mechanism). The provisions for carbon trading and the Clean Development Mechanism have provided useful practical experience on how to manage such mechanisms, which are likely to be part of future agreements on climate change.

The Kyoto Protocol represents a major attempt by the international community to come to grips with climate change, and by signaling future policy actions to reduce GHG emissions, it may encourage investors to adopt more efficient technologies. But it has been subject to many criticisms. The sharp cuts in emissions required of some participating countries restrained some countries from signing, particularly as no constraints were imposed on other countries where emissions will be growing fastest in the foreseeable future. The transaction costs involved in the Clean Development Mechanism and the Joint Implementation Framework make it difficult for countries to meet their obligations at the lowest global cost. It is too early to judge compliance (emission curtailment obligations are legally binding only for the 2008–2012 period). But emissions from transition economies are well below their Kyoto targets owing to the major decline in economic activity after 1990, while emissions from most industrial country signatories exceed their targets.[21] The penalties for noncompliance are not likely to change behavior. Countries that fail to meet their targets during 2008–12 must make up for this shortfall in the subsequent commitment period, plus a 30 percent penalty. A country liable for the penalty could fail to ratify the extension, or insist on raising its emissions limit as a condition of participation. Unlike the World Trade Organization (WTO) agreement, other countries are not provided with the means of enforcing compliance (Aldy, Barrett, and Stavins 2003).

Country and local efforts. Individual countries, as well as some local governments, have taken steps to limit carbon emissions. While these have not yet had a major impact on the size of total emissions, they do help to encourage similar initiatives, provide some momentum to efforts to limit climate change, and provide useful information on the feasibility of different approaches. Finland, the Netherlands, Norway, and Sweden adopted a carbon tax in the 1990s, and the United Kingdom has imposed a "climate change tax" on electricity generated by using fossil fuels since 2001.

In the United States, the California legislature recently passed a law that would cut carbon gas emissions 25 percent by 2020; Oregon has mandated cuts of 75 percent by 2050; 279 cities have signed a commitment to comply with the Kyoto targets; northeast states have set up the Regional Greenhouse Gas Initiative to control emissions; and 22 states have adopted so-called renewable portfolio standards to encourage renewable energy sources (Rabe 2006). Of course, a host of policies affect emissions, including many not designed to contain climate change. For example, high taxes on gasoline can help to reduce gasoline consumption and thus reduce emissions.

Carbon trading. The Kyoto Protocol and regional initiatives have created a carbon market that trades reductions in GHG emissions, supported by efforts from the government of the Netherlands and the World Bank (notably through the Prototype Carbon Fund, which began operations in April 2000). The overall market rose from about 13 million tons of CO_2-equivalent in 2001 to 704 million tons in 2005 (figure 5.7), when its value totaled $11 billion. The value of the market continues to rise—it was $7.5 billion in the first quarter of 2006 alone. The vast majority of transactions are aimed at complying with the Kyoto Protocol, and the market is dominated by the European Union's Emissions Trading Scheme. Developing countries accounted for almost half of global transactions in 2005 through the Clean Development Mechanism. Given the huge uncertainties about the post-2012 climate policy regime, the volume of project-based transactions may decline, as the window of

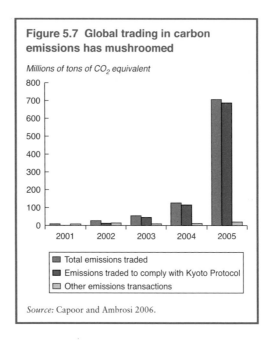

Figure 5.7 Global trading in carbon emissions has mushroomed

Millions of tons of CO_2 equivalent

■ Total emissions traded
■ Emissions traded to comply with Kyoto Protocol
□ Other emissions transactions

Source: Capoor and Ambrosi 2006.

opportunity to develop projects and validate their reduction credits under the Kyoto Protocol will soon start to close.

The way forward

Because the establishment of institutions to address climate change requires considerable lead time, it would be desirable to start building such institutions immediately. And because lack of agreement on international cost distribution remains an important impediment to policy implementation, reaching a compromise on this question is a high priority. Progress in international negotiations concerning optimal climate policies would strengthen private incentives for energy efficiency and government incentives for appropriate policies. Progress would be encouraged by an agreement that the results of such efforts will be recognized in any future revisions of contractual obligations.

Proposals for a new agreement to succeed the Kyoto Protocol should be evaluated according to several criteria (Aldy, Barrett, and Stavins 2003). The emissions targets should reduce climate change to an acceptable level. Participation should be as broad as possible. The policies should be efficient, either by maximizing the net benefits to society compared with alternatives, or at a minimum, by representing the least costly means of achieving an agreed-upon goal. The obligations and results of the policies should be viewed as equitable, both across countries and, given the long-term issues surrounding climate change, across generations. (A conflict currently exists between different notions of equity: the industrial countries are most responsible for climate change and have the greatest ability to pay, while developing countries are likely to be most affected.) Policies should be flexible enough to take account of new information; this is critical given the time scale involved and the potential impact of technological developments on emissions, mitigation efforts, and countries' ability to adapt. Finally, the design of the rules and the institutions established must effectively address the substantial difficulties involved in monitoring performance and ensuring compliance with treaty provisions.

Obviously there are important trade-offs among these goals. Targets that achieve large reductions in GHG emissions may not attract sufficient participation, and flexible arrangements may not reflect sufficient commitment to environmental targets. And the criteria for judging some targets are subjective. Individuals and governments may have different views of what level of climate change is acceptable, or how much future generations should pay for mitigation. So, designing an optimal agreement to limit climate change is ultimately a political, rather than a technical, exercise.

Negotiations for a successor to the Kyoto Protocol have already started within the framework of the United Nations Framework Convention on Climate Change. Failure to seize this opportunity to come up with an effective treaty curtailing the risk of climate change may seriously endanger not only the benefits of achieving the Millennium Development Goals, but also the welfare of entire future generations in industrial and developing countries alike.

Conclusions and policy recommendations

Avian flu, the depletion of marine fisheries, and climate change are very different issues representing different threats to global welfare. But in some respects, they are similar. All could involve substantial economic and human costs. In all cases, the risks posed have been intensified by globalization and the related acceleration in growth and technological progress. And in all cases, the necessary solutions will require a high degree of international policy coordination. No one country can, by itself, stem the rise of GHGs sufficiently to avoid a continued increase in global temperatures and potentially catastrophic effects. Similarly, cooperation by all countries is required to contain a potential flu pandemic that could result in millions of fatalities. And ensuring the sustainability of marine fisheries requires cooperation on sustainable management and observance by many countries of agreed-on fishing limits.

Institutional effectiveness varies from case to case

The effectiveness of the current institutional frameworks for addressing these issues varies. International efforts to contain the short-term threats of the SARS epidemic and avian flu virus have been swift and effective, although avian flu remains endemic in several countries and thus a continuing threat. The generally adequate legal framework governing the management of marine fish stocks is often rendered ineffective by inadequate enforcement and inappropriate incentive systems. The international institutions required to confront the longer-term threat posed by climate change have been generally ineffective. The Kyoto Protocol represents an initial effort to limit GHG emissions, and it has provided valuable experience in the implementation of controls. However, it lacks the participation of major current and future GHG emitters, enforcement of its provisions is problematic, and, in its present form, it is neither an effective nor an efficient response to the climate change problem. There is at present no international institution able to coordinate an effective response to climate change.

Achieving strong international coordination to address threats to global welfare is easiest where there is a general consensus on the nature of the problem and what to do, where the threat is immediate, where individuals and countries have strong private incentives to address the problem in ways that have external benefits, and where the number of countries that must be involved in negotiations is limited (table 5.2).

The greatest difficulties in achieving effective international cooperation are presented by climate change. Although scientific understanding of the relationship between GHG emissions and global warming is sufficient to justify action, the implications for welfare of both problems and solutions are difficult to forecast. The most severe damages from climate change will likely take several decades to occur, leading to disagreements on the appropriate discount rate to apply to welfare calculations and the equitable division of costs among generations. No one country gains much relief from the threat of climate change through its own efforts to control emissions. And an effective response requires gaining agreement from all major polluters. It is no surprise that international institutions have made little headway, despite the potentially catastrophic costs of failure. By contrast, there is general agreement on the short-term threat posed by a flu pandemic, and individuals and individual countries gain substantial private

benefits from prevention efforts, so international efforts to contain (some) infectious diseases have been relatively effective. The threat to the sustainability of marine fisheries occupies an intermediate position: there is little disagreement over the dangers of overexploitation of marine fish stocks, while the extent to which individual government efforts to manage fisheries generate private benefits varies depending on the species involved—and particularly on whether fish tend to migrate to the high seas or between exclusive economic zones.

Some policy priorities are clear

Climate change. Understanding how the lack of effective international institutions impedes an effective response to climate change focuses attention on policy priorities. Discussions are already under way under the aegis of the UN Framework Convention on Climate Change to replace the Kyoto Protocol, which expires in 2012, with a more comprehensive and ambitious agreement. Meanwhile, it may be useful for the global community to start putting in place the pertinent institutions, such as a global system for trading emission permits, as well as improved means of monitoring emissions (particularly in developing countries), which will allow a rapid implementation of effective policies once these are agreed upon.

Negotiations over the next agreement must take into account the position of developing countries. Since industrial countries are the major source of the current stock of GHGs in the atmosphere, there is a compelling

Table 5.2 Uncertainty and incentives affect international institutions

Threat	Time scale of threat	Degree of scientific consensus	Benefit of country's own mitigation efforts	Number of countries involved in solution	Effectiveness of institutions
Flu pandemic	Short-term	High	High	Many	High
Marine fisheries	Medium-term	High	High/moderate	Many or limited (depends on species)	Moderate
Climate change	Medium- to long-term	Moderate	Limited	Many	Low

Source: Authors.

argument that they should assume the lion's share of the costs. Nevertheless, future growth in emissions will occur mainly in developing countries. Industrial countries taking on a larger burden can be reconciled with achieving universal participation through a system of appropriate transfers, for example through the allocation of emission permits.

While international agreement is critical to limiting GHG emissions, individual countries need not delay action. A large number of measures could be adopted to limit atmospheric GHG concentrations while simultaneously raising current welfare. For example, eliminating subsidies on fossil fuels could reduce the energy intensity of production and thus unnecessarily high GHG emissions. These efforts could also have a substantial role in improving health by reducing local pollution. For industrial countries, the health benefits from reduced pollution may offset a large share of mitigation costs (see Burtraw and others 2003; Proost and Regemorter 2003; Aunan and others 2004; McKinley and others 2005). Choosing energy-efficient technology for the tens of trillions of dollars in global infrastructure investment will have irreversible impacts on GHG emission paths throughout the century (Grubb 2006a).

The focus on international coordination is essential, given the nature of the problem. But international negotiations typically proceed at the slow pace required to achieve consensus, while there is an urgent need for action *now* to slow the accumulation of GHGs. Further delays in addressing climate change would increase the costs of future, necessary mitigation efforts and greatly increase the risks of severe damage to global welfare. The scientific consensus is sufficient to demonstrate that prudence lies on the side of addressing climate change. Achieving policy consensus is more difficult, but it is now urgent.

Avian flu. Research remains a priority in combating future pandemics, particularly efforts to speed the development of vaccines in response to the next mutation of the flu virus, or—even better—to develop vaccines with broader application against groups of viruses. Because uncertainty concerning use, the large sunk costs involved, and lack of effective demand from many potential consumers in developing countries limit private investment in vaccines, this is an urgent area for public investment by the industrial countries.

Individual governments should focus on the distribution of vaccines, arrangements for quarantine, financial incentives for reporting disease, and sanctions for failure to report within their own jurisdictions. Industrial countries might consider it in their interest to subsidize such activities in developing countries, which may lack financial resources adequate to the task. And international discussions could be useful to provide for appropriate burden-sharing among the countries able to assume a portion of such costs.

Marine fisheries. Strengthening the system of regional fisheries management organizations, and establishing them where none exist, may merit further contributions by industrial countries. The UN General Assembly fund to aid developing countries in implementing the Fish Stocks Agreement appears to have gotten off to a slow start, with some developing countries calling for increased contributions and others noting that the fund is underused owing to a lack of knowledge by many potential recipients (Fiji UN Mission 2006). A reduction in fish subsidies, a redirection of subsidies toward assisting with exit from the industry, and the financing of general support to fishing through taxation of the fishing industry would help limit overcapacity and overfishing. Limits on the exploitation of the environment at the bottom of the sea are sensible until more knowledge has accumulated on how fishing and other activities affect that environment. Sustainability would be enhanced by implementing an ecosystem-based approach to fisheries management, which focuses on sustainable exploitation while safeguarding the ecosystem's structure, function, and productivity. The uncertainties involved in determining sustainable levels of fish stocks argue for allowing a safe margin of error when setting management regimes and catch limits.

The need for international cooperation will grow

The scenario presented in chapter 2 envisions some acceleration in global growth and trade over the next quarter century. A deepening of globalization will lead to faster poverty reduction and a general improvement in global welfare. But continuing globalization will also increase the risks that countries face. This chapter has highlighted the short-term risks from infectious disease, the medium-term risk of depletion of marine fish resources, and the medium- to long-term risk posed by climate change. Of these, only climate change appears capable of seriously derailing global growth over the next quarter century. The strength of global institutions designed to meet these problems will have important implications for the likelihood of achieving this growth path.

Many other problems will, to differing degrees, require a global solution—among them preserving biodiversity, achieving an intellectual property regime that encourages innovation while limiting excessive monopoly rents, and reducing the transmission of macroeconomic instability. The countries involved in each case, the importance of the risks and benefits, and the scope for international action will vary considerably. But the interrelated phenomena of growth, technological progress, and globalization will intensify the need to find cooperative international solutions to all of these problems, while diminishing the ability of any single country to resolve critical issues on its own.

Notes

1. The Antonine Plague, either smallpox or measles, is estimated to have killed 5 million people in the second century A.D., and major episodes of bubonic plague occurred in the 6th and 14th centuries, the latter killing a quarter of Europe's population.

2. Subsequent investigations established that the disease originated in Guangdong province in China in late 2002, but news of the early cases of the sickness had not been made public by the Chinese government.

3. In China alone over the last 40 years the human population has increased by two-thirds, while the poultry population has expanded more than 10-fold. Similar increases in both human and animal populations have occurred in other Asian countries (Osterholm 2005). Additional concerns arise from the presence of the H5N1 virus in migratory birds (without showing clinical symptoms), which can lead to the transmission of the disease between continents, and the virus's ability to adapt to other species (including various mammals).

4. The disease outbreaks have been found to be strongly linked to the cold season, and the behavior of the disease over the coming months will be critical.

5. The one successful case of global eradication was smallpox, which succeeded in part because of the nature of the disease: no nonhuman host, potential for effective diagnosis and surveillance, ability to interrupt person-to-person transmission, and vaccination (Barrett 2004).

6. Bottom trawling, where the trawling rig is dragged along the sea floor, can damage vulnerable ecosystems on the sea bottom. Studies in Australia indicate that the sea floor ecosystem had not recovered from bottom trawling 15 years after an area is closed to fishing (FAO 2004). The use of explosives has damaged coral reefs, and poisons have killed nontarget species (Whole Systems 2006). The FAO estimates that marine fish discards (fish caught other than the target fish and thrown away) total about 10 million metric tons per year (Kura and others 2005), although discards declined since the early 1990s (FAO 2004).

7. For example, improved ships and freezer facilities enable ships to stay at sea for long periods. Sonar, satellite navigation systems, depth sensors, and air surveillance, combined with detailed maps of the ocean floor, help locate fish and improve the accuracy of net casting (Parsell 2002).

8. All subsidies do not threaten the sustainability of fish stocks, and few studies have attempted to link the value of subsidies quantitatively to their effect on fish stocks (FAO 2000). For example, subsidies to artisanal fishing may not raise catch levels enough to endanger sustainability, and some subsidies already are designed to facilitate exit from the industry. Quantitative modeling is extremely difficult owing to the lack of adequate data on subsidies and the multiple causes of changes in fisheries stocks (Tallontire 2004). The impact of subsidies will also depend on the effectiveness of management of fish stocks.

9. The Convention also provides that the freedom to fish on the high seas is subject to the general duty to cooperate in conservation and management and to

maintain or restore populations so as to obtain the maximum yield.

10. Examples of other approaches, rarely used in regional fisheries management organizations, are a total ban on fishing for several years to allow replenishment of fish stocks, restrictions on the capture of females or immature fish (to allow them reproduce), and closure of the fishery during spawning season.

11. Note that these data include China, which many believe has overstated fish captures (FAO 2004).

12. When industrial fishing fleets move close to shore they can damage the sea-bottom habitat, damage local fish nets, and drastically reduce fish species on which local craft fishers depend.

13. Climate change refers to the *incremental* effect of anthropogenic GHG emissions on the average global surface temperature and related changes in weather patterns. The natural greenhouse effect, caused by the pre–Industrial Revolution contents of GHGs in the atmosphere, is estimated to raise average global surface temperature by some 32 degrees Celsius from what it would be without natural radiative forcing, allowing human life to exist. So far anthropogenic emissions of CO_2, the most important GHG, have raised atmospheric concentration of CO_2 from 280 parts per million (ppm) at the start of the Industrial Revolution to 380 ppm, coinciding with an increase of average global surface temperature by about 0.6 degrees Celsius.

14. Given existing stocks of fossil fuels relative to current and projected economic growth, the past close link between output and fossil-fuel use could continue for a sufficiently long period to lead to a multiple increase in the atmospheric GHG concentrations that prevailed before the Industrial Revolution. The carbon contents of estimated fossil-fuel reserves are approximately five times the current atmospheric carbon content (in the form of CO_2) and more than 600 times current annual anthropogenic carbon emissions.

15. These estimates are clearly subject to multiple uncertainties (Grubb 2006b). In addition to the usual caveats for forecasts of growth and population, the economic and welfare impact of climate change is difficult to measure. Many market effects are not included owing to lack of data. The valuation of nonmarket effects is problematic and can raise ethical issues (life is typically valued in terms of the willingness to pay to preserve it, thus leading to high valuations in rich countries and low valuations in poor countries). Transition costs are typically not included, and the sensitivity of existing systems to transitional rises in temperature is largely unknown.

16. These may include, among other ideas, wind scrubbers to filter carbon dioxide from the air, "fertilization" of oceans with iron to encourage growth of plankton, petrification of carbon dioxide, and deflection of sunlight from the Earth through the use of a giant space mirror (Hall 2005). While considered of little practical relevance only a decade ago, geoengineering is gaining more serious consideration today (Broad 2006).

17. The existence of various GHGs requires that they be taxed in proportion to their contributions to climate change. Similarly, subsidies for alternative activities that reduce climate change potential (such as reforestation) should be proportional to their effect. While easy to formulate, the implementation of this principle is not a trivial task.

18. In a world without uncertainty, setting a price for emissions is equivalent to setting a quota. If the cost of reducing emissions is uncertain, the welfare effects of either setting prices or quantities of emission may differ (Weitzman 1974).

19. The present value of benefits from a coordinated solution may be negative for some countries (including the United States), thus further undermining incentives for participation (Nordhaus and Yang 1996). While side payments might be envisioned to encourage participation by those who suffer from a coordinated solution, the fairness involved in paying the world's largest GHG emitter to restrain emissions is problematic.

20. While the problem of carbon leakage is generally recognized, there remains disagreement concerning its quantitative importance: alternative model simulations come to different results as to the amount of carbon leakage likely to occur in response to a given policy for a given subregion (Burniaux and Oliveira Martins 2000).

21. Emissions from the European Union (EU15) countries are estimated at 0.8 percent below 1990 levels, compared with a target of −8 percent. Japan's emissions are estimated to be 7.4 percent, and Canada's 29 percent, above 1990 levels, compared to a target of −6 percent (UNFCCC 2006).

References

Aldy, Joseph E., Scott Barrett, and Robert N. Stavins. 2003. "Thirteen Plus One: A Comparison of Global Climate Policy Architectures." Available at www.nicholas.duke.edu/solutions/documents/.

APEC (Asia-Pacific Economic Cooperation). 2000. "Study into the Nature and Extent of Subsidies in the Fisheries Sector of APEC Member Economies." Available at www.APEC.org.

Aunan, K., J. Fang, H. Vennemo, K. Oye, and H. M. Seip. 2004. "Co-Benefits of Climate Policy: Lessons Learned from a Study in Shanxi, China." *Energy Policy* 32 (4): 567–81.

Barrett, Scott. 2004. "Critical Factors for the Successful Provision of Transnational Public Goods."

Background Study for the International Task Force on Global Public Goods. Available at www.gpgtaskforce.org.

Bell, Clive, and Maureen Lewis. 2004. "The Economic Implications of Epidemics Old and New." *World Economics* 5 (4): 137–74.

Berrill, M. 1997. *The Plundered Seas: Can the World's Fish be Saved?* Vancouver, BC: Greystone Books.

Bolton, D. A. 2005. "Managing Living Marine Resources Multilaterally: Some Threshold Questions." In *Deep Sea 2003: Conference on the Governance and Management of Deep-Sea Fisheries,* ed. Ross Shotton. Rome: Food and Agriculture Organization.

Broad, William J. 2006. "How to Cool a Planet (Maybe)." *New York Times,* June 27, F1.

Burniaux, Jean-Marc, and Joaquim Oliveira Martins. 2000. "Carbon Emission Leakages: A General Equilibrium View." OECD Economics Department Working Paper No. 242, Organisation for Economic Co-operation and Development, Paris.

Burtraw, D., A. Krupnick, K. Palmer, A. Paul, M. Toman, and C. Bloyd. 2003. "Ancillary Benefits of Reduced Air Pollution in the U.S. from Moderate Greenhouse Gas Mitigation Policies in the Electricity Sector." *Journal of Environmental Economics and Management* 45: 650–73.

Capoor, Karan, and Philippe Ambrosi. 2006. "State and Trends of the Carbon Market." Unpublished paper, World Bank, Washington, DC.

CDC (Centers for Disease Control). 2004. "Interim Recommendations for Infection Control in Health-Care Facilities Caring for Patients with Known or Suspected Avian Influenza." Available at www.cdc.gov/flu/avian/professional/infect-control.htm.

Cunningham, Steve, and Dominique Greboval. 2001. *Managing Fishing Capacity: A Review of Policy and Technical Issues.* FAO Fisheries Technical Paper No. 409, Food and Agriculture Organization, Rome.

Ellerman, A. Denny, Henry D. Jacoby, and Annelene Decaux. 1998. "The Effects on Developing Countries of the Kyoto Protocol and Carbon Dioxide Emissions Trading." World Bank Policy Research Working Paper No. No. 2019, Washington, DC.

Esty, Daniel H., and Maria H. Ivanova. 2002. "Revitalizing Global Environmental Governance: A Function Driven Approach." In *Global Environmental Governance: Options and Opportunities,* ed. Daniel H. Esty and Maria H. Ivanova. New Haven, CT: Yale School of Forestry and Environmental Studies.

FAO (Food and Agriculture Organization). 2000. "Report of the Expert Consultation on Economic Incentives and Responsible Fisheries." FAO, Rome.

_____. 2004. "The State of World Fisheries and Aquaculture." FAO, Rome.

Fiji UN Mission. 2006. "Report on the Review Conference on the Agreement for the Implementation of the Provisions of the United Nations Convention on the Law of the Sea of 10 December 1982 relating to the Conservation and Management of Straddling Fish Stocks and Highly Migratory Fish Stocks." United Nations, New York. May.

Gianni, Matthew. 2004. "High Seas Bottom Trawl Fisheries and Their Impacts on the Biodiversity of Vulnerable Deep-Sea Ecosystems: Options for International Action." World Conservation Union, Gland, Switzerland.

Grubb, Michael. 2006a. "Framing the Economics of Climate Change: An International Perspective." Submission to the Stern Review on the Economics of Climate Change, HM Treasury and Cabinet Office, London.

_____. 2006b. "Climate Change Impacts, Energy and Development." Paper presented at the Annual World Bank Conference on Development Economics, Tokyo, May 30.

Hall, Wayne. 2005. "Climate Change and Geoengineering." Available at www.globalresearch.ca.

Honohan, Patrick, and Luc Laeven. 2005. *Systemic Financial Crises: Containment and Resolution.* Cambridge, U.K.: Cambridge University Press.

IEA. 2004. *World Energy Outlook.* Paris: International Energy Agency.

_____. 2005. *World Energy Outlook.* Paris: International Energy Agency.

IPCC (Intergovernmental Panel on Climate Change). 2001. *Third Assessment Report—Climate Change 2001.* Geneva. Available at www.ipcc.ch.

Kura, Yumiko, Carmen Revenge, Eriko Hoshino, and Greg Mock. 2005. "Fishing for Answers: Making Sense of the Global Fish Crisis." World Resources Institute Report, Washington, DC.

Lodge, Michael W. 2005. "Improving International Governance in the Deep Sea." In *Deep Sea 2003: Conference on the Governance and Management of Deep-Sea Fisheries,* ed. Ross Shotton. Rome: Food and Agriculture Organization.

Lomborg, Bjorn, ed. 2004. *Global Crises, Global Solutions.* Cambridge, U.K.: Cambridge University Press.

McKinley, G., M. Zuk, M. Hojer, M. Avalos, I. Gonzalez, R. Iniestra, I. Laguna, M. Martinez, P. Osnaya, L. M. Reynales, R. Valdes, and J. Martinez. 2005. "Quantification of Local and Global Benefits from Air Pollution Control in Mexico City." *Environmental Science and Technology* 39: 1954–61.

Milazzo, Matteo. 1998. "Subsidies in World Fisheries: A Reexamination." World Bank Technical Paper No. 406, Fisheries Series, Washington, DC.

Nordhaus, William D., and Zili Yang. 1996. "A Regional Dynamic General-Equilibrium Model of Alternative Climate-Change Strategies." *American Economic Review* 86 (4): 741–65.

OECD (Organisation for Economic Co-operation and Development). 2005. *Why Fish Piracy Persists: The Economics of Illegal, Unreported and Unregulated Fishing.* Paris: OECD.

Osterholm, Michael T. 2005. "Preparing for the Next Pandemic." *New England Journal of Medicine* 352 (18): 1839–42. Available at www.nejm.org.

Parsell, D. L. 2002. "High-Tech Fishing is Emptying Deep Seas, Scientists Warn." *National Geographic News,* February 26. Available at news.nationalgeographic.com/news/2002/02/0225_0226_fishcrisis.html.

Pauly, Daniel, Villy Christensesn, Sylvie Guenette, Tony J. Pitcher, U. Rashid Sumaila, Carl J. Walters, R. Watson, and Dirk Zeller. 2002. "Toward Sustainability in World Fisheries." *Nature* 418 (August 8): 689–95.

Proost, S., and D. V. Regemorter. 2003. "Interaction between Local Air Pollution and Global Warming and Its Policy Implications for Belgium." *International Journal of Global Environmental Issues* 3 (3): 266–86.

Rabe, Barry. 2006. "Race to the Top: The Expanding Role of U.S. State Renewable Portfolio Standards." Pew Center on Global Climate Change, Arlington, VA.

Rischard, Jean-François. 2002. *High Noon: Twenty Global Problems, Twenty Years to Solve Them.* New York: Basic Books.

Schmidt, Carl-Christian. 2002. "Fish Crisis: A Problem of Scale." *OECD Observer* 233 (August).

Sender, Elena. 2006. "Les retards du plan grippe aviare" (Bird flu plan delayed). *Science et Avenir* (March): 57–59.

Shotton, Ross. 2006. *Deep Sea 2003: Conference on the Governance and Management of Deep-Sea Fisheries.* FAO Fisheries Proceedings 3/2. Rome: Food and Agriculture Organization.

Sierra, Katherine. 2006. "An Investment Framework for Clean Energy and Development." Presentation at the Dialogue on Climate Change, Clean Energy, and Sustainable Development, October 3–4. Monterrey, Mexico.

Sturm-Ramirez, Katharine. 2006. Unpublished briefing memorandum, St. Jude's Children's Hospital, Memphis, TN.

Tallontire, Anne. 2004. "Trade Issues Background Paper: The Impact of Subsidies on Trade in Fisheries Products." Food and Agriculture Organization, Rome.

Tol, R. S. J. 2002. "New Estimates of the Damage Costs of Climate Change, Part I: Benchmark Estimates." *Environmental and Resource Economics* 21 (1): 47–73.

U.K. Government. 2006. "The Stern Review: The Economics of Climate Change." Available at www.hm-treasury.gov.uk/independent_reviews.

UNFCCC (United Nations Framework Convention on Climate Change). 2006. "National Inventory Submissions 2006" (data on emissions by country). Available at unfccc.int/national_reports/annex_i_ghg_inventories/national_inventories_submissions/items/3734.php.

Van Vuuren, Detlef P., and Brian C. O'Neill. 2006. "The Consistency of IPCC's SRES Scenarios to 1990–2000 Trends and Recent Projections." *Climatic Change* 75 (1–2): 9–46.

Warren, Rachel. 2006. "Impacts of Global Climate Change at Different Annual Mean Global Temperature Increases." In *Avoiding Dangerous Climate Change,* ed. J. Schellnhuber, W. Cramer, N. Nakicenovic, G. Yohe, and T. M. L. Wigley. New York: Cambridge University Press.

Webster, D. G. 2006. "Leveraging Competitive Advantages: The Role of Developing Countries in International Fisheries Management." Available at biology.usc.edu/PDF/WebsterDevcos.pdf.

Weitzman, Martin. 1974. "Prices vs. Quantities." *Review of Economic Studies* 61 (4): 477–91.

Weyant, John P. 2000. "An Introduction to the Economics of Climate Change Policy." Pew Center on Global Climate Change, Arlington, VA.

WHO (World Health Organization). 2005. *Avian Influenza: Assessing the Pandemic Threat.* http://www.who.org.

————. 2006. "Avian Influenza, Including Influenza A (H5N1), in Humans: WHO Interim Infection Control Guideline for Health Care Facilities Alert." Available at www.who.int/csr/disease/avian_influenza/guidelines/infectioncontrol1/en.

Whole Systems. 2006. "Ocean Fish Production." Available at www.whole-systems.org/fisheries. html.

World Bank. 2004. "Saving Fish and Fishers: Toward Sustainable and Equitable Governance of the Global Fishing Sector." Agriculture and Rural Development Department, World Bank, Washington, DC.

————. 2006. *Global Development Finance.* Washington, DC: World Bank.

WWF (World Wildlife Fund). 2001. "Hard Facts, Hidden Problems: A Review of Current Data on Fishing Subsidies." World Wildlife Fund Technical Paper. Washington, DC.

Appendix
Regional Economic Prospects

Table A.1 East Asia and the Pacific forecast summary
Annual percent change (unless otherwise indicated)

	1991–2000[a]	2003	2004	2005	Estimate 2006	Forecast 2007	2008
GDP at market prices (2000 US$)[b]	8.3	8.8	9.0	9.0	9.2	8.7	8.1
GDP per capita (units in US$)	6.9	7.8	8.1	8.1	8.3	7.8	7.2
PPP GDP[c]		8.9	9.2	9.2	9.3	8.8	8.2
Private consumption	7.3	6.1	7.3	7.7	6.0	6.5	7.3
Public consumption	7.3	5.3	6.3	5.9	4.0	6.3	6.4
Fixed investment	9.7	17.0	11.8	9.6	8.9	11.7	9.0
Exports, GNFS[d]	12.4	17.8	22.4	17.7	16.1	12.7	11.9
Imports, GNFS[d]	12.0	17.0	19.4	12.5	13.1	14.0	12.8
Net exports, contribution to growth	1.2	5.3	7.0	9.6	11.4	11.3	11.2
Current account balance/GDP (%)	0.4	3.5	3.4	5.8	7.0	6.4	5.9
GDP deflator (median, LCU)	6.6	3.4	4.2	3.0	2.7	4.7	3.4
Fiscal balance/GDP (%)	−0.8	−2.5	−1.8	−1.3	−1.1	−1.1	−1.0
Memo items: GDP							
East Asia, excluding China	5.9	5.5	6.1	5.4	5.4	5.7	5.9
China	9.5	10.0	10.1	10.2	10.4	9.6	8.7
Indonesia	3.3	4.9	5.1	5.6	5.5	6.2	6.5
Thailand	3.6	7.0	6.2	4.5	4.5	4.6	5.0

Source: World Bank.

a. Growth rates over intervals are compound averages; growth contributions, ratios, and the GDP deflator are averages.
b. GDP is measured in constant 2000 U.S. dollars.
c. GDP is measured at PPP exchange rates.
d. Exports and imports of goods and nonfactor services.

Table A.2 East Asia and the Pacific country forecasts

Annual percent change (unless otherwise indicated)

					Estimate	Forecast	
	1991–2000[a]	2003	2004	2005	2006	2007	2008
Cambodia							
GDP at market prices (2000 US$)[b]		7.0	10.0	13.4	8.9	6.5	7.0
Current account balance/GDP (%)		−3.6	−3.9	−6.4	−13.7	−10.7	−7.7
China							
GDP at market prices (2000 US$)[b]	9.5	10.0	10.1	10.2	10.4	9.6	8.7
Current account balance/GDP (%)	1.5	2.8	3.6	7.1	8.5	7.5	7.0
Fiji							
GDP at market prices (2000 US$)[b]	2.1	3.0	5.3	0.7	3.1	2.2	2.5
Current account balance/GDP (%)	−3.1	−8.3	−17.0	−17.1	−10.3	−6.1	−1.9
Indonesia							
GDP at market prices (2000 US$)[b]	3.3	4.9	5.1	5.6	5.5	6.2	6.5
Current account balance/GDP (%)	−0.4	3.5	0.6	0.3	0.8	0.2	−0.5
Lao PDR							
GDP at market prices (2000 US$)[b]		6.1	6.4	7.0	7.3	6.6	6.9
Current account balance/GDP (%)		−8.2	−14.3	−19.9	−14.6	−24.9	−23.6
Malaysia							
GDP at market prices (2000 US$)[b]		5.4	7.2	5.2	5.5	5.5	5.5
Current account balance/GDP (%)		12.9	12.9	15.6	14.8	14.8	15.2
Papua New Guinea							
GDP at market prices (2000 US$)[b]	3.9	2.7	2.9	3.0	3.8	4.0	4.0
Current account balance/GDP (%)	2.3	11.2	2.2	13.5	8.0	7.0	4.9
Philippines							
GDP at market prices (2000 US$)[b]	3.1	3.6	6.2	5.0	5.5	5.7	6.0
Current account balance/GDP (%)	−0.2	4.4	1.9	2.5	2.6	1.8	1.5
Samoa							
GDP at market prices (2000 US$)[b]	2.7	−1.0	3.1	3.0	3.0	3.5	3.5
Current account balance/GDP (%)	−8.4	5.0	−4.5	−7.3	0.1	0.2	0.0
Thailand							
GDP at market prices (2000 US$)[b]	3.6	7.0	6.2	4.5	4.5	4.6	5.0
Current account balance/GDP (%)	−1.2	5.5	2.9	−1.5	0.2	2.2	2.5
Vietnam							
GDP at market prices (2000 US$)[b]	7.0	7.3	7.8	8.4	8.0	7.5	7.5
Current account balance/GDP (%)		−4.9	−2.0	−0.4	2.4	0.1	−1.7

Source: World Bank.

Note: Growth and current account figures presented here are World Bank projections and may differ from targets contained in other Bank documents. Kiribati, Dem. Rep. of Korea, N. Mariana Islands, Marshall Islands, the Federated States of Micronesia, Mongolia, Myanmar, Palau, American Samoa, Solomon Islands, Timor-Leste, and Tonga are not forecast owing to data limitations.
a. Growth rates over intervals are compound averages; growth contributions, ratios, and the GDP deflator are averages.
b. GDP is measured in constant 2000 U.S. dollars.

Table A.3 Europe and Central Asia forecast summary

Annual percent change (unless otherwise indicated)

	1991–2000[a]	2003	2004	2005	Estimate 2006	Forecast 2007	Forecast 2008
GDP at market prices (2000 US$)[b]	−0.2	5.9	7.2	6.0	6.4	5.7	5.5
GDP per capita (units in US$)	−0.4	5.9	7.2	6.0	6.3	5.6	5.5
PPP GDP[c]	−0.4	6.2	7.4	5.9	6.5	5.8	5.6
Private consumption	1.2	6.0	8.1	7.9	7.8	6.3	5.8
Public consumption	0.5	2.9	2.3	2.9	3.1	3.0	2.9
Fixed investment	−4.6	10.4	12.7	11.7	10.9	8.9	7.9
Exports, GNFS[d]	3.8	12.7	13.4	7.3	10.0	9.5	9.9
Imports, GNFS[d]	2.8	15.7	17.7	10.5	12.8	10.6	10.2
Net exports, contribution to growth	0.5	2.2	0.5	−1.1	−2.5	−3.2	−3.5
Current account balance/GDP (%)		−1.0	0.3	0.9	0.8	−0.6	−1.4
GDP deflator (median, LCU)	104.7	4.3	6.2	4.0	6.0	5.1	5.0
Fiscal balance/GDP (%)		−2.6	−0.6	1.4	1.9	2.2	1.5
Memo items: GDP							
Transition countries	2.6	4.8	6.7	5.5	5.8	5.2	5.2
Central and Eastern Europe	2.2	4.3	5.5	4.6	5.7	5.3	5.3
Commonwealth of Independent States	−3.7	7.7	8.0	6.7	7.3	6.4	6.0
Poland	4.5	3.8	5.3	3.4	5.4	5.1	5.2
Russia	−3.4	7.3	7.2	6.4	6.8	6.0	5.5
Turkey	3.5	5.8	8.9	7.4	6.0	5.0	5.0

Source: World Bank.

a. Growth rates over intervals are compound averages; growth contributions, ratios, and the GDP deflator are averages.
b. GDP is measured in constant 2000 U.S. dollars.
c. GDP is measured at PPP exchange rates.
d. Exports and imports of goods and nonfactor services.

Table A.4 Europe and Central Asia country forecasts

Annual percent change (unless otherwise indicated)

	1991–2000[a]	2003	2004	2005	Estimate 2006	Forecast 2007	Forecast 2008
Albania							
GDP at market prices (2000 US$)[b]	4.7	6.0	5.9	5.5	5.0	6.0	5.8
Current account balance/GDP (%)	−5.6	−8.1	−5.5	−7.8	−8.1	−7.1	−6.5
Armenia							
GDP at market prices (2000 US$)[b]	−2.6	13.9	10.5	14.0	9.5	8.5	7.5
Current account balance/GDP (%)		−6.8	−4.5	−3.9	−4.7	−4.6	−4.5
Azerbaijan							
GDP at market prices (2000 US$)[b]	−5.1	11.2	10.2	26.2	22.7	25.7	19.9
Current account balance/GDP (%)		−27.8	−30.0	1.1	15.1	25.6	34.1
Belarus							
GDP at market prices (2000 US$)[b]	−1.1	7.0	11.0	9.2	9.3	4.5	3.3
Current account balance/GDP (%)		−2.2	−5.2	1.5	−0.2	−3.2	−3.9
Bulgaria							
GDP at market prices (2000 US$)[b]	−0.9	4.5	5.7	5.6	5.6	5.6	5.6
Current account balance/GDP (%)	−2.3	−5.5	−5.8	−11.3	−12.5	−12.0	−11.3
Croatia							
GDP at market prices (2000 US$)[b]	0.8	5.3	3.8	4.3	4.5	4.0	4.0
Current account balance/GDP (%)		−7.2	−5.4	−6.6	−6.7	−5.1	−5.0
Czech Republic							
GDP at market prices (2000 US$)[b]	1.5	3.2	4.2	6.1	6.8	6.0	6.3
Current account balance/GDP (%)		−6.4	−6.2	−2.1	−3.0	−3.1	−3.0

(continued)

Table A.4 (*continued*)

Annual percent change (unless otherwise indicated)

	1991–2000[a]	2003	2004	2005	Estimate 2006	Forecast 2007	2008
Estonia							
GDP at market prices (2000 US$)[b]	0.0	6.7	7.8	9.8	9.2	8.0	6.8
Current account balance/GDP (%)		−12.1	−13.0	−11.0	−11.8	−11.2	−10.5
Georgia							
GDP at market prices (2000 US$)[b]	−7.2	11.1	6.2	8.5	7.5	6.5	6.0
Current account balance/GDP (%)		−7.2	−8.3	−8.4	−9.9	−11.5	−11.0
Hungary							
GDP at market prices (2000 US$)[b]	2.1	3.4	5.2	4.1	3.8	2.5	3.2
Current account balance/GDP (%)	−5.4	−8.7	−8.6	−7.4	−8.0	−6.7	−6.0
Kazakhstan							
GDP at market prices (2000 US$)[b]	−2.5	9.3	9.6	9.4	9.0	9.0	8.9
Current account balance/GDP (%)		−0.9	1.1	−0.9	7.0	2.4	−1.9
Kyrgyz Republic							
GDP at market prices (2000 US$)[b]	−3.2	7.0	7.1	−0.6	4.3	5.5	4.8
Current account balance/GDP (%)		−5.2	−3.4	−8.3	−11.0	−9.8	−7.7
Latvia							
GDP at market prices (2000 US$)[b]	−1.6	7.2	8.5	10.2	9.8	7.5	6.0
Current account balance/GDP (%)		−8.2	−12.9	−12.4	−13.5	−12.0	−11.5
Lithuania							
GDP at market prices (2000 US$)[b]	−2.8	9.7	7.0	7.5	7.0	6.5	6.0
Current account balance/GDP (%)		−7.0	−7.7	−7.0	−8.5	−8.4	−8.0
Macedonia, FYR							
GDP at market prices (2000 US$)[b]	−0.3	2.8	4.1	4.0	4.0	4.0	4.5
Current account balance/GDP (%)		−3.3	−7.7	−1.4	−3.1	−3.9	−3.9
Moldova							
GDP at market prices (2000 US$)[b]	−8.2	6.6	7.4	7.1	3.0	3.0	5.0
Current account balance/GDP (%)		−7.1	−2.0	−9.8	−21.2	−17.6	−9.8
Poland							
GDP at market prices (2000 US$)[b]	4.5	3.8	5.3	3.4	5.4	5.1	5.2
Current account balance/GDP (%)	−3.5	−2.1	−4.2	−1.4	−1.5	−1.9	−2.4
Romania							
GDP at market prices (2000 US$)[b]	−0.3	5.2	8.3	4.1	5.8	6.2	6.3
Current account balance/GDP (%)	−6.7	−5.8	−8.2	−8.7	−11.4	−12.9	−13.6
Russian Federation							
GDP at market prices (2000 US$)[b]	−3.4	7.3	7.2	6.4	6.8	6.0	5.5
Current account balance/GDP (%)		8.2	10.2	10.9	9.7	5.2	2.9
Slovak Republic							
GDP at market prices (2000 US$)[b]	1.9	4.5	5.4	6.1	6.7	7.1	5.7
Current account balance/GDP (%)		−0.9	−3.1	−8.5	−7.2	−4.2	−3.5
Turkey							
GDP at market prices (2000 US$)[b]	3.5	5.8	8.9	7.4	6.0	5.0	5.0
Current account balance/GDP (%)	−1.1	−3.4	−5.2	−6.4	−8.0	−7.5	−6.4
Ukraine							
GDP at market prices (2000 US$)[b]	−7.2	9.4	12.1	2.6	6.0	4.5	5.5
Current account balance/GDP (%)		5.8	10.5	3.1	−1.0	−3.4	−4.1
Uzbekistan							
GDP at market prices (2000 US$)[b]	−0.2	4.2	7.7	7.0	6.0	4.0	4.0
Current account balance/GDP (%)		8.7	9.9	14.3	17.0	17.2	14.8

Source: World Bank.

Note: Growth and current account figures presented here are World Bank projections and may differ from targets contained in other Bank documents. Bosnia and Herzegovina, the Republic of Montenegro, the Republic of Serbia, Tajikistan, and Turkmenistan are not forecast owing to data limitations.
a. Growth rates over intervals are compound averages; growth contributions, ratios, and the GDP deflator are averages.
b. GDP is measured in constant 2000 U.S. dollars.

Table A.5 Latin America and the Caribbean forecast summary

Annual percent change (unless otherwise indicated)

	1991–2000[a]	2003	2004	2005	Estimate 2006	Forecast 2007	2008
GDP at market prices (2000 US$)[b]	2.9	2.0	6.0	4.5	5.0	4.2	4.0
GDP per capita (units in US$)	1.4	0.5	4.5	3.1	3.7	2.8	2.7
PPP GDP[c]	3.5	2.1	5.6	4.3	4.9	4.1	4.0
Private consumption	2.5	2.5	5.3	4.7	5.0	3.8	3.6
Public consumption	1.5	5.9	0.9	3.4	3.3	1.9	1.1
Fixed investment	5.2	−3.2	14.6	7.7	9.0	8.1	6.9
Exports, GNFS[d]	7.4	2.7	12.4	7.8	6.2	5.7	6.8
Imports, GNFS[d]	8.9	2.0	14.4	11.3	9.0	7.6	7.2
Net exports, contribution to growth	−0.6	1.6	1.3	0.6	−0.1	−0.6	−0.7
Current account balance/GDP (%)	−2.8	0.5	1.0	1.6	1.9	1.4	1.0
GDP deflator (median, LCU)	10.1	7.2	8.3	9.1	7.3	6.1	6.1
Fiscal balance/GDP (%)		−0.1	0.2	0.2	0.7	0.1	−0.4
Memo items: GDP							
Latin Amer. & the Carib., excluding							
Argentina	2.8	1.0	5.5	3.8	4.6	3.9	4.0
Caribbean	3.1	3.2	2.5	6.5	7.6	5.0	4.8
Central America	3.1	1.6	4.3	3.2	4.5	3.6	3.6
Argentina	3.3	8.8	9.0	9.2	7.7	5.6	4.0
Brazil	2.6	0.5	4.9	2.3	3.5	3.4	3.8
Mexico	3.0	1.4	4.4	3.0	4.5	3.5	3.5

Source: World Bank.

a. Growth rates over intervals are compound averages; growth contributions, ratios, and the GDP deflator are averages.
b. GDP is measured in constant 2000 U.S. dollars.
c. GDP is measured at PPP exchange rates.
d. Exports and imports of goods and nonfactor services.

Table A.6 Latin America and the Caribbean country forecasts

Annual percent change (unless otherwise indicated)

	1991–2000[a]	2003	2004	2005	Estimate 2006	Forecast 2007	Forecast 2008
Antigua and Barbuda							
GDP at market prices (2000 US$)[b]	3.1	4.9	5.2	5.0	7.1	3.9	4.1
Current account balance/GDP (%)	−5.3	−10.1	−18.7	−15.9	−20.4	−18.4	−16.7
Argentina							
GDP at market prices (2000 US$)[b]	3.3	8.8	9.0	9.2	7.7	5.6	4.0
Current account balance/GDP (%)	−3.1	6.2	1.9	2.7	2.2	1.4	0.9
Belize							
GDP at market prices (2000 US$)[b]	4.8	9.4	4.6	3.1	2.6	2.6	3.3
Current account balance/GDP (%)	−7.2	−20.3	−17.6	−18.5	−18.8	−24.9	−24.9
Bolivia							
GDP at market prices (2000 US$)[b]	3.2	2.8	3.6	4.1	3.1	3.1	3.2
Current account balance/GDP (%)	−6.1	0.8	3.5	5.2	5.3	4.0	3.9
Brazil							
GDP at market prices (2000 US$)[b]	2.6	0.5	4.9	2.3	3.5	3.4	3.8
Current account balance/GDP (%)	−2.1	0.8	2.0	1.9	1.4	1.1	0.8
Chile							
GDP at market prices (2000 US$)[b]	5.6	3.7	6.1	6.3	5.0	5.3	5.3
Current account balance/GDP (%)	−2.8	−1.5	1.7	0.6	3.5	2.7	2.0
Colombia							
GDP at market prices (2000 US$)[b]	2.3	4.1	4.8	5.1	4.7	4.2	4.0
Current account balance/GDP (%)	−1.9	−1.2	−1.0	−1.9	−2.3	−3.0	−3.7
Costa Rica							
GDP at market prices (2000 US$)[b]	5.0	6.5	4.1	5.9	5.0	4.6	4.1
Current account balance/GDP (%)	−3.6	−5.3	−4.6	−4.9	−5.7	−4.1	−4.4
Dominica							
GDP at market prices (2000 US$)[b]	1.8	0.0	3.6	2.4	3.0	3.0	3.0
Current account balance/GDP (%)	−16.3	−19.5	−23.0	−23.2	−24.2	−24.5	−24.0
Dominican Republic							
GDP at market prices (2000 US$)[b]	5.9	−0.4	2.0	9.3	8.5	5.5	5.0
Current account balance/GDP (%)	−3.2	6.3	5.3	−0.4	−3.2	−4.1	−3.6
Ecuador							
GDP at market prices (2000 US$)[b]	1.3	2.7	7.9	4.7	3.5	3.0	3.0
Current account balance/GDP (%)	−2.3	−1.7	−0.9	−0.3	0.7	−1.1	−2.7
El Salvador							
GDP at market prices (2000 US$)[b]	4.2	1.8	1.5	2.8	3.2	3.1	3.1
Current account balance/GDP (%)	−2.0	−5.1	−3.9	−4.4	−5.7	−4.7	−4.3
Guatemala							
GDP at market prices (2000 US$)[b]	3.7	2.1	2.7	3.2	4.1	4.0	4.0
Current account balance/GDP (%)	−4.6	−4.2	−4.3	−4.4	−4.1	−4.0	−3.4
Guyana							
GDP at market prices (2000 US$)[b]	4.3	−0.6	1.6	−3.0	3.5	3.3	3.6
Current account balance/GDP (%)	−19.9	−6.3	−8.9	−19.9	−26.1	−22.3	−15.4
Honduras							
GDP at market prices (2000 US$)[b]	3.0	3.5	4.6	4.2	4.5	4.5	4.0
Current account balance/GDP (%)	−7.7	−4.6	−5.3	−0.5	−1.5	−1.3	−1.2
Haiti							
GDP at market prices (2000 US$)[b]	−1.7	0.4	−3.8	1.5	2.5	2.7	3.0
Current account balance/GDP (%)	−1.6	−0.4	0.4	0.7	−1.2	−1.4	−1.5
Jamaica							
GDP at market prices (2000 US$)[b]	0.7	2.3	0.9	2.0	3.0	3.5	3.0
Current account balance/GDP (%)	−2.7	−9.4	−5.8	−8.8	−10.4	−8.4	−5.0

Table A.6 (*continued*)
Annual percent change (unless otherwise indicated)

	1991–2000ᵃ	2003	2004	2005	Estimate 2006	Forecast 2007	2008
Mexico							
GDP at market prices (2000 US$)ᵇ	3.0	1.4	4.4	3.0	4.5	3.5	3.5
Current account balance/GDP (%)	−3.7	−1.4	−1.0	−0.6	0.1	−0.2	0.4
Nicaragua							
GDP at market prices (2000 US$)ᵇ	3.4	2.3	5.1	4.0	3.7	4.2	4.6
Current account balance/GDP (%)	−28.6	−18.1	−18.7	−18.8	−18.1	−19.4	−19.9
Panama							
GDP at market prices (2000 US$)ᵇ	4.1	4.3	7.6	6.4	6.3	5.7	5.5
Current account balance/GDP (%)	−4.8	−3.9	−7.8	−5.2	−4.6	−5.0	−6.2
Peru							
GDP at market prices (2000 US$)ᵇ	3.7	4.0	4.8	6.7	6.6	5.5	5.0
Current account balance/GDP (%)	−5.5	−1.5	0.0	1.4	1.1	0.5	−0.4
Paraguay							
GDP at market prices (2000 US$)ᵇ	1.7	2.6	4.1	3.0	3.2	3.0	3.1
Current account balance/GDP (%)	−2.0	2.2	0.3	−0.2	−0.3	−0.4	−0.3
St. Kitts and Nevis							
GDP at market prices (2000 US$)ᵇ	4.1	2.1	6.4	4.9	3.7	4.0	4.1
Current account balance/GDP (%)	−18.8	−51.8	−24.4	−21.6	−21.0	−20.0	−20.0
St. Lucia							
GDP at market prices (2000 US$)ᵇ	2.4	3.0	4.0	5.4	5.5	3.4	3.3
Current account balance/GDP (%)	−11.3	−18.6	−13.0	−25.2	−15.3	−10.0	−10.0
St. Vincent and the Grenadines							
GDP at market prices (2000 US$)ᵇ	2.0	4.5	4.3	4.9	4.3	4.1	4.2
Current account balance/GDP (%)	−19.0	−15.5	−19.4	−23.6	−24.3	−25.0	−25.8
Trinidad and Tobago							
GDP at market prices (2000 US$)ᵇ	2.9	13.2	6.5	7.0	12.0	6.2	6.5
Current account balance/GDP (%)	0.2	9.4	15.4	18.9	23.2	17.2	17.3
Uruguay							
GDP at market prices (2000 US$)ᵇ	2.7	2.5	12.3	6.6	5.5	4.4	3.8
Current account balance/GDP (%)	−1.5	−0.5	0.3	−0.5	−1.7	−2.2	−2.5
Venezuela, R. B. de							
GDP at market prices (2000 US$)ᵇ	1.1	−7.7	17.9	9.3	8.5	6.0	5.5
Current account bal/GDP (%)	2.6	13.7	12.6	18.1	17.1	12.6	7.6

Source: World Bank.

Note: Growth and current account figures presented here are World Bank projections and may differ from targets contained in other Bank documents. Barbados, Cuba, Grenada, and Suriname are not forecast owing to data limitations.
a. Growth rates over intervals are compound averages; growth contributions, ratios, and the GDP deflator are averages.
b. GDP is measured in constant 2000 U.S. dollars.

Table A.7 Middle East and North Africa forecast summary

Annual percent change (unless otherwise indicated)

	1991–2000[a]	2003	2004	2005	Estimate 2006	Forecast 2007	2008
GDP at market prices (2000 US$)[b]	3.8	4.4	4.8	4.4	4.9	4.9	4.8
GDP per capita (units in US$)	1.9	2.7	3.0	2.6	3.1	3.0	3.1
PPP GDP[c]	3.9	4.6	4.8	4.4	5.2	4.9	4.9
Private consumption	3.5	3.7	6.3	4.8	5.0	5.0	6.5
Public consumption	3.6	3.1	2.8	6.2	9.2	5.3	5.2
Fixed investment	3.2	5.9	10.0	5.4	10.1	9.5	3.7
Exports, GNFS[d]	3.8	3.8	6.2	4.8	6.6	4.7	5.2
Imports, GNFS[d]	−0.9	3.8	12.9	7.2	12.5	8.7	7.2
Net exports, contribution to growth	−4.1	0.0	−1.9	−2.6	−4.4	−5.7	−6.4
Current account balance/GDP (%)	−0.5	0.0	2.5	6.6	6.8	3.6	2.3
GDP deflator (median, LCU)	7.7	4.4	6.9	14.5	8.7	4.1	4.8
Fiscal balance/GDP (%)	−4.3	−0.9	−2.4	−1.2	−0.4	0.1	0.1
Memo items: GDP							
MENA Geographic Region[e]	3.1	5.7	5.0	5.3	5.5	5.2	5.0
Resource poor-labor abundant[f]	4.8	4.0	4.8	4.0	5.0	5.1	5.3
Resource rich-labor abundant[g]	2.8	5.1	4.9	4.7	4.7	4.6	4.4
Resource rich-labor importing[h]	2.3	7.4	5.3	6.7	6.5	5.7	5.2
Algeria	1.8	6.8	5.2	5.3	3.0	4.5	4.3
Egypt, Arab Rep. of	4.4	3.1	4.2	4.9	5.8	5.6	5.8
Iran, Islamic Rep. of	2.9	5.0	5.1	4.4	5.8	5.0	4.7

Source: World Bank.

a. Growth rates over intervals are compound averages; growth contributions, ratios, and the GDP deflator are averages.
b. GDP is measured in constant 2000 U.S. dollars.
c. GDP is measured at PPP exchange rates.
d. Exports and imports of goods and nonfactor services.
e. Geographic region includes high-income countries: Bahrain, Kuwait, and Saudi Arabia.
f. Egypt, Jordan, Lebanon, Morocco, and Tunisia.
g. Algeria, Iran, the Syrian Arab Republic, and the Republic of Yemen.
h. Bahrain, Kuwait, Oman, and Saudi Arabia.

Table A.8 Middle East and North Africa country forecasts

Annual percent change (unless otherwise indicated)

	1991–2000[a]	2003	2004	2005	Estimate 2006	Forecast 2007	Forecast 2008
Algeria							
GDP at market prices (2000 US$)[b]	1.8	6.8	5.2	5.3	3.0	4.5	4.3
Current account balance/GDP (%)	3.3	13.0	13.1	21.2	24.2	17.5	15.8
Egypt, Arab Rep. of							
GDP at market prices (2000 US$)[b]	4.4	3.1	4.2	4.9	5.8	5.6	5.8
Current account balance/GDP (%)	0.9	4.5	4.3	3.3	1.7	1.5	−0.7
Iran, Islamic Rep. of							
GDP at market prices (2000 US$)[b]	2.9	5.0	5.1	4.4	5.8	5.0	4.7
Current account balance/GDP (%)	1.2	−7.8	0.9	7.5	5.6	2.2	2.0
Jordan							
GDP at market prices (2000 US$)[b]	4.9	4.1	8.4	7.3	6.3	5.0	5.0
Current account balance/GDP (%)	−4.3	11.6	−0.2	−18.2	−21.6	−20.3	−16.2
Lebanon							
GDP at market prices (2000 US$)[b]		4.9	6.3	1.0	−5.5	4.5	2.9
Current account balance/GDP (%)		−27.5	−23.7	−21.7	−21.5	−23.1	−23.5
Morocco							
GDP at market prices (2000 US$)[b]	1.6	5.5	4.2	1.7	7.0	3.5	4.5
Current account balance/GDP (%)	−1.4	3.5	1.9	2.4	1.2	0.7	0.9
Oman							
GDP at market prices (2000 US$)[b]	4.0	1.3	3.1	4.8	6.5	5.5	5.0
Current account balance/GDP (%)	−3.7	4.0	2.2	14.6	25.2	19.1	14.4
Syrian Arab Republic							
GDP at market prices (2000 US$)[b]	4.1	1.1	3.9	5.1	4.0	3.7	3.5
Current account balance/GDP (%)	1.0	3.4	1.1	−4.0	−2.5	−4.9	−6.7
Tunisia							
GDP at market prices (2000 US$)[b]	4.3	5.6	6.0	4.2	5.3	5.6	6.0
Current account balance/GDP (%)	−4.3	−2.9	−1.7	−1.1	−1.2	−1.4	−1.2
Yemen, Republic of							
GDP at market prices (2000 US$)[b]	5.3	3.1	2.6	3.8	3.9	2.5	3.0
Current account balance/GDP (%)	−4.3	1.4	2.0	5.0	−4.9	−8.4	−11.5

Source: World Bank.

Note: Growth and current account figures presented here are World Bank projections and may differ from targets contained in other Bank documents. Djibouti, Iraq, Libya, and the West Bank and Gaza are not forecast owing to data limitations.
a. Growth rates over intervals are compound averages; growth contributions, ratios, and the GDP deflator are averages.
b. GDP is measured in constant 2000 U.S. dollars.

Table A.9 South Asia forecast summary

Annual percent change (unless otherwise indicated)

	1991–2000[a]	2003	2004	2005	Estimate 2006	Forecast 2007	2008
GDP at market prices (2000 US$)[b]	5.0	7.8	8.0	8.1	8.2	7.5	7.0
GDP per capita (units in US$)	3.2	6.1	6.3	6.4	6.7	5.9	5.6
PPP GDP[c]	5.6	8.0	8.1	8.2	8.3	7.5	7.1
Private consumption	3.8	6.7	6.3	8.2	7.8	7.0	6.3
Public consumption	5.1	4.6	8.4	4.4	5.3	4.2	4.2
Fixed investment	5.8	11.5	8.2	10.9	12.6	12.1	10.3
Exports, GNFS[d]	9.4	11.5	12.9	19.0	22.3	15.5	13.8
Imports, GNFS[d]	10.2	11.3	21.9	19.6	23.6	16.9	13.3
Net exports, contribution to growth	−2.4	0.4	−1.1	−1.3	−1.7	−2.2	−2.2
Current account balance/GDP (%)	−1.6	1.4	−0.8	−1.4	−2.2	−2.5	−2.5
GDP deflator (median, LCU)	8.1	4.5	7.6	6.3	8.1	7.4	6.5
Fiscal balance/GDP (%)	−7.6	−7.8	−7.2	−7.1	−7.1	−6.7	−6.1
Memo items: GDP							
South Asia, excluding India	3.9	5.1	6.1	6.9	6.5	6.6	6.4
Bangladesh	4.5	5.3	6.3	6.2	6.7	6.2	6.5
India	5.4	8.6	8.5	8.5	8.7	7.7	7.2
Pakistan	3.4	5.0	6.4	7.8	6.6	7.0	6.5

Source: World Bank.

a. Growth rates over intervals are compound averages; growth contributions, ratios, and the GDP deflator are averages.
b. GDP is measured in constant 2000 U.S. dollars.
c. GDP is measured at PPP exchange rates.
d. Exports and imports of goods and nonfactor services.

Table A.10 South Asia country forecasts

Annual percent change (unless otherwise indicated)

	1991–2000[a]	2003	2004	2005	Estimate 2006	Forecast 2007	2008
Bangladesh							
GDP at market prices (2000 US$)[b]	4.5	5.3	6.3	6.2	6.7	6.2	6.5
Current account balance/GDP (%)	−0.4	0.3	−0.4	−0.9	0.9	0.4	−0.6
India							
GDP at market prices (2000 US$)[b]	5.4	8.6	8.5	8.5	8.7	7.7	7.2
Current account balance/GDP (%)	−1.2	1.1	−0.8	−1.3	−2.2	−2.5	−2.4
Nepal							
GDP at market prices (2000 US$)[b]	4.4	3.1	3.8	2.7	1.9	3.7	4.5
Current account balance/GDP (%)	−6.3	2.1	2.9	2.2	2.4	3.9	2.9
Pakistan							
GDP at market prices (2000 US$)[b]	3.4	5.0	6.4	7.8	6.6	7.0	6.5
Current account balance/GDP (%)	−3.7	4.3	−0.8	−3.1	−3.9	−4.4	−5.3
Sri Lanka							
GDP at market prices (2000 US$)[b]	4.7	6.0	5.4	6.0	7.0	6.5	6.0
Current account balance/GDP (%)	−4.6	−0.6	−3.2	−2.8	−4.9	−4.1	−3.5

Source: World Bank.

Note: Growth and current account figures presented here are World Bank projections and may differ from targets contained in other Bank documents. Afghanistan, Bhutan, and the Maldives are not forecast owing to data limitations.
a. Growth rates over intervals are compound averages; growth contributions, ratios, and the GDP deflator are averages.
b. GDP is measured in constant 2000 U.S. dollars.

Table A.11 Sub-Saharan Africa forecast summary

Annual percent change (unless otherwise indicated)

	1991–2000[a]	2003	2004	2005	Estimate 2006	Forecast 2007	Forecast 2008
GDP at market prices (2000 US$)[b]	2.3	4.2	5.2	5.5	5.3	5.3	5.4
GDP per capita (units in US$)	0.0	1.9	3.0	3.2	3.3	3.3	3.5
PPP GDP[c]	3.2	3.8	5.4	5.7	5.6	5.7	5.7
Private consumption	1.9	0.6	5.6	5.8	5.3	4.5	4.6
Public consumption	2.9	7.2	5.7	5.7	5.0	5.9	5.9
Fixed investment	3.8	7.7	13.6	9.0	13.6	8.7	8.7
Exports, GNFS[d]	4.3	7.5	6.0	6.8	5.7	7.2	7.1
Imports, GNFS[d]	4.3	7.3	9.5	9.2	10.3	7.7	7.7
Net exports, contribution to growth	0.7	−1.7	−3.0	−3.9	−5.6	−5.9	−6.3
Current account balance/GDP (%)	−2.1	−1.0	−0.2	0.8	0.3	−0.2	−0.9
GDP deflator (median, LCU)	10.0	5.7	6.4	6.7	5.8	4.6	5.0
Fiscal balance/GDP (%)	−4.4	−2.6	−2.4	−1.3	−1.0	−1.2	−0.9
Memo items: GDP							
Sub-Saharan Africa, excluding South Africa	2.6	5.0	5.7	5.9	5.8	6.2	6.1
Oil exporters	2.4	6.7	6.6	7.0	6.9	7.5	7.2
CFA countries	2.5	3.5	5.0	4.3	4.1	3.6	4.4
Kenya	1.7	3.0	4.9	5.8	4.9	5.1	4.9
Nigeria	2.2	10.7	6.5	6.2	4.8	5.1	5.4
South Africa	1.9	3.0	4.5	4.9	4.6	3.9	4.3

Source: World Bank.

a. Growth rates over intervals are compound averages; growth contributions, ratios and the GDP deflator are averages.
b. GDP is measured in constant 2000 U.S. dollars.
c. GDP is measured at PPP exchange rates.
d. Exports and imports of goods and nonfactor services.

Table A.12 Sub-Saharan Africa country forecasts

Annual percent change (unless otherwise indicated)

	1991–2000[a]	2003	2004	2005	Estimate 2006	Forecast 2007	2008
Angola							
GDP at market prices (2000 US$)[b]	0.9	3.4	11.1	18.7	16.9	22.3	15.7
Current account balance/GDP (%)	−6.0	−5.0	3.5	8.7	11.9	15.3	13.1
Benin							
GDP at market prices (2000 US$)[b]	4.3	3.9	3.1	3.5	4.3	4.2	4.1
Current account balance/GDP (%)	−6.8	−9.8	−7.9	−7.3	−7.4	−7.4	−7.4
Botswana							
GDP at market prices (2000 US$)[b]	4.4	6.7	4.9	4.0	5.2	4.3	4.1
Current account balance/GDP (%)	8.4	6.0	9.9	14.0	14.0	12.1	9.5
Burkina Faso							
GDP at market prices (2000 US$)[b]	3.2	8.0	4.6	7.1	6.5	4.9	5.2
Current account balance/GDP (%)	−5.6	−12.2	−13.2	−12.2	−6.9	−6.5	−5.0
Burundi							
GDP at market prices (2000 US$)[b]	−2.2	−1.2	4.8	0.9	5.3	5.7	5.4
Current account balance/GDP (%)	−3.4	−4.8	−8.1	−10.5	−15.6	−14.3	−13.7
Cameroon							
GDP at market prices (2000 US$)[b]	1.8	4.2	3.6	2.4	4.1	3.9	4.1
Current account balance/GDP (%)	−3.6	−6.3	−3.1	−2.0	0.5	0.2	0.2
Cape Verde							
GDP at market prices (2000 US$)[b]	5.6	5.0	4.4	5.9	5.8	5.9	5.6
Current account balance/GDP (%)	−8.3	−11.1	−14.6	−4.5	−9.0	−8.6	−8.2
Central African Republic							
GDP at market prices (2000 US$)[b]	1.7	−4.6	1.8	2.8	3.6	3.9	4.3
Current account balance/GDP (%)	−4.3	−2.2	−4.5	−2.8	−3.1	−2.9	−3.0
Chad							
GDP at market prices (2000 US$)[b]	1.2	14.3	33.2	8.4	3.9	2.8	2.7
Current account balance/GDP (%)	−5.5	−43.9	−3.8	4.1	8.7	7.0	4.8
Comoros							
GDP at market prices (2000 US$)[b]	1.8	2.1	−0.2	4.2	1.3	2.1	2.7
Current account balance/GDP (%)	−6.7	−4.1	−4.1	−4.6	−4.7	−4.2	−3.7
Congo, Rep. of							
GDP at market prices (2000 US$)[b]	1.3	0.8	3.6	7.7	6.8	1.1	6.5
Current account balance/GDP (%)	−16.5	14.1	20.7	19.6	25.5	25.4	25.6
Côte d'Ivoire							
GDP at market prices (2000 US$)[b]	2.3	−1.5	1.5	1.8	1.7	2.2	2.7
Current account balance/GDP (%)	−4.0	2.0	1.6	−0.1	1.7	2.5	2.3
Equatorial Guinea							
GDP at market prices (2000 US$)[b]	18.5	14.0	29.4	8.1	8.2	8.3	12.3
Current account balance/GDP (%)	−33.0	−147.6	−23.8	−13.4	−7.0	−8.4	−8.6
Eritrea							
GDP at market prices (2000 US$)[b]		3.0	2.8	4.5	1.7	1.9	2.4
Current account balance/GDP (%)		11.0	5.9	−0.6	−1.1	−1.7	−1.9
Ethiopia							
GDP at market prices (2000 US$)[b]	3.8	−3.9	12.3	8.7	5.8	5.6	5.5
Current account balance/GDP (%)	−0.9	−2.6	−4.4	−7.6	−7.7	−5.5	−4.9
Gabon							
GDP at market prices (2000 US$)[b]	1.8	2.2	1.4	2.9	2.7	1.9	2.7
Current account balance/GDP (%)	5.6	9.5	10.9	15.9	21.3	19.7	17.2
Gambia, The							
GDP at market prices (2000 US$)[b]	3.0	6.9	5.1	5.0	4.4	3.8	3.6
Current account balance/GDP (%)	4.5	−5.7	−11.8	−12.7	−9.1	−6.9	−5.9

Table A.12 *(continued)*

Annual percent change (unless otherwise indicated)

	1991–2000[a]	2003	2004	2005	Estimate 2006	Forecast 2007	Forecast 2008
Ghana							
GDP at market prices (2000 US$)[b]	3.8	5.2	5.8	5.4	5.6	5.7	5.8
Current account balance/GDP (%)	−6.5	1.9	−2.7	−7.6	−7.6	−7.1	−6.9
Guinea							
GDP at market prices (2000 US$)[b]	3.8	1.2	2.6	3.1	4.1	4.7	3.9
Current account balance/GDP (%)	−5.7	−2.9	−5.2	−2.9	−4.0	−3.2	−3.1
Guinea-Bissau							
GDP at market prices (2000 US$)[b]	1.0	0.6	1.6	2.4	3.8	2.9	3.1
Current account balance/GDP (%)	−24.0	−10.9	3.1	−7.1	−5.2	−7.8	−7.0
Kenya							
GDP at market prices (2000 US$)[b]	1.7	3.0	4.9	5.8	4.9	5.1	4.9
Current account balance/GDP (%)	−1.6	0.4	−2.7	−2.2	−3.5	−5.5	−4.7
Lesotho							
GDP at market prices (2000 US$)[b]	3.0	3.3	2.7	1.3	1.7	1.8	2.1
Current account balance/GDP (%)	−13.3	−10.7	−2.3	13.4	16.3	17.9	19.6
Madagascar							
GDP at market prices (2000 US$)[b]	2.4	9.8	5.2	4.6	4.9	5.3	5.5
Current account balance/GDP (%)	−7.8	−8.0	−9.3	−11.2	−10.6	−9.6	−8.3
Malawi							
GDP at market prices (2000 US$)[b]	2.6	3.9	5.1	2.1	8.1	4.7	5.1
Current account balance/GDP (%)	−8.5	−7.9	−9.7	−8.1	−4.7	−6.3	−5.8
Mali							
GDP at market prices (2000 US$)[b]	3.9	7.6	2.3	6.8	5.7	5.0	4.8
Current account balance/GDP (%)	−5.7	−13.0	−6.1	−7.9	−6.6	−5.8	−5.4
Mauritania							
GDP at market prices (2000 US$)[b]	4.5	6.4	5.2	5.4	17.9	9.8	14.7
Current account balance/GDP (%)	−0.6	−9.4	−19.2	−40.0	4.7	−1.5	3.7
Mauritius							
GDP at market prices (2000 US$)[b]	4.6	4.4	4.7	2.5	3.8	2.9	2.7
Current account balance/GDP (%)	−1.6	1.7	−1.6	−3.9	−4.8	−6.2	−6.4
Mozambique							
GDP at market prices (2000 US$)[b]	5.1	7.8	7.5	6.6	6.9	6.5	6.7
Current account balance/GDP (%)	−17.2	−14.1	−8.6	−10.8	−12.3	−13.9	−13.7
Namibia							
GDP at market prices (2000 US$)[b]	3.4	3.5	6.0	3.3	3.5	3.9	4.1
Current account balance/GDP (%)	4.1	5.4	8.6	8.8	9.0	5.9	2.3
Niger							
GDP at market prices (2000 US$)[b]	1.5	3.8	−0.6	7.1	4.1	4.0	4.0
Current account balance/GDP (%)	−6.9	−12.2	−12.2	−10.8	−7.7	−7.4	−6.6
Nigeria							
GDP at market prices (2000 US$)[b]	2.2	10.7	6.5	6.2	4.8	5.1	5.4
Current account balance/GDP (%)	0.7	16.3	17.7	23.1	18.5	17.6	15.2
Rwanda							
GDP at market prices (2000 US$)[b]	0.4	0.9	4.0	6.5	5.1	6.1	5.7
Current account balance/GDP (%)	−3.5	−7.5	−2.7	−3.6	−9.3	−10.2	−9.7
Senegal							
GDP at market prices (2000 US$)[b]	3.0	6.5	5.6	5.5	3.8	5.1	5.2
Current account balance/GDP (%)	−6.0	−7.6	−7.1	−9.9	−9.9	−8.9	−8.0
Seychelles							
GDP at market prices (2000 US$)[b]	4.3	−6.3	−2.0	−2.3	−1.8	0.4	0.9
Current account balance/GDP (%)	−7.4	−2.3	−4.2	−13.1	−4.1	−3.9	−3.7

(continued)

Table A.12 (*continued*)

Annual percent change (unless otherwise indicated)

	1991–2000[a]	2003	2004	2005	Estimate 2006	Forecast 2007	2008
Sierra Leone							
GDP at market prices (2000 US$)[b]	−5.6	9.3	7.4	7.2	6.9	6.1	6.2
Current account balance/GDP (%)	−9.0	−7.1	−4.3	−8.4	−6.9	−6.0	−5.6
South Africa							
GDP at market prices (2000 US$)[b]	1.9	3.0	4.5	4.9	4.6	3.9	4.3
Current account balance/GDP (%)	−0.2	−1.4	−3.5	−4.2	−5.9	−5.7	−5.3
Sudan							
GDP at market prices (2000 US$)[b]	4.9	6.0	5.2	7.9	11.8	10.1	9.2
Current account balance/GDP (%)	−6.8	−5.4	−3.4	−11.0	−5.1	−3.7	−3.5
Swaziland							
GDP at market prices (2000 US$)[b]	2.8	2.4	2.1	1.8	1.2	1.1	0.9
Current account balance/GDP (%)	−2.6	1.7	1.4	−1.9	−2.5	−3.1	−4.0
Tanzania							
GDP at market prices (2000 US$)[b]	2.7	5.7	6.7	6.9	5.5	7.1	6.8
Current account balance/GDP (%)	−12.5	−0.6	−3.0	−4.7	−7.3	−7.2	−7.6
Togo							
GDP at market prices (2000 US$)[b]	2.3	−1.3	4.6	1.5	2.8	2.7	3.1
Current account balance/GDP (%)	−8.5	−9.9	−7.6	−11.0	−9.0	−7.2	−7.0
Uganda							
GDP at market prices (2000 US$)[b]	6.2	6.5	5.5	6.3	5.1	5.7	5.8
Current account balance/GDP (%)	−7.0	−5.1	−1.7	−2.8	−6.5	−7.4	−7.0
Zambia							
GDP at market prices (2000 US$)[b]	0.7	5.1	5.4	4.8	5.1	4.9	4.6
Current account balance/GDP (%)	−10.5	−8.1	−10.3	−7.8	−6.1	−6.9	−7.3
Zimbabwe							
GDP at market prices (2000 US$)[b]	0.4	−10.4	−3.8	−6.5	−3.3	−2.9	−2.1
Current account balance/GDP (%)	−7.5	−6.1	−19.4	−20.6	−7.6	−8.7	−9.4

Source: World Bank.

Note: Growth and current account figures presented here are World Bank projections and may differ from targets contained in other Bank documents. The Democratic Republic of Congo, Liberia, Mayotte, São Tome and Principe, and Somalia are not forecast owing to data limitations.

a. Growth rates over intervals are compound averages; growth contributions, ratios, and the GDP deflator are averages.
b. GDP is measured in constant 2000 U.S. dollars.